PROOFREADING: Skills for Success

SHARON ANN SOUDER
Muskingum Area Technical College

CHÉRIE C. WHITE
Muskingum Area Technical College

Houghton Mifflin Company BOSTON TORONTO

Geneva, Illinois Palo Alto Princeton, New Jersey

This textbook is dedicated to our families and friends—Joe and Missie White, Joe and Marty White, Lynn Souder, Roy and Loujuana Worstall, and David McKay—for all their support and, most of all, their patience while we worked on the book.

Senior Associate Editor: Joanne M. Dauksewicz
Project Editor: Helen F. Bronk
Production/Design Coordinator: Jennifer Waddell
Manufacturing Coordinator: Christine McGriff
Marketing Manager: Bob Wolcott

Cover: James Gibson, DESIGNHEADS; Tony Scarpetta, photography.

Printed in the U.S.A.

Student Edition ISBN: 0-395-66038-6

Instructor's Edition ISBN: 0-395-73720-6

Library of Congress Catalog Card Number: 94-76552

123456789–CS–99 98 97 96 95

Contents

Preface

This text is designed to help you become successful in proofreading, whether that proofreading is for someone else's communications or for your own written work, on the job, in school, or at home. We believe that written work should be professional and error-free in order to reflect the writer's true abilities and his or her time spent writing, editing, and proofreading. We also believe that the only way to become proficient at proofreading is through *practice.* Just as with sports, music, or anything else, it takes practice to become skilled. Working carefully through this text, you will receive plenty of practice proofreading.

This text features exercises that are based on the kind of writing that people proofread on a daily basis: letters, reports, resumes, memorandums, news releases, in-house publications, itineraries, etc. We believe these exercises to be far superior to the type based on a collection of unrelated sentences. After all, people don't usually write or read such collections of random sentences. We have also sifted through volumes of grammar rules and listed only those rules we thought would be used most often. All of the rules are demonstrated through examples to guide you through this maze called the English language.

In the exercises, you will note that a variety of topics are covered to maintain your interest as well as to open new avenues of information. The historical and general-information reports are true. You will also notice some real proofreading "demons" that we built into the exercises to stretch your abilities. These proofreading challenges will require you to really think about what you are reading, helping to develop and sharpen your skills all the more.

Please note that paragraphs within the text may be hyphenated at the first line or last full line. While this is contrary to the rules presented in this book, it is a standard practice for book publishers. However, hyphenation within the exercises follows the rules applied to business documents; hyphenating the first line or the last full line should be considered an error. In addition, margins within exercises will appear much smaller than normal. This has been done to allow the type to be set as large as possible and allow room to add proofreaders' marks.

Special Features

The book contains many special features to enhance learning:

- Exercises are arranged according to a cumulative approach, building upon skills already mastered and allowing for continual review and plenty of practice.
- Three out of four unit reviews are designed as mini-simulations. Packets of related business documents, such as letters, memos, news releases, and itineraries, are provided so you can refer to them for accuracy. These mini-simulations also give a realistic view of typical business communications.
- All correspondence is dated for the year 1999, and a calendar is provided inside the back cover so that you can verify dates and days in checking for accuracy.
- Different typefaces and type sizes are used for the exercises to simulate the kinds of materials that would require proofreading in real life.
- Throughout the text, proofreading pointers highlight proofreading trouble spots and provide helpful hints for dealing with them.
- Rules are listed at the beginning of each chapter for easy reference.
- Each exercise contains a numbered ruler so that errors can be quickly located during class.

Acknowledgments

We would like to thank the Muskingum Area Technical College "family," especially the administration for its support and the students for class testing this text. We would also like to thank Joanne Dauksewicz and Helen Bronk at Houghton Mifflin Company for their guidance, patience, and suggestions. A special thank you to Martha Mahan who got us both into this in the first place.

We wish to acknowledge the following people in particular for their special assistance in reviewing the manuscript: Susan M. Avila, South Hills Business School; Barbara Blaisdell, Bryant & Stratton Business Institute; Lynne M. Erickson, Davenport College/Lansing Community College; Emily Eubanks, Aquinas College at Milton; Joy Hanel, South Central Technical College; Ruth M. Mackiewicz, Katherine Gibbs School; Glenna Oakley, Francis Tuttle Vo-Tech Center; Joyce Albin Poskozim, Northwestern Business College; and Pam Winkler, Hammel College.

S.A.S.
C.C.W.

CHAPTER 1

Proofreading Skills and Symbols

CHAPTER OUTLINE

We never get a second chance to make a first impression. People often form their first impressions of us in response to some written communication—perhaps a letter of inquiry, an application form, or a memo. Our daily communications are extensions of who we are, and for that reason we need to be careful to present ourselves in the very best light. Inaccurate communications give others the impression that we either don't care or are incapable of doing better. Neither impression is desirable, socially or professionally.

Consider the countless job applications that are discarded because of careless mistakes. Would an employer be justified in feeling that a sloppy application blank is an indication of careless work? Apparently so, if we can extend the findings of a recent study: People who did not use standard English competently in a job interview had shorter interviews and fewer job offers than those who did. If the job was offered, the salary was sometimes 35 percent less.

Let's say that you do land the job of your dreams; you still need to remember that your written memo, cover letter, or report will cross the "big" desk only once for the first-time impression. A finished piece of writing reflects the ability, accuracy, attitude, and dependability of its creator. How many promotions would be available to an employee who was inaccurate in a memo concerning a critical due date for a government contract bid? How far could an individual advance if he or she had difficulty in projecting a professional image in a written report? For that matter, how far would the very idea get if the report was ill-prepared and confused the reader?

Proofreading allows us to polish carefully any written communication. It gives us a chance to make a good first impression every time.

Poor proofreading is a reflection on every person connected with the document. The ability, accuracy, attitude, and dependability of the writer are certainly in question. The same can be said of the secretary who types it; the boss who supervises the employee who wrote it; the president of the company, who is ultimately responsible for the employees; and the chairman of the board of directors, who hires the president. Errors in written communication can affect even the integrity of the business itself.

Consider, for example, an enterprising student who wants to earn extra money by typing papers. The student prepares an advertisement that appears on the bulletin board and offers to do typing:

Typing at reasonable rates.
No job to big or to small.

Some students may not catch the errors in the advertisement, but those who do would be wise to avoid this typist. Reasonable rates would be welcome, but the accuracy of the typist would be questionable.

Definition of Proofreading

The traditional job of the proofreader was to read a document looking for typographical errors by comparing it against an original version. Today, the duties of a proofreader go beyond that. Proofreading, by definition, is finding and correcting *errors of any type* in a document.

A proofreader is responsible for identifying errors in content, grammar, usage, mechanics (such as punctuation, word division, capitalization, and number usage), omission, and spelling.

Proofreading is not editing copy for style (the way the ideas are presented). The writing style is the responsibility of the writer, not the proofreader. A writer who is also the proofreader should first edit the document for style and then check it for accuracy. As you work through this text, you will be asked to locate proofreading errors, not make stylistic changes.

Preparing to Proofread: Tools of the Trade

Every trade has a set of tools, and proofreading is no exception. Before you start, you should have these items within easy reach.

Calculator	A calculator is useful for checking totals and calculations in documents.
Calendar	A calendar is essential for verifying dates in documents.
Colored Pens	Proofreaders use colored pens instead of pencils or black pens because proofreading marks need to be easily seen. Black ink or pencil will

PROOFREADING POINTER

Keep all your proofreading tools together in a convenient location in your desk. Your employer will appreciate the time you save, and you will appreciate the aggravation you avoid.

blend in with the typed text already on the page. Errors need to stand out so that the person making corrections will not miss them.

Dictionary	Any standard desk dictionary will give information on word usage, spelling, and word division.
Files and Catalogs	In organizations that frequently use catalog numbers or stock numbers, it is important to have access to those numbers to check their accuracy.
Index Cards	Some proofreaders use an index card in much the same manner as a ruler. Index cards are a little wider and effectively block information below the line being read.
Reference Manual	All proofreaders need to master as many of the rules associated with mechanics and usage as possible, but there will always be questions. A good reference manual is a must when you're not absolutely sure.
Removable Self-Adhesive Notes	These notes are handy for writing a question to the writer if the copy is otherwise clean. Many proofreaders also use them to remind themselves to check something in the copy.
Ruler	A colored ruler is helpful in marking the place when proofreading.
Thesaurus	A thesaurus is helpful when you are trying to find alternative wording.
Word-Division Book	Looking up word division is much quicker in a small word-division book such as *The Word Book II.*
ZIP Code Directory	A correct ZIP Code is an essential part of an address. The U.S. Postal Service estimates that correspondence could take from two days to a week longer to reach its destination if no ZIP Code is given.

Methods of Proofreading

There are many methods of proofreading, but three especially effective techniques are **comparison proofreading, team proofreading,** and **typewriter proofreading.** Most successful proofreaders find that no one system is totally effective for every type of material and that one reading will not catch all errors. When you polish a piece of furniture or a car, you go over the surface many times until you get the desired result; the same is true with proofreading.

Comparison Proofreading The most commonly used method of proofreading is comparison. When comparing, you place the original and the second version side by side. The copy you will be correcting should be on the side of the hand you use for writing. Read each word or punctuation mark in the original and then check to see that the word or punctuation mark is in the other version. Follow this procedure for the entire document, going back and forth from the original to the second copy.

Some proofreaders like to use one finger, an index card, or a ruler to mark their place in the original while they mark corrections with a colored pen on the copy.

Team Proofreading The team technique is used in proofreading as a way to check technical materials. One person reads the copy aloud word by word, including the punctuation marks, while a second person checks the document for accuracy. Team proofreading is a very accurate way to check copy, but it has some drawbacks. Because it involves the time of two proofreaders, it doubles the cost of proofreading time. In addition, the noise it generates can be a major factor in a crowded, busy office.

Typewriter Proofreading Another method of proofreading is used on a typewriter. The paper bail, which usually has a ruler printed on it, is used as a place marker as the typist reads through the typed document, checking it line by line. Since it is difficult to align the type after the paper is removed from the typewriter, it is important to check the document carefully while it is still in the machine.

These three methods of comparing one document with another will help the proofreader to achieve accuracy, provided the original is correct. Keep in mind, however, that finding and correcting errors in the original are also the responsibility of the proofreader. It doesn't matter whether the writer or the proofreader missed the error; it's still an error!

Proofreading on the Screen

With the widespread use of word processing software and equipment, proofreading on the computer screen has become a major concern. Proofreading on a screen is an extremely difficult skill to master since the images on the screen are not sharp, only part of the document is visible, and the human eye can read only a portion of the screen at a time. Even experienced proofreaders find they are not always accurate when proofreading on the screen.

Spell-checking programs have further complicated proofreading on the screen. Writers use these programs and feel secure that they are leaving few errors in their documents. Unfortunately, this sense of security is often misleading. Consider the following passage:

```
Several employees want to reed there pro-
duction results before the formal presenta-
tion two the Bored of Trustees. Therefore,
the manger asked that for copies be pre-
pared for oily distribution. The company
will than publish it's findings sew that
the general public will no the results.
```

The spell checker did not find anything wrong with this passage. (There are 11 errors.)

The key to successful proofreading while using a computer is not to rely on checking only the screen. Certainly the writer should scan the screen for obvious errors and correct them. The screen scan, however, does not eliminate the need for printing a copy of the document and *proofreading the paper copy for final accuracy.*

Proofreaders' Marks

Proofreaders' symbols are used to mark errors in copy, and, through the years, a set of standard proofreading marks has evolved. By mastering and using these marks, a proofreader ensures that other employees will be able to correct the copy if the original proofreader is unable to do the revision.

CHART 1.1

ACTION	SYMBOL	MARKED TEXT	CORRECTED TEXT
Transpose letter *(change the order)*	∼	hte	the
Transpose words		the in	in the
Stet *(leave as original)*	....	June 12, 1992 stet	June 12, 1992
Editor's query *(ask the editor)*	ed?	Tuesday at 9 p.m. / Tuesday at 9 a.m. (ed. a.m. or p.m.)	Tuesday at 9 p.m.
Boldface	∼∼∼	Cheryl Smith	**Cheryl Smith**
Paragraph	¶	hope you will be able to attend the ceremony.¶ I have also been invited.	hope you will be able to attend the ceremony. I have also been invited.
Capitalize a letter	≡	wednesday	Wednesday
Capitalize an entire word	═	Planning	PLANNING
Lowercase a letter	/	Average	average
Lowercase an entire word	/‾‾	ESSENTIALLY	essentially
Run in, no return	⁀	I would like to / send you	I would like to send you
Spell out	○	Nov.	November

EXERCISE 1–A

Directions: Compare the memorandum on this page with the memorandum on the next page. Using the standard proofreaders' marks listed in Chart 1.1, indicate the needed changes on the comparison copy. The memorandum on this page is correct.

TO: All Full-time Faculty

FROM: Dr. Elizabeth Justice, Vice President of Instruction

DATE: August 2, 1999

SUBJECT: Training Session for Fall Advising

Please report for a full day's training session for fall advising on August 15. We will be having a continental breakfast of fruit, rolls, juices, coffee, and teas from 8:30 to 9:30 a.m. During this time we will also introduce the new faculty.

The morning guest speakers and their topics are as follows:

Sam Donnelly	**Increased Fees**
Jerry Mather	**Financial Assistance**
Martha Cook	**Beginning the Application Process**
Juanita Ferrer	**The Role of Student Services**
Grace Peng	**New and Old Forms**
Steve Wessel	**Placement Testing and Advising**
Sarah Knight	**Special Problems**

Lunch at noon will be on your own.

At 1 p.m. David Wells will be conducting the afternoon workshop after President Harding opens the session. We hope that the closing remarks will occur around 3 p.m.

In preparation for this important meeting, please read the enclosed materials. Also remember to bring your copy of *The Adviser's Handbook,* which was updated and sent to you this past spring.

We here at the college hope you have had a restful summer and are looking forward to another new school year. See you at 9 a.m. on August 15!

ll

Enclosure

COMPARISON COPY 1-A

TO: All Full-time Faculty

FROM: Dr. Elizabeth Justice, Vice President of Instruction

DATE: August 2, 1999

SUBJECT: Training Session for Fall Advising

Plaese report for a full day's training session for fall advising on Aug. 15. We will be having a continental breakfast of fruit, rolls, juices, coffee, and teas from 8:30 to 9:30 a.m. During this time we will also introduce the new faculty.

The morning guest speakers and their topics are as follows:

Sam Donnelly	Increased fees
Jerry Mather	Financial Assistance
Martha Cook	Beginning the Application Process
Juanita Ferrer	The Role of Student Services
Grace Peng	New and Old forms
Steve Wessel	Placement Testing and Advising
Sarah Knight	Special Problems

Lunch at NOON will be on your own.

At 1 p.m. David Wells will be conducting the afternoon workshop after President Harding opens the session. we hope that the closing remarks will occur around 3 p.m.

In preparation for this important meeting, read please teh enclosed materials. Also remember to bring your copy of *The Adviser's Handbook,* which was updated and sent to you this past Spring.

We here at the college hope you have had a restful Summer and are looking forward to another new school year. See you at 9 a.m. on Aug. 15!

ll

Enclosure

CHART 1.2

ACTION	SYMBOL	MARKED TEXT	CORRECTED TEXT
Insert letter	x ^	maling (i inserted)	mailing
Insert word	xxxx ^	at time (the inserted)	at the time
Insert period	⊙	Mr⊙Smith	Mr. Smith
Insert required space	□	on April □ 21	on April 21
Insert comma	^,	If we go, we will find	If we go, we will find
Insert semicolon	^;	Sue Jane, president, Bill Combs, vice president	Sue Jane, president; Bill Combs, vice president
Insert colon	(:)	7(:)30 p.m.	7:30 p.m.
Insert a line space	#—	Winnington, Delaware # Moretown, Texas	Winnington, Delaware Moretown, Texas
Insert space	# ^	inthe	in the

EXERCISE 1-B

Directions: Compare the report on this page with the report on the next page. Using the standard proofreaders' marks listed in Chart 1.2, indicate the needed changes on the comparison copy. The report on this page is correct.

PLATE TECTONICS

Plate tectonics is a geological theory that explains the shifting of the earth's masses. This theory, developed in the 1960s, explains that the earth is formed on enormous shifting slabs called plates. There are three types of plates: divergent boundaries, convergent boundaries, and transform fault boundaries. In the divergent boundary areas, molten rock is rising up between slowly separating plates; the molten rock then hardens and forms new oceanic crusts along the already present oceanic ridges. Convergent boundaries, the second type of plates, are found at the edge of deep oceanic trenches; the edge of the massive plates simply breaks off and falls so far down that it melts and becomes a part of the molten rock. Finally, transform fault boundaries are rather passive and are described as plates merely rubbing and shifting past each other.

Plate tectonics is the basis of modern geology and helps explain the presence of the great ocean basins as well as the layers of the earth. Even the explanation of the migration of humans and animals along the ancient pathways between the continents can be more completely explained by the theory of plate tectonics.

COMPARISON COPY 1–B

PLATE TECTONICS

Plate tectonics is a geological theory that explains shifting of the earth's masses. This theory developed in the 1960s, explains that the earth is formed on enormous shifting slabs called plates. There are threetypes of plates divergent boundaries, convergent boundaries, ad transform fault boundaries. In the divergent boundary areas, molten rock is rising up between slowly separating plates the molten rock then hardens and forms new oceanic crusts along the already present oceanic ridges. Convergent boundaries, the second type of plates are found at the edge of deep oceanic trenches; the edge of the massive plates simply breaks of and falls so far down that it melts and becomes part of the molten rock Finally, transform fault boundaries are rather passive and are described as plates merely rubbing and shifting past each other.

Platetectonics is the basis of modern geology and helps explain the presence of the great ocean basins as well as the layers of the earth. Even the explanation of the migration of humans and animals alng the ancient pathways between the continents can be more completely explained by the thery of plate tectonics.

EXERCISE 1–C

Directions: Compare the bibliography on this page with the one on the next page. All underlined material in the handwritten copy should be italicized *(slanted)* in the comparison copy. Using the standard proofreaders' marks listed in Charts 1.1 and 1.2, indicate the needed changes in the comparison copy. This page is correct.

BIBLIOGRAPHY

Ansel, Mary Beth. *The Care and Feeding of Your Computer.* Boston: Houghton Mifflin, 1998.

Banard, Westley, and Julia Jenkins, eds. *To PC or Not to PC: That Is the Question.* Englewood Cliffs: Prentice-Hall, 1994.

Dillon, Maria. *Which Word Processing Package Is for You?* Vol. 2. New York: Macmillan, 1997.

Goodale, Ralph, and Sam Lamont. "Controlling Viruses." *The New York Times* April 1, 1999: 2.

Manoff, Willis. *The War Against Big Blue.* New York: Harper & Row, 1998.

Priest, Pat, and Marsha Reynolds. "Have You Had a Mac Attack Today?" *Consumer Reports* September 1999: 791–798.

Timmons, Joseph. *Reasoning Behind the Options.* Boston: Houghton Mifflin, 1998.

———. "What You Really Need Now and in the Future." *The Bulletin for Computer Lovers.* 72:3 (March 13, 1998): 201–203.

West, Cranston L. "A Future Look Into the World of Computers." *Smithsonian* 27 (May 1997): 47–51.

COMPARISON COPY 1-C

Bibliography

Ansel, MaryBeth. *The Care and Feeding fo Your Computer*. Boston: Houghton Mifflin, 1998.

Banard, Westley, and Julia Jenkins, ed. *To PC or Not to PC That Is the Question*, Englewood Cliffs: PrenticeHall, 1994.

Dillon, Maria, *Which Word Processing Package is for You?* Vol. 2. New York: Macmillan, 1997.

Goodale, Ralph and Sam Lamont, "Controlling Viruses." *the New York Times* April 1, 1999: 2.

Manoff, Willis. *The War Against Big Blue.* New York: Harper Row, 1998.

Priest, Pat, and Marsha Reynolds. "Have You Had a Mac Attack Today?" *Consumer Reports* September 1999: 791-789.

Timmons, Joseph. *Reasoning Behind the Options*. Boston: Houghton Mifflin, 1998.

———, "What You Really Need Now and the Future," *The Bulletin For Computer Lovers*. 72:3 (March 3, 1998): 201-203.

West, Cranston L., "A Future Look into the World of Computers." *Smithsonian*. 29 (May 1997): 47-51.

CHART 1.3

ACTION	SYMBOL	MARKED TEXT	CORRECTED TEXT
Insert question mark		Will you call me	Will you call me?
Insert exclamation mark		Caution	Caution!
Insert hyphen		7 foot fence	7-foot fence
Insert dash		Red, blue, green these colors will	Red, blue, green—these colors will
Insert quotation marks		article entitled Never on Sunday	article entitled "Never on Sunday"
Insert underscore		The word never is never used.	The word <u>never</u> is never used.
Insert italics	ital	The word never is never used.	The word *never* is never used.
Insert parentheses		Can we afford the expense?	(Can we afford the expense?)
Insert apostrophe		its	it's

EXERCISE 1-D

Directions: Compare the résumé on this page with the résumé on the next page. Using the standard proofreaders' marks listed in Chart 1.3, indicate the needed changes on the comparison copy. The résumé on this page is correct.

Mary Wilson

2386 Winstona Place, Zanesville, Ohio 43701 Ph: (111) 555-3465

Career Objective

Eager, energetic **Office Specialist** desires to climb ladder into management

Education

A.A.B. Business Administration—Microcomputer Applications
Mason Area Technical College, Zanesville, Ohio
GPA 3.65
23 credit hours in computer-related courses

Experience

6/91–8/93 Work-study, Business Division, MATC
Duties: 1. DTP—Aldus PageMaker
2. WP—WordPerfect

6/91–9/91 McDonald's (Cambridge, Ohio)—full-time customer service representative
Duties: 1. customer service
2. food preparation

5/87–8/88 McDonald's—promoted to assistant manager
Duties: 1. assign crew positions
2. prepare cash flow reports
3. prepare closing reports

8/85–5/87 Maternity Leave

8/84–8/85 McDonald's—customer service representative
Duties: 1. customer service
2. closing procedures

Activities

10/91–6/93 Business Professionals of America
Active Member
President MATC chapter (92–93)

1/91–6/92 Selected for Student Ambassadors Club to promote the college.

1993 Who's Who in American Junior Colleges

Honors and Awards

Named to Dean's List—MATC
Placed in Business Professionals of America Competitions

State 1993	1st Emblem Building Team
	2nd Parliamentary Procedure Team
	2nd Employment Skills
Nationals 1993	2nd Emblem Building Team
	6th Parliamentary Procedure Team

Community Service

Volunteer for Red Cross Bloodmobile—O'Leary Branch (1990–93)
Basketball Coach for Special Olympics Team

References Available on Request

COMPARISON COPY 1-D

Mary Wilson 2386 Winstona Place, Zanesville, Ohio 43701 Ph: (111) 555-3465

Career Objective

Eager, energetic **Office** Specialist desires to climb latter into management

Education

A.A.B. Business Administration—Microcomputer Applications
Mason Area Technical College, Zanesville, Ohio
GPA 3.65
23 credit hours in computer-related courses

Experience

6/91–8/93 Work-study, Business Division, MATC
Duties: 1. DTP—Aldus PageMaker
2. WP—WordPerfect

6/91–9/91 McDonald's, (Cambridge, Ohio)—fulltime customer service representative
Duties: 1. customer service
2. food preparation

5/87–8/88 McDonald's—promoted to assistant manager
Duties: 1. assign crew positions
2. prepare cash flow report
3. prepare closing reports

8/85–5/87 Matemity Leave

8/84–8/85 McDonald's—customer service represenative
Duties: 1. customer service
2. closing procedures

Activities

10/91–6/93 Business Professionals of America
Active Member
President MATC chapter (92–93)

1/91–6/92 Selected for Student Ambassadors Club to promote the College.

1993 Who's Who in American Junior Colleges

Honors and Awards

Named to Dean's List—MATC
Placed in Business Professionals of America Competitions
State 1993 1st Emblem Building Team
2nd Parlimentary Procedure Team
2nd Employment Skills
Nationals 1993 2nd Emblem Building Team
6th Parlimentary Procedure Team

Community Service

Volunteer for Red Cross Blood Mobile—O'Leary Branch (1990–93)
Basketball Coach for Special Olympics Team

References available on Request

EXERCISE 1-E

Directions: Compare the report on this page with the report on the next page. Using standard proofreaders' marks listed in Charts 1.1 through 1.3, indicate the needed changes on the comparison copy. The report on this page is correct.

SUDDEN INFANT DEATH SYNDROME

Sudden Infant Death Syndrome (SIDS), more commonly referred to as "crib death," is a baffling and incurable disease. What happens is tragic: The parents carefully put the infant to bed, and the next morning the child is found dead. Research suggests that infants whose parents are under twenty are at greater risk, and it seems that most cases occur in the winter with the child's possibly having a slight cold.

Even with the many cases that have been documented, the medical world is not certain what causes SIDS. One theory, called the viral disease theory, suggests that the common cold acts on the nervous system, causing the vocal chords to have spasms and cut off the air supply. A sleep-apnea or breath-holding theory suggests that the developing central nervous system fails to send properly spaced breathing signals. The result is that the child simply stops breathing.

To date, the most common procedure to treat this disease is to use an electronic device. The apparatus is attached to the sleeping child to help monitor the child's breathing. An alarm will sound to wake the parents when the child's measured breathing stops. This only alerts the parents to proceed with CPR and does nothing to help deter the causes or help cure the disease.

Can you imagine going to bed each night, desperately listening for a buzzer to alert you that your child is no longer breathing? Let us hope that the medical community can quickly find a cure for this tragic disease!

COMPARISON COPY 1-E

SUDDEN INFANT DEATH SYNDROME

Sudden Infant Deth Syndrome SIDS, more commonly refered to as crib death, is a baffling and incurable disease. What happens is tragic: The parents carefully put the infant to bed and the next morning the child is found dead. Research suggests that infants whose parents are under twenty are at greater risk, and seems that most cases occur in the winter with the child's possibly having a slight cold.

Even with the many cases that have been documented, the medical world is not certain what causes sids. One theory, called the viral disease theory, suggests that the common cold acts on the nervous system,causing the vocal chords to have spasms and cut off the air supply. A sleep-APNEA ro breath-holding theory suggests that the developing central nervous system fails to send properly spaced breathing signals. The result is that the child simply stops breathing

To date the most common procedure to treat this disease is to use an electronic device. The Apparatus is attached the to sleeping child to help monitor the child's breathing. An alarm will sound to wake the parents when the child's measured breathing stops. This only alerts the parents to proceed with cpr and does nothing to help deter the causes or help cure the disease.

Can you imagine going to bed each night, desperately listening for a buzzer to alert you that you child is no longer breathing Let us hope that the medical community can quickly find a cure for this tragic disease

CHART 1.4

ACTION	SYMBOL	MARKED COPY	CORRECTED COPY
Delete a character		where	where
Delete a line		Washington University Davis College	Washington University Davis College
Delete a space		bed room	bedroom
Delete a word		the very helpful teacher	the helpful teacher
Delete an underscore		Marsington, Maine	Marsington, Maine
Delete a letter and substitute a new letter		Allen Gray	Allen Grey
Delete a word and substitute a new word		with the help of David Nichols	with the help of Marvin Nichols
Delete space(s) but leave one space		at the time	at the time
Delete and close up		Master Plan	MasterPlan

EXERCISE 1-F

Directions: Compare the memo on this page with the memo on the next page. Using the standard proofreaders' marks listed on Chart 1.4, indicate needed changes on the comparison copy. The memo on this page is correct.

MEMORANDUM

TO: Allen Jocobsen

FROM: Kristy Dalley

DATE: June 30, 1999

SUBJECT: New Employees

I am pleased to announce the addition of Millie Brokowski to the staff of the *Daily Independent*. A former employee of the *Detroit Free Press* with 16 years of experience in advertising layout, Millie will be in charge of the layout of our new advertising insert appearing in the Wednesday evening edition.

Also joining the staff is Ed Ames, a recent graduate of Clovis Technical College. Ed will be in charge of the graphic design of the new insert. Ed majored in graphic design at Clovis, and he has worked for our firm for the past three years on a part-time basis.

Both of these employees should help make the new advertising insert a success.

COMPARISON COPY 1-F

MEMORANDUM

TO: Allen Jocobsen

FROM: Kristy Dalley

DATE: June 30, 1999

SUBJECT: New Employees

I am pleased to announce the adddition of Millie Brokowski to the staff of the *Daily Independant.* A former employee of the *Detroit Free Press* with 16 years of experience in advertising layout, Millie will be in charge of the layout of our new advertising insert appearing in the Wednesday evening eddition.

Also joining the staff is Ed Ames, a recent graduate of Clovis Techniical College. Ed will be in charge of the graphic design of the new insert. Ed majored in graphic design at Clovis, and he has worked for our firm for the past three years on a part-time basis.

Both of these employees should help make the new advertising insect a success.

EXERCISE 1-G

Directions: Compare the letter on this page with the letter on the next page. Using the standard proofreaders' marks listed on Charts 1.1 through 1.4, indicate needed changes on the comparison copy. The letter on this page is correct.

July 24, 1999

Mr. Brian Teague
Handyman's Haven
348 Briar Avenue
Copaigue, NY 11726

Dear Mr. Teague:

In the past, I have completely believed in the durability of your Handyman's Helper garden tools. In fact, I have almost the complete line! However, my belief is weakening.

Two weeks ago I received your improved roto-weasel hoe, and upon the third use one of the tines broke off completely. There were no rocks in the path, and I certainly did not misuse the hoe in any way. If that weren't enough, my Handyman's sprinkler head sprang a leak. Although I have used this for four years, it has a ten-year guarantee, as you recall.

I would like both items replaced. I am enclosing a copy of the original sales receipts as well as copies of the warranties. Please note that the part number for the sprinkler head is 47925L, and it is the XL204 series. The hoe is 67203(RWH).

When you send the replacements, I do not expect to pay any additional shipping costs. If you wish to inspect the damaged items, I would be glad to take them to the local authorized dealer here in Deer Park; but if you wish me to mail them, you will need to pay for the shipping.

I look forward to their prompt replacement and hope to be able, once again, to favorably "advertise" your line of garden implements to my friends and neighbors. Thank you!

Sincerely,

Ms. Susan B. Clark

Enclosure

COMPARISON COPY 1-G

July 24, 1999

Mr. Brian Teague
Handyman's Haven
348 Briar Avenue
Copaigue, NY 11726

Dear Mr. Teague

In the past, I have completely believed in the durability of your Handymans Helper Garden Tools. In facts, I have almost the complete line. However, my beleif is weakening.

Two weeks ago I received your improved roto- weasel hoe, and upon the third use one of the tines broke completely off. There were no rocks in the path and I certainly did not mis use the hoe in any way. If that werent enough, my Handiman's Sprinkler head sprang a leak. All though I have used this four for years, it has a ten-ear guarantee , as you recall.

I would like both items replaced. I am enclosing a copy of the original sales receipts as well as copies of the warranties. Please note that the part number four the sprinkler head is 47925L, and it is the XL204 series. The Hoe is 67203RWH.

When you send the replacements, I do not expect to pay any additional shippping costs. If you wish to inspect the damaged items, I would be glad to take them to the local authorized dealer here in Deer Pk. but if you wish me to mail them, you will need to pay for the shipping.

I look forward to their prompt replacement and hope to be able, ounce again, to favorably advertise your line of garden implements to my friends and neighbors.

Thank you

Sincerely,

Susan B. Clark

CHART 1.5

ACTION	SYMBOL	MARKED TEXT	CORRECTED COPY
Indent	☒	Now is the opportunity we have all	Now is the opportunity we have all
Move left	[	[Otterbein College Smith College Muskingum College	Otterbein College Smith College Muskingum College
Move right	]	] Otterbein College Smith College Muskingum College	Otterbein College Smith College Muskingum College
Center text]	[	] Red River Song [	Red River Song
Raise text ***(Superscript)***	✓	Footnotes are placed at the end of the text.1	Footnotes are placed at the end of the text.[1]
Lower text ***(Subscript)***	^	Some elements are found in H20.	Some elements are found in H_2O.
Align	||	Carter Training Center University of Kansas Allen Career Center	Carter Training Center University of Kansas Allen Career Center
Single space	SS	WORDS SS A Matter of Meaning	WORDS A Matter of Meaning
Double space	DS	WORDS DS A Matter of Meaning	WORDS A Matter of Meaning
Triple space	TS	WORDS TS A Matter of Meaning	WORDS A Matter of Meaning
Quadruple space	QS	WORDS QS A Matter of Meaning	WORDS A Matter of Meaning

EXERCISE 1-H

Directions: Compare the second column with the first column, marking any changes with standard proofreaders' marks listed in Chart 1.5. The text in the left column is correct.

1.

Thank you for your order for 7 dozen Meridan Smaltz portraits. We will be happy to notify you when the material arrives in our distribution center.

2.

Martha Davisen, executive director of Klingerhoff, Inc., has announced that the following individuals have been promoted to supervisory positions:

Kit Anderson
Allen Jadwin
Arthur Merrezandra
Linda Smith

3.

Wanted: Mature individual for house sitting in Victorian home on Cape Cod. Responsibilities include the following:

Lawn Care
Pool Cleaning
General Maintenance
Dog Walking and Feeding

4.

Marion Duane, noted financier, remarried in 1993 to Ellen Janiston of Harrisville, Texas. According to <u>Know-It-All Encyclopedia</u>, Duane is the wealthiest man in Arkansas.[1]

1.

Thank you for your order for 7 dozen Meridan Smaltz portraits. We will be happy to notify you when the material arrives in our distribution center.

2.

Martha Davisen, executive director of Klingerhoff, Inc., has announced that the following individuals have been promoted to supervisory positions:

Kit Anderson
Allen Jadwin
Arthur Merrezandra
Linda Smith

3.

Wanted: Mature individual for house sitting in Victorian home on Cape Cod. Responsibilities include the following:

Lawn Care
Pool Cleaning
General
Maintenance
Dog Walking and
Feeding

4.

Marion Duane, noted financier, remarried in 1993 to Ellen Janiston of Harrisville, Texas. According to Know-It-All Encyclopedia, Duane is the wealthiest man in Arkansas.1

EXERCISE 1-1

Directions: Compare the manuscript on this page with the manuscript on the next page. Using the standard proofreaders' marks listed previously in this chapter, mark any needed changes on the comparison copy. This page is correct.

ARCHERY

The phrase *bow and arrow* brings to mind either the Old West and the Native American or Robin Hood and his Merry Men. However, the origin of the bow and arrow goes farther back in history than Medieval England (476–1453); references to the bow and arrow are found in the Bible as well as in the literature and art remaining from ancient civilizations. The Greeks and Romans used the bow as a standard military weapon. The Egyptians were best known for their mounted archers, but other groups of the time were also versed in "horse archery." Native American groups were known for their skills in the use of the bow and arrow for hunting, and their hunting skill was enhanced by their ability to track game.

Although there are several types of bows, the plain hand bow is by far the best known. The bow is a single piece of wood shaped so a string can be tied between the ends. The arrow has a notch on the end that fits onto the string. The string is pulled back with the arrow notched on the string and then released. The amount of force it takes to draw the arrow back so just the tip of the arrow extends beyond the bow is called the "pounds pull."

Before the Norman Conquest in Europe, bows and arrows were considered unimportant as military weapons. Most of the bows were short—3 to 5 feet—and were used primarily for hunting. It wasn't until late in the twelfth century that the longbow evolved. Up to 6 feet long with a pull between 80 and 140 pounds, the longbow was used extensively by the legendary Robin Hood. The longbow was considered an important military weapon and continued to maintain its popularity until the mid-1500s.

While the bow and arrow have been replaced by other weapons in today's military arsenal, archery as a sport has grown in popularity. The strength of the bow can be modified to match the strength of the archer, making archery a sport for people of all ages and strengths. Competitions in both target archery and field (hunting) archery are popular with enthusiasts and keep the "romance" of the bow and arrow alive today.

COMPARISON COPY 1-1

ARCHERY

The phrase *bow and arrow* brings to mind either the old west and the Native American Indians or Robin Hood and his Merry Men. However, the origin of the bow and arrow goes farther back in history than Medieval England (476-1453); references to the bow and arrow are found in the Bible as well as in the literature and art remaining from ancient civilizations. The Greeks and Romans used the bow as a standard military weapon. The Egyptians were the best known for their mounted archers, but other groups of the time were also versed in "horse archery." Native American groups were known for their skills in the use of the bow and arrow for huntings, and their "hunting skill" was enhanced by their ability to track game.

Although there are several types of bows, the plain hand bow is by far the best known. The bow is a single piece of wood shaped so a string can be tied between the ends. The arrow has a notch on the end to fit onto the string. The string is then pulled back with the arrow notched on the string and released. The amount of force it takes to draw the arrow back so just the tip of the arrow extends beyond the bow is called the "pounds pull."

Before the Norman Conquest in Europe, bows and arrows were considered unimportant as military weapons. Most of the bows were short—3 to 5 feet—and were used primarily for hunting. It wasn't until late in the twelfth century that the longbow had developed. Up to 6 feet long with a pull between 80 and 140 pounds, the longbow was used extensively by the legendary Robin Hood. The long bow was considered an important military weapon and continued to maintain its popularity until the mid 1500s.

While the bow and arrow have been replaced by other weapons in today's military arsenal, archery as a sport has grown in popularity. The strength of the bow can be modified to match the strength of the archer, making archery a sport for people of all ages and strengths. Competitions in both target archery and field (hunting) archery are popular with enthusiasts and keep the "romance" of the bow alive today.

CHAPTER

2

Reading for Meaning

CHAPTER OUTLINE

When we communicate, we want our messages to be received as accurately as possible—we want the receivers to understand and to remember, even if only briefly, what we have communicated. Our chances of achieving this goal are significantly better if we are logical. For example, a manager could request a review of Reports 101, 103, 102, and 104, but the message would click in the employee's mind more clearly and accurately (to say nothing of more quickly) if the manager requested a review of Reports 101 through 104. Similarly, if someone asked us to describe a piece of equipment, we would have a much better chance of gaining shared meaning if we described that piece of equipment by using some type of logical order—how it looked from top to bottom or how it operated from the beginning of the process to the end. We could draw a more complete picture of our favorite room in someone else's brain if we described the room by using a systematic pattern rather than by skipping randomly from object to object and from side to side. In other words, good communications require the use of logic and organization. Proofreaders polish communications by reading for meaning.

Consistency, Logic, and Order

Proofreaders must be on guard for more than merely an accurate duplication of an original document. Remember, proofreading goes beyond comparing two copies to find typographical errors. As a proofreader, you must step back and inspect the finished writing from many angles. The writing must be correct in grammar and usage, and it must be accurate in content. It also must be consistent, logical, and orderly. Everything must work together if the reader is to receive a positive first impression and comprehend the message accurately and completely. You don't want the reader to become confused or side-tracked.

Reading for meaning means watching for errors in three general categories: consistency, logic, and order. Errors in consistency present a special challenge to the proofreader when reading for meaning. These errors could include inconsistent use of abbreviations, unmatched headings, and styles in dates and phone numbers. Errors in logic are pieces of information that simply don't make sense, such as February 30 or a two-hundred-year-old man's celebrating a birthday. Errors in order could be lists given in incorrect numerical or alphabetical order.

Avoiding Sexist Language

Reading for meaning also means reading with an "ear" open for sexist or biased wording. We live in a society struggling to overcome prejudices, and each of us can contribute by being sensitive to the feelings of others. We need to be aware that words are powerful instruments that affect personal and professional lives. When used negatively, words can limit, define, and even lower our impressions of people, careers, and actions. As members of society, we have an opportunity and an obligation to use words that are free of prejudice. A good proofreader develops an eye for these errors. Changing *salesman* to *sales representative, chairman* to *chairperson,* and *mailman* to *mail carrier* does not modify a writer's intentions. Changing phrases like *men and girls* to *men and women* allows a clear balance in the relationship. In a description of a family tree, *ancestors* is a better word than *forefathers.* (After all, "foremothers" shared equally in our ancestry.)

It is important to use judgment when you make proofreading changes in errors involving prejudice. Remember, a proofreader does not change the style of another's writing. If you know the writing contains sexist or other prejudiced terms and you are not sure of the writer's willingness to change, you might mark those words with an editor's query. Be sure to offer a tactful, well-worded solution when you discuss the question with the author. Many people have no trouble accepting a suggested change; they simply haven't been aware of the problems words may cause.

Common Errors in Content

Reading for meaning is an active process. Your mind has to be completely "on line" if you are to focus your attention on the many types of content errors that could occur in any given document. The following list contains a few of the more common errors you may encounter as you proofread for meaning.

Alphabetical Order — A list of names in a letter should be in alphabetical order. This includes the names in the copy notation at the end of the letter.

Chronological Order — A series of dates should be listed in chronological order.

PROOFREADING POINTER

Be consistent from beginning to end. Make sure that letters end in the same style as they begin. If there is no punctuation after the salutation, for example, there should be no punctuation after the closing.

Consistency in Format The appearance of a document—its letter and punctuation styles—should be consistent. If a letter's date starts at the center, the closing lines must also start at the center. If there is punctuation after the salutation, there also must be punctuation after the complimentary close. If the page number is placed on line 4 on one continuation page, it must be placed on line 4 on all other continuation pages.

Courtesy Titles Avoid using courtesy titles inconsistently. Don't call a physician *Dr.* in one paragraph and *Mr.* in another paragraph. Also avoid listing men's names without courtesy titles and women's names with titles. Treat all names in a consistent manner.

Date Accuracy Check dates in documents to be sure they are consistent. Mentioning a meeting on July 14 in one paragraph and the same meeting on July 16 in another paragraph should be spotted by the proofreader. If you don't know the exact date of the meeting, an editor's query is appropriate.

Date Style Be consistent with the style of dates. Both 7-12-97 and 7/12/97 could be correct, but only one style should be used in a document.

Day, Date Agreement A common error is lack of agreement between the date and the day of the week. Check a calendar to be sure the two agree. If they don't, query the editor.

Handling of Book Titles Book titles are italicized. If italic type is not available, use underscoring. Book titles should be handled in the same manner throughout the document.

Impossible Facts Read the document to make sure it makes sense. Pay particular attention to dates. A man born in 1726 would not be celebrating his retirement this year. Also remember that not all months have the same number of days. June never has 31 days, so a letter mentioning June 31 requires an editor's query to determine the correct date.

Math Accuracy Check all documents for mathematical accuracy. For example, a book that originally sold for $25 and has been reduced by $10 cannot be advertised for $20. The actual sale price should be $15.

Names and Addresses Always double-check names and addresses. Be careful that names are spelled the same way throughout the document.

Numerical Order Numbers in a series should be listed in numerical order whenever possible.

Phone Number Style Be sure the style of phone numbers is correct. Either 614-555-7823 or (614) 555-7823 could be correct, but the style should be consistent within a document or a table.

Punctuation Style Use parentheses, brackets, and abbreviations consistently in the same document. In general, avoid using abbreviations, but if they are used, the usage should be consistent. Don't spell out a word in one place and abbreviate it in another.

Redundancies Watch for redundancies, which are unintentional repetitions. Avoid phrases like *refer back* to the memo. *Refer* means to look back, so the word *back* is redundant and unnecessary. The following list contains some commonly used redundancies:

Redundancy	Correct Form
consensus of opinion	consensus
different kinds	kinds
each and every time	each time every time
end result	result
individual person	individual
period of time	period
refer back	refer
repeat again	repeat

Sexist Terms Avoid terms that convey bias. For example, the word *policeman* is considered biased. A better word choice would be *police officer.*

Wrong Words Sometimes a word is correctly spelled but incorrectly used in a document. A computer spell checker would not pick up this kind of error, even though the word is wrong. For example, "A book was fold by the bookstore" has no meaning. The word *fold* should be *sold.*

PROOFREADING POINTER

If you find errors of fact or logic in your text and you can't find the answer yourself, consult an authority or mark the error with an editor's query.

Watch Out for Errors

To help you check dates for accuracy, we have provided a calendar on the inside back cover of this textbook. Use this calendar for exercises throughout the remainder of the book.

Finding errors in meaning and consistency requires practice and attention to detail. These errors are best found by reading the document for meaning only after all the other errors have been located and corrected. *Throughout the remainder of the book,* **any** *exercise may contain errors of bias, consistency, logic, order, or redundancy.*

EXERCISE 2-A

Directions: Read the following memorandum, checking for "reading for meaning" errors. Using standard proofreaders' marks, either correct the errors or mark them with an editor's query.

July 6, 1999

Randolph Jacobsen, Sales Manager

RECOGNITION OF SALES LEADERS

Returning to work this Monday is a pleasure since I have the opportunity to write this memorandum recognizing our top three sales leaders in the Seasonal Novelties Division. As of last Friday, the final day of our contest, we had a tie in sales of Halloween masks. The leading salesmen are Ms. Megan Miller, Keith Jones, and Dwight Dunnerson.

It was certainly a delight to find that three people not only had surpassed their quotas for sales but had tied with one another in the contest. That left me with the dilemma of deciding who should receive the sales incentive award. Referring back to the contest announcement on March 24, I found the answer on what to do in case of a tie. The person with the highest sales of Ghastly Ghost masks wins the trip to the Mardi Gras in New Orleans, Louisiana. Congratulations to Keith Jones, who will be traveling to New Orleans.

Megan Miller and Dwight Dunnersen will receive one paid vacation day for their outstanding performances in the contest. It is a pleasure to have these fine salesmen on the staff here at Signs of Celebration.

Joseph Edwards, CEO

df

EXERCISE 2-B

Directions: Read the following memorandum, checking for "reading for meaning" errors. Either correct the errors or mark them with an editor's query.

TO: Marion Junniper

FROM: Edward Winston

DATE: July 22, 1999

SUBJECT: Help in Tracking Down Invoices

Kerry Williams from the Purchasing Department has just completed his semi-monthly house-cleaning chores. It seems that purchase orders 43556, 43987, 43721, 43876, and 43999 have not cleared Kerry's office. All purchase orders must, of course, be returned to Kerry so the invoices can be filed and sent to the Accounting Department for payment.

The numbers, names, dates, and departmental telephones of the missing purchase orders are listed below:

Invoice	Requested by	Date	Description
43556	Edward Routen	April 27, 1999	Signature pencils
43986	Ms. Marla Shoemaker	April 29, 1999	Font Software
43721	Mrs. Ethel Eden	April 30. 1999	Cranberry Notes
43876	Marcus Baldwin	May 17, 1989	3 1/2" Disks
43999	Richard Evans	May 23, 1999	Mouse Mat

Could you help me track down these items so we can remove them from our "most wanted" list. We don't want to be placed on our creditors' "most wanted" list!

ml

EXERCISE 2-C

Directions: Read the following letter, checking for "reading for meaning" errors. Using standard proofreaders' marks, either correct the errors or mark them with an editor's query.

April 23, 1999

Mr. Randolph Rarick
89 Yeyerian Road
New Smyrna Beach, FL 32069

Dear Mr. Rarick

Yes, we do allow high school physics students to tour our facilities here at the Miller Nuclear Power Authority (MNPA). As it turns out, only one of the dates you listed for possible tours is available on our schedule for the month of May—Friday the 15th.

The tour lasts four hours and includes lunch in our cafeteria. We will expect your group to arrive at the main entrance to the plant at 10 p.m. The security personnel will call our office immediately upon your arrival, and I will then meet you at the visitors' center. Students will be issued protective badges, helmets, and coats to wear during the tour.

Prior to the actual tour, Mr. Rareck, the students will receive a brief lecture on the history and operation of the MPNA. This is done before the tour so students will know what to look for during the tour; some of the areas are so noisy that conversation is impossible. Your students will also receive a printed guidebook and will be able to read about each of the stops in case they have questions. After every five stops, we schedule a short break for questions in a quiet room.

Lunch will be served to the students in the cafeteria, where they will dine with members of the staff who are part of the Nuclear Education Task Force here at the plant. Normally the tour would end after lunch, but we have arranged for your group to have a special presentation on the safety and track record of nuclear power plants. Our task force is putting the presentation together with special emphasis on consumer safety. The tour will end at 3 p.m.

We hope this meets with your approval. We'll expect to see your students on May 14 at 10 a.m.

Sincerely

Kingsford Embers III

EXERCISE 2-D

Directions: Proofread the following letter, comparing the copy with the original. Mark any errors in the comparison copy with standard proofreaders' marks. Remember, you are always responsible for locating "reading for meaning" errors in the original as well as in the comparison copy.

February 12, 1999

Mr. Wesley DaFoe, CEO
Cozy Corner Reading Centers
1530 Manford Place
Boston, MA 02109

Dear Mr. DaFoe:

We have exciting news for you! Barbara Hess has agreed to visit selected bookstores in the Boston and New York City areas during her latest promotional tour. She has agreed to two afternoon book-signing sessions in the Boston area and four sessions in the greater New York area (one morning and three afternoons). As you are well aware, Ms. Hess has written the following bestsellers: *Digging Dirt*, *Seeing Through Smoke*, *Behind Closed Curtains*, and *Hollywood From the Inside Out*. Her latest book, *The Last Word on Hollywood*, will be out in time for the autograph sessions.

Your chain of bookstores was selected because of its excellent reputation and metropolitan locations. You may select any two sites in Boston and also any three sites in New York. Ms. Hess has requested that the morning's location be the same as the afternoon's so that she may have a lengthy lunch break and will not have to travel. All the other afternoon sessions need to be at different stores. Ms. Hess prefers her afternoon publicity sessions to start at 2:30 a.m. and to last no longer than four hours, including two 15-minute breaks. She also requests limousine service to and from her hotel. Her secretary will be making her dining and evening plans.

We know you will want to make publicity plans for this exciting event. Ms. Hess will be in the Boston area for two weeks starting Monday, April 18, and you may schedule her two afternoon sessions during either week. Her visit to New York City will begin the following Monday, May 3, and last for ten days.

Please call her secretary, Sam Carpenter, at (724) 555-7932 or (724) 555-7933 to finalize the dates, times, and locations. We feel sure that this will be profitable for both Kozy Corner Reading Centers and Ms. Ness.

Sincerely,

Ms. Lorena Caldwell, CEO
Emu Publications

COMPARISON COPY 2-D

February 12, 1999

Mr. Wesley Dafoe, COE
Cozy Corner Reading Centers
1530 Manford Pl.
Boston, MA 02109

Dear Mr. DaFoe:

We have exciting news for you; Barbara Hess has agreed to visit selected bookstores in the Boston and New York city areas during her last promotional tour. She has agreed to two afternoon book-signing sessions in the Boston area and four sessions in the greater New York Area (one morning and three afternoons). As you are well aware, Ms. Hess has written the following bestsellers: *Digging Dirt*, *Seeing through Smoke*, *Behind Closed Curtains*, and *Hollywood From the Inside Out*. Her latest book, The Last Word on Hollywood, will be out in time for the autograph sessions.

Your chain of book stores was selected because of its excellent reputation nad metropolitan locations. You may select any two sites in Boston and also any two sites in New York. Ms. Hess has requested that the mornings location be the same as the afternoons so that she may have a lengthy lunch break and will not have too travel. All the other afternoon sessions need to be at different stores. Ms. Hess refers her afternoon publicity sessions to start at 2:30 a.m. and to last no longer than four hours including two 15 minute breaks. She also requests limousine service to and form her hotel. Her secretary will be making her dinning and evening plans.

We know you will want to make publicity plans for this exciting event. Ms. Hess will be in the Boston are for two weeks starting Monday, April 18, and you may schedule her two afternoon sessions during that week. Her visit to New York City will begin the following Monday, May 3 and last for ten days.

Please call her secretary, Sam Carpenter, at (724)-555-7932 or (724) 555-7933 to finalize the date, times and locations. We feel sure that this will be profitable for Kozy Corner Reading Centers and Ms. Ness.

Sincerely,

Ms. Lorena Caldwell, CEO
Emu Publications

EXERCISE 2–E

Directions: Proofread the following letter, comparing the copy with the original. There also may be mistakes in the original. Mark any errors in the comparison copy with standard proofreaders' marks. The 1998 date on this letter is correct.

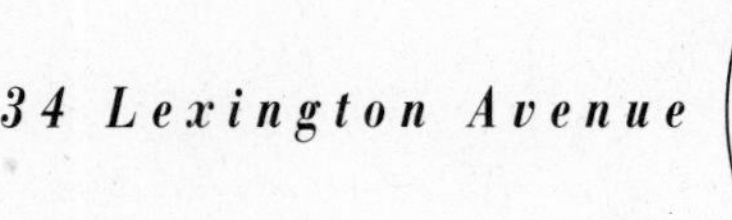

Lawrence, KS 66044

July 10, 1998

Ms. Loujuana Danniston
1278 Carthiginian Way
Shawnee Mission, KS 66210

Dear Ms. Danniston

I was pleased to hear that you had agreed to "keynote" next year's annual convention of the American Florist Association to be held in Kansas City on Friday, September 2, through Sunday, September 5, 1999. We will be sending you more information as the time for the convention draws near.

Although we are just now putting the finishing touches on this year's conference in Orlando, Florida, we are also preparing to submit the 1999 preconference materials to the printer. We always like to let the conference delegates know the conference theme a year in advance. As you are probably aware, the perennials are being featured at this year's conference. Next year we plan to feature annuals.

Your topic, "Planting a Flower Garden—Once a Year, Every Year," should fit in well with the theme. Annuals are such a favorite. They tend to give the gardener such pleasure, and they don't require replanting from year to year.

As the keynote speaker, you will arrive in Kansas City the day before the conference actually begins. Your expenses will, of course, be covered by our organization. The $1000 honorarium will be donated to the two charities you listed: $400 to the Orchid Guild, $300 to the Wildflower Preservation Foundation, and $200 to the Endangered Herb Society. A contribution acknowledgment will be sent directly to you.

You will be our guest during the conference, and we hope you will learn as much from the delightfully innovative flower enthusiasts our conference attracts as they will learn from you speech. Thanks again for agreeing to keynote our 1998 conference. See you in Orlando this spring and in Kansas City next spring.

Sincerely,

Eldridge Shumacher, President
American Floral Association

ly

COMPARISON COPY 2-E

34 Lexington Avenue *Lawrence, KS 66044*

July 10, 1998

Ms. Loujuana Dannison
1278 Carthiginian Way
Shawnee Mission, KS 66120

Dear Ms. Dannison

I was pleased to hear that you had agreed to "keynote" next year's annual convention of the American Florist Association to be held in Kansas City on Friday, September 2 through Sunday, September 5, 1999. We will be sending you more information as the time for the convention draws near.

Although we are just now putting the finishing touches on this year's conference in Orlando, Florida, we are also preparing to submit the 1999 preconference materials to the printer. We always like to let the conference delegates know the conference theme a year in advance. As you are aware, the perennials are being featured at this year's conference. Next year we hope to feature annuals.

Your topic, "Planting a Garden—Once a Year, Every Year," should fit in well with the theme. Annuals are such a favorite. They tend to give the gardener such pleasure; and they don't require replanting from year to year.

As the keynote speaker, you will arrive in Kansas City the day before the confrence actually begins. Your expenses will, of course, be covered by our organization. The $1000 honorarium will be donated to the two charities you listed: $400 to the Orchid Guild, $300 to the Wildflower Preservation Foundation, and $200 to the Endangered Herb Society. Contribution acknowledgements will be sent directly to you.

You will be our guest during the conference. and we hope you will learn as much from the delightfully innovative flower enthusiasts our conference attracts as they will learn from you speech. Thanks again for agreeing to keynote our 1998 conference. See you in Orlando this spring and in Kansas City next spring.

Sincerely,

Eldridge Shumacher, President
American Floral Associaton

ly

CHAPTER

3

Spelling, Sound-Alikes, and Divisions

Based on the beginning of this letter, what chance do you think this person will have of even reaching the interview stage, not to mention receiving the actual job offer?

```
Dear Sir:

I am aplying for the assistent manger's job that was
advertized in last Wensdays paper. I work good with
people and I'm a hard worker. I was going to call
you latter but I didnt want to loose the job
opportunity ...
```

Although the writer may not have wanted to "loose" the job, his letter probably lost it for him. Employers believe that job applicants who make mistakes in a cover letter would make mistakes on the job, and few employers would be willing to take that risk.

Some of the most common writing errors are spelling errors. Spelling errors include not only transposed letters (typos) and actual misspelled words but also the misuse of words that sound alike. Incorrect division of words, phrases, and lines can also cause a piece of writing to look less than polished and final. Proofreading is the key to catching these errors.

Spelling

A position for a media technician became available at a small technical college. As the job-search committee carefully checked through the required cover letters, résumés, references, and transcripts, it became obvious that one applicant seemed particularly well-qualified to repair and install media equipment and work in the media lab. His experience and training were extensive. However, his cover letter contained misspelled and crossed-out words, as well as a variety of simple grammatical errors. Although the job required only a small number of communication duties (some internal forms to be processed), this individual's writing abilities were of such concern that the committee recommended hiring him with a three-month probationary period. During that time, he would have to improve his writing skills; if he failed to do so, his employment would be terminated.

This example serves as a good reminder that no matter what the job duties are, the application materials make a critical first impression. The most glaring mistake for this individual was his inability to spell.

Spelling is a tough problem, so if you're not absolutely 100 percent sure of a spelling, *look it up!* Some people have a feeling that a word looks "funny," and they know they have to check it. Others mentally develop a list of "demon" words that always seem to give them problems, and they then conquer those words. Unfortunately, a few people spell so poorly that, even though it is extremely time consuming, they must look up practically everything. Eventually these poor spellers improve and find they spend less time searching and correcting.

Although the English language is full of inconsistencies, it does have some spelling rules that can be memorized and applied. A reputable English handbook usually contains many of these rules as well as a list of spelling demons.

No matter how you decide to approach the spelling problem, you first need to appraise your present spelling skills. Exercise 3–A is designed to help you do just that. The directions ask you not to use a dictionary. Please don't, no matter how tempted you are. See what your "spelling sense" really is. Good luck!

PROOFREADING POINTER

There's *a rat* in *separate!* Take your most commonly misspelled words and make up a saying or sentence to help yourself remember the correct spelling. For example, there is *a rat* in sep*arat*e.

EXERCISE 3–A

Directions: Circle all the incorrectly spelled words in the following list. *Do not use a dictionary.*

academically
accommodate
accumulate
acknowledgment
acquaintance
acquisition
additionally
adolescent
advantageous
amateur
among
analyze
annually
appraisal
approximate
athlete
baccalaureate
bachelor
bankruptcy
belligerent
beneficiary
benefited
biscuit
breadth
brilliant
bureaucracy
business
calendar
cashier
catalog
category
chassis
chief
colonel
column
commemorate
commitment
committee
comparative

competitive
complement
concede
condescend
controlling
corps
correlate
courteous
credible
criterion
defendant
deferred
dependant
desirable
desperation
development
dilemma
disseminate
dissent
ecstasy
efficiency
eliminate
embarrass
endeavor
environment
exaggerate
exhibition
extraordinary
February
fluorescent
forego
foreseeable
freight
fulfill
genuine
government
grammar
grateful
guarantee

guidance
harass
height
heroine
hindrance
homogeneous
illegitimate
impasse
independence
initiative
interrupt
investor
jewelry
judgment
kindergarten
knowledgeable
laboratory
language
ledger
lenient
library
maintenance
maneuver
mathematics
mileage
miniature
miscellaneous
mortgage
necessary
necessitate
nevertheless
noticeable
nuisance
occasionally
occurrence
omission
pamphlet
parallel
parliamentary

permanent
permissible
permitted
personnel
prescribe
privilege
profession
prominent
prompt
quantity
questionnaire
receipt
receive
recommendation
remembrance
remittance
repossess
requisition
restaurant
rhythm
separate
sergeant
subpoena
subtle
superintendent
supersede
taxable
tendency
thoroughly
truly
vacuum
valuable
vengeance
verbatim
villain
withdrawal
writing
written
yield

Sound-Alikes

When we read, we use our "inner ear" to sound out words; we often comment after reading a sentence, "That sounds OK to me." In fact, we rely on our verbal ability so strongly that it often overshadows the written ability's memory banks. We are tempted to think that if we don't hear a mistake, it must not be there (or their or they're).

Similar-Sounding Words This fallacy—believing that there are no mistakes because we hear no mistakes—produces its own special set of problems. As we write quickly, and sometimes without too much concern for details, we often write a word that sounds the same as another. In many cases, we probably use the one with which we are most familiar, regardless of its correctness. To compound the problem, we proofread hurriedly, and, of course, the word still sounds OK to the brain. This sound-alike problem typically occurs with **homophones**—words that sound the same but are spelled differently. A simple example would be the "bear" that lives in the woods versus "bare" naked.

PROOFREADING POINTER

Red-Flag Words You should become so familiar with the commonly misused sound-alikes that you recognize them as "red-flag" words. When you see them, slow down and double-check.

Mispronunciation Sometimes this sound-alike problem is not caused by true homophones; sloppy or incorrect pronunciation seems to give our brain license to treat many words as if they were sound-alikes. In fact, this dropping off and slurring of sounds can create a spelling nightmare. Some individuals spell *February* as *Febuary, library* as *libary,* and *government* as *goverment,* all because of incorrect pronunciation. A sensitive ear, a careful check in a dictionary for the pronunciation of a word, and repeated verbal practice are the best defenses against this particular problem.

Inadequate Vocabulary As if sound-alikes and mispronunciations weren't enough to trip us, a lack of vocabulary knowledge frequently adds to the confusion. Words like *proceed* and *precede* or *intrapersonal* and *interpersonal* get misused. Knowing the meaning of common prefixes, roots, and suffixes can greatly improve spelling and word sense. One of the many increase-your-vocabulary books, a dictionary, or an English handbook can go a long way toward ending vocabulary deficiency.

These three problems frequently translate to spelling errors in written communications. Therefore, spelling can be improved by developing an eye and an ear for correct pronunciation, enhanced vocabulary, and careful inspection for sound-alikes. English handbooks also contain lists of sound-alikes. Although these lists vary from text to text, they usually include the most common words.

This text does not contain spelling rules and lists, nor does it provide exercises for building vocabulary. It does, however, list below some of the more common sound-alikes to help you refresh your memory since these words create frequent problems in proofreading. *For the rest of this book, sound-alike problems and misspelled words may occur in* **any** *of the exercises.*

PROOFREADING POINTER

Don't get caught in a proofreading trap by using these "words":

Alot

Irregardless

Thru

They are not words and should never be used.

A

A/An

a — used before a word beginning with a consonant sound

an — used before a word beginning with a vowel sound

Accept/Except

accept — to receive; to agree

except — exclude; but

Access/Excess

access — admittance

excess — surplus

Ad/Add

ad	abbreviation for *advertisement*
add	to increase by joining

Adapt/Adept/Adopt

adapt	to adjust; to modify
adept	skilled
adopt	to take by choice

Addition/Edition

addition	mathematical procedure
edition	a particular version of printed material

Advice/Advise

advice	*n.*, recommendation; guidance
advise	*v.*, to give information; to suggest

Affect/Effect

affect	*v.*, to influence
effect	*n.*, consequence or result *v.*, to cause to happen

Aisle/Isle

aisle	passageway
isle	island

Alot/Allot/A lot

alot	Not a word! Do not use.
allot	to distribute or assign a portion
a lot	a great deal

All ready/Already

all ready	completely prepared
already	previously

All right/Alright

all right	the opposite of all wrong
alright	Not a word! Do not use.

Allowed/Aloud

allowed	permitted
aloud	speaking out loud

Altar/Alter

altar	structure used for worship
alter	to change

Alumna/Alumnae/Alumni/Alumnus

alumna	a female graduate
alumnae	female graduates
alumni	male graduates or a combination of male and female graduates
alumnus	male graduate

Allusion/Delusion/Illusion

allusion	an indirect reference
delusion	a false belief
illusion	a misconception

Among/Between

among	used when discussing more than two persons or things
between	used when discussing two persons or things

Amount/Number

amount	used for items that cannot be counted
number	used for items that can be counted

Angel/Angle

angel	winged heavenly being
angle	geometric term

Anxious/Eager

anxious	desirous but with fear
eager	desirous with delight

B

Bare/Bear

bare	naked
bear	*n.*, animal *v.*, to carry; to produce

Between see *Among*

Beside/Besides

beside	next to
besides	in addition; furthermore

Billed/Build

billed	to present a statement of charges or costs
build	to construct

Board/Bored

board	*n.*, a flat piece of wood; meals *v.*, to go aboard a ship or plane
bored	tired from tediousness

Brake/Break

brake	*n.*, a stopping device
break	*n.*, an opening; an opportunity *v.*, to separate into parts

Breadth/Breath/Breathe

breadth	width
breath	respiration
breathe	*v.*, to inhale and exhale air

Bred/Bread

bred	reproduced or brought up
bread	food item

Buy/By

buy	to purchase
by	*prep.*, next to; close to

C

Can not/Cannot

can not	rarely used
cannot	negative form of *can*

Capital/Capitol

capital	city that is the official seat of government; wealth in the form of money or property
capitol	the building in which a legislature assembles

Casual/Causal

casual	informal
causal	originating from a cause

Ceiling/Sealing

ceiling	upper surface of a room; maximum limit
sealing	closing securely

Cemetery/Symmetry

cemetery	graveyard
symmetry	an arrangement with balanced proportions

Cents/Sense/Since

cents	pennies
sense	meaning; hearing, sight, smell, touch, or taste
since	between then and now

Choose/Chose

choose	to select or make a choice
chose	past tense of *choose*

Cite See *Sight*

Coarse/Course

coarse	rough
course	unit of learning; plan; part of a meal

Coma/Comma

coma	an unconscious state
comma	a punctuation mark

Complement/Compliment

complement	to complete
compliment	to praise

Confidant/Confident

confidant	a trusted friend
confident	self-assured

Conscience/Conscientious/Conscious

conscience	the sense of right and wrong
conscientious	thorough
conscious	aware of; awake; intentional

Continual/Continuous

continual	continuing (with breaks)
continuous	continuing (without breaks)

Council/Counsel

council	governing body
counsel	*n.*, an attorney; *v.*, to give advice

Currant/Current

currant	a food
current	*adj.*, present-day; *n.*, flow of electricity or water

Curser/Cursor

curser	one who curses
cursor	a visual indicator showing position on a computer

D

Defer/Differ

defer	to put off
differ	to be unlike; to disagree

Delusion — See *Allusion*

Discreet/Discrete

discreet	having or showing good judgment in speech or behavior
discrete	individually distinct; separate

Dew/Do/Due

dew	water droplets condensed from the air
do	to perform or execute
due	owed as a debt; expected

Dual/Duel

dual	composed of two parts
duel	prearranged fight between two people

Dyeing/Dying

dyeing	coloring with a dye
dying	ceasing to live

E

Eager — See *Anxious*

Edition — See *Addition*

Effect — See *Affect*

Eligible/Illegible

eligible	qualified
illegible	not readable

Eminent/Imminent

eminent	outstanding
imminent	about to occur

Envelop/Envelope

envelop	to cover; to surround
envelope	container for a letter

Ensure/Insure

ensure	to make certain
insure	to protect against financial loss

Except — See *Accept*

Excess — See *Access*

F

Fair/Fare

fair	*n.*, light in color; just; *adj.*, a public exhibition
fare	*n.*, transportation charge

Farther/Further

farther	a greater distance (measurable)
further	more; in addition; to a greater extent

Formally/Formerly

formally	ceremoniously
formerly	in the past

Forth/Fourth

forth	forward in time, place, and order
fourth	ordinal number occurring after *third*

G

Guarantee/Guaranty

guarantee	*v.*, make sure; pledge
guaranty	*n.*, contract; certificate

H

Hear/Here

hear	to receive by ear
here	at or in this place

Higher/Hire

higher	taller; greater
hire	to employ

Hole/Whole

hole	an opening
whole	entire; complete

Holly/Holy/Wholly

holly	a tree or shrub
holy	sacred
wholly	entirely; completely

Hour/Our

hour	sixty minutes
our	pronoun indicating possession

Human/Humane

human	a person
humane	benevolent; kindly

I

Illegible See *Eligible*

Illusion See *Allusion*

Imminent See *Eminent*

Imply/Infer

imply	to suggest
infer	to conclude; to assume

Incidence/Incidents

incidence	frequency; occurrence
incidents	events; episodes

Incite/Insight

incite	to provoke to action
insight	an understanding of

Instance/Instants

instance	example; case
instants	moments

Interstate/Intrastate

interstate	between states
intrastate	within one state

Irregardless/Regardless

irregardless	Not a word! Do not use.
regardless	in spite of everything; anyway

Its/It's

its	possessive pronoun
it's	it is

K

Knew/New

knew	was aware of
new	recent; unfamiliar

Know/No

know	to understand
no	not so; not; not any

L

Ladder/Later/Latter

ladder	device used for climbing
later	after the usual or expected time
latter	being the second of two

Lead/Led

lead	*n.*, heavy metal *v.*, to guide
led	guided (past tense of *lead*)

Learn/Teach

learn	to gain knowledge
teach	to give knowledge to others; to instruct

Lessen/Lesson

lessen	to make or become less
lesson	instructional exercise

Lightening/Lightning

lightening	to brighten; to lessen
lightning	a natural electric discharge in a storm

Loose/Lose

loose	not tight
lose	to misplace

M

Made/Maid

made	constructed, forced
maid	a servant; an unmarried female

Mail/Male

mail	postal material
male	masculine

Marital/Marshal/Martial

marital	pertaining to marriage
marshal	a legal officer
martial	military

May Be/Maybe

may be	is permitted, possible
maybe	perhaps; possibly

Moral/Morale

moral	legal; ethical
morale	spirit; state of mind

Morning/Mourning

morning	before noon
mourning	period of grieving

Muscle/Mussel

muscle	tissue responsible for body movement
mussel	edible sea animal

N

New	See *Knew*
No	See *Know*
Number	See *Amount*

O

Of/Off

of	*prep.*, from
off	distant; removed

Our	See *Hour*

Overdo/Overdue

overdo	to do too much
overdue	past the agreed time

P

Pair/Pare/Pear

pair	two of a kind
pare	to peel
pear	a fruit

Passed/Past

passed	*v.*, overtook; moved ahead
past	*n.*, an earlier time *adj.*, over

Patience/Patients

patience	tolerance
patients	those under medical care

Peak/Peek

peak	the top
peek	to glance quickly

Persecute/Prosecute

persecute	to mistreat
prosecute	to sue in court

Personal/Personnel

personal	private
personnel	employees; staff

Plain/Plane

plain	*adj.*, undecorated *n.*, prairie land
plane	*n.*, a level surface; an airplane *v.*, to make level

Practicable/Practical

practicable	feasible; possible
practical	sensible; useful

Pray/Prey

pray	to offer a prayer
prey	*n.*, victim *v.*, to hunt; to victimize

Precede/Proceed

precede	to go before
proceed	to continue

Precedents/Precedence/Presidents

precedents	established rules
precedence	priority
presidents	chief officers

Presence/Presents

presence	attendance
presents	gifts

Principal/Principle

principal	*n.*, the head of a school; a sum of money *adj.*, first in importance
principle	a basic truth; a rule

Q

Quiet/Quite
- quiet — silent
- quite — really; completely

R

Raise/Rise
- raise — *v.*, to lift; to improve in status; *n.*, an increase in salary
- rise — *v.*, to move up by itself

Read/Red
- read — comprehended the meaning of
- red — a color

Reality/Realty
- reality — truth
- realty — real estate

Regardless — See *Irregardless*

Road/Rode
- road — a highway
- rode — traveled

Role/Roll
- role — a part or character
- roll — *v.*, to turn over and over; *n.*, a list; a food

S

Sail/Sale
- sail — *n.*, part of a ship; *v.*, to travel by water; to glide
- sale — the exchange of goods or services for an amount of money

Scene/Seen
- scene — the setting of an action; a display of anger; a part of a play
- seen — perceived with the eye

Sealing — See *Ceiling*

Seams/Seems
- seams — lines formed by sewing material together
- seems — appears

Sense — See *Cents*

Sew/So
- sew — to stitch
- so — thus; to such an extent; therefore

Shone/Shown
- shone — gave off light; glistened
- shown — displayed, instructed, revealed

Sight/Site/Cite
- sight — to see
- site — a location
- cite — to quote

Since — See *Cents*

Sit/Set
- sit — to occupy a seat
- set — to put; to position; to arrange

Speak/Speech
- speak — to talk
- speech — a presentation

Stationary/Stationery
- stationary — in the same place
- stationery — writing paper

Strait/Straight
- strait — a narrow passage of water
- straight — not crooked

Symmetry — See *Cemetery*

T

Teach — See *Learn*

Than/Then
- than — compared with
- then — at that time

Their/There/They're

their	belonging to them
there	in that place
they're	they are

Thorough/Threw/Through/Thru

thorough	complete
threw	tossed
through	by way of; by means of; in one side and out the other
thru	Not a word. Do not use!

To/Too/Two

to	in the direction of
too	in addition to; also; very
two	a number

U

Undo/Undue

undo	to reverse; to untie
undue	excessive

W

Ware/Wear/Where

ware	material goods
wear	to have or put on
where	at or in what place

Waist/Waste

waist	middle of the body
waste	*n.*, unusable material; *v.*, to consume uselessly

Wait/Weight

wait	to delay; to remain inactive in anticipation
weight	a measure of heaviness of a specific object

Waive/Wave

waive	to give up
wave	*n.*, a gesture; a signal *v.*, to move back and forth

Weak/Week

weak	lacking strength
week	seven days

Weather/Whether

weather	condition of the atmosphere
whether	if; either

We're/Were

we're	we are
were	an auxiliary verb

Whole See *Hole*

Wholly See *Holly*

Who's/Whose

who's	who is
whose	belonging to whom

Wood/Would

wood	lumber
would	a verb form

Y

You're/Your

you're	you are
your	belonging to you

EXERCISE 3–B

Directions: Find the sound-alikes in the following sentences and use standard proofreaders' marks to indicate any needed changes.

1. The magician's advertisement claimed that he would present the world's greatest delusion.
2. The clock in the Alumni Center of Jocelyn's School for Women has run continually for 100 years.
3. A duel often occurred when two rivals for a made's affections fought each other; this is a fine argument for the acquisition of marital arts skills.
4. The amount of people attending the concert will determine weather the principle will allow future concerts to be held.
5. They adopted the script, with only minor modifications, so that my daughter could play an angel in the Christmas play.
6. We planned to send the notices to the new members of the executive bored in company envelops.
7. Molly, Eddie, and I found we were up to hear in organizational duties, which we planned to divide between us.
8. Lynn planned to insure that she had a date for the homecoming dance, so she excepted three dates.
9. Robert Andrews stressed to the Personnel Department that he needed a secretary who could be discreet.
10. Who's part in the play seams to be the most difficult to cast?

EXERCISE 3-C *Directions:* Use standard proofreaders' marks to indicate any needed changes (sound-alikes) in the following article.

BUILDING SELF-CONFIDANCE

There is no guaranty on how hour lives will turn out. There is no guaranty that the rode of life will be smooth or that we can even say life will be fare. At times it may seam that we can not control our own destiny and that we must except whatever lessens in life role hour way. Sometimes it may seam that its all ready to late to climb life's latter of success.

But weight just a minute before you waive success good-bye and precede toward the symmetry. Realty isn't that bleak, and we can do something to put on the breaks and get that train back on the track. We might not be able to undue the passed, but we can certainly set our sites on a new coarse that leads to success.

Weather we are successful depends a great deal on us. We need to develop both patients and energy. We can not afford to remain stationery if we want to be successful. There are many ways to become successful, and people need to find there own paths. However, it does seem that successful people due have something in common: self-confidence. In fact, successful people seam to radiate self-confidence. Perhaps it is the confidance that makes them successful.

The good knews is that no one is born with self-confidence. It is developed, sew that means we can all billed a measure of self-confidence. How? By thinking and acting confidently. There are many different ways to think and act confidently, but just five very basic and simple techniques can help improve you're level of self-confidence.

One simple method of building self-confidence is to be a front-seater. This means being in the front row of the classroom or any place where you're listening participation is required. Unfortunately, many people practicably sprint to the back of the classroom or slide into the back pew. Irregardless of why you might be doing this, think about what this really says: that you don't want to be involved, that you want an easy getaway, or that you don't want to be noticed. Sure, sitting up front is a little more conspicuous, but their is nothing inconspicuous about success. It may be humane nature to hide, but being a front-seater builds confidence.

Another good way to build your self-confidence is to use good eye contact. This does not mean you have to go into a staring match, but you do have to become conscience about maintaining good eye contact. A person who's eye contact is poor is saying, "I'm afraid. I lack confidence. I'm hiding my true inner self." If looking eye to eye with someone else is uncomfortable, try to adopt this procedure by looking at the bridge of the person's nose, right between the eyes. Good eye contact will also have a positive affect on your communications. Raise the angel of you're sites and look a little hire!

A third affective way to build self-confidence is simply by walking faster. People who wander or drag there feet are nonverbally showing others that they have no real plans or place to go. They become easy pray for attackers. Police already advice people that by walking in an upright, brisk fashion, they may discourage wood-be muggers. Confidant walkers look as though they are practically sprinting. So stand up strait and go, go, go!

A fourth basic method of building self-confidence is to speek up. The person whose whispering is actually saying, "My opinion isn't worth much. I lack confidence." The more you speak up, the more you ad to you're level of self-confidence. And remember this—the more you speak up, the easier it is to speak up the next time. In fact, why not take a speach coarse? Work that jaw mussel!

A fifth and last technique for building self-confidence is to smile. A big smile is excellent medicine for a confidence deficiency. A smile takes away your worries and helps to overcome your fears. In edition, it takes alot more muscles to make a frown than it does to make a smile. Make an effort to smile. It will boost your moral. Remember, chances are good that you'll receive a smile as a return for every time you chose to smile.

Although these five methods are simple ones, they will take practice if you really wish to master them. Practice these techniques continually. Be conscience of your actions. In the beginning it may seem that your only giving the allusion of self-confidence, but in realty you will be developing it. So be a front-seater, use good eye contact, walk faster, speek up, and smile. Life is to short and offers to many rewards to go through it lacking self-confidence.

Word Division

The general rule in business writing is to avoid dividing words at the end of lines whenever possible. Word processing packages automatically wrap the text, dropping it down to begin a new line. A common mistake is to allow the software to wrap the text without hyphenating words. If text is justified (left and right margins are straight and even) and if words are not divided, the computer will insert additional space between the words to allow the lines to end evenly. The result may be large white spaces between words.

Some word processing packages contain a hyphenation feature that inserts hyphens at the end of lines. Unfortunately, most of these programs divide words at any syllable, rather than at the correct syllable. Proofreaders should check all syllable breaks for accuracy.

Some words present a particular challenge to proofreaders because they are spelled alike but pronounced differently. Unfortunately, these words are also divided differently, based on their grammatical use. Some examples are listed below.

proj-ect (noun)	pro-ject (verb)
rec-ord (noun)	re-cord (verb)
pres-ent (noun)	pre-sent (verb)
des-ert (noun)	de-sert (verb)

Knowing that words should be divided at the end of a line is one thing; knowing where to divide them is another. There are rules that should be followed when deciding where to divide words.

WORD-DIVISION RULES

One-Syllable Words

3.1 Words of one syllable should never be divided.

stopped	dough
true	drive

Words of Five or Fewer Letters

3.2 Never divide a word of five or fewer letters.

car	honor
honey	south

Contractions

3.3 Don't divide contractions, abbreviations, or figures.

can't	won't
NBEA	25,000

Divide Words Between Syllables

3.4 Divide words only between syllables. A word division book or dictionary will provide information on syllables. A proofreader should always be careful to check for accuracy of division. If you're not sure, look it up.

Incorrect	**Correct**
org-an-ize	or-gan-ize
lakefr-ont	lake-front
bus-iness	busi-ness

Leave at Least Three Characters on Each Line

3.5 Don't divide a word unless you can leave a syllable of at least three characters on both lines. The hyphen on the first line counts as one of the three characters.

Incorrect	**Correct**
feder-al	fed-eral
threat-en	threaten
a-sleep	asleep

Hyphenated Words

3.6 Divide a hyphenated word only at the hyphen.

Incorrect	**Correct**
self-por-trait	self-portrait
voice-o-ver	voice-over
up-per-class	upper-class

Words Containing Single-Vowel Syllables

3.7 When a word contains a single-vowel syllable, divide the word after the single-vowel syllable rather than before.

Incorrect	**Correct**
sep-arate	sepa-rate
compar-ison	compari-son
concil-iate	concili-ate

Other Division Considerations

Some phrases should always be kept together to avoid difficulty in reading. For example, *November 15* should never be typed so *November* is on one line and *15* is on another line. Most word processing software packages contain a feature called a required space (hard space) that forces the computer to look at the two-word phrase as one word and prevents the computer from breaking the line inappropriately. The following example contains an additional proofreading mark used to indicate that a phrase should not be divided from line to line. The second illustration shows the way the passage would look after the correction has been made.

> I will be sending all of the information on home
> ownership that you requested on or about November ⊏⊐
> 15. Please be sure to return the enclosed form.

> I will be sending all of the information on home
> ownership that you requested on or about
> November 15. Please be sure to return the enclosed
> form.

In addition to deciding where to divide words and phrases, a proofreader also needs to decide where in a sentence the line is divided or where in the paragraph or page the lines are divided. The following rules cover the other kinds of division a proofreader should be sure to check.

LINE, PARAGRAPH, AND PAGE DIVISIONS

Single-Unit Phrases

3.8 Avoid dividing phrases that should be read as one unit, such as the following:

page 67	356 days
September 16	Gate 7
David Milan Sr.	6 p.m.
Ms. Jenkins	5 percent

Dates

3.9 If a date must be divided at the end of a line, break it between the day and the year.

Incorrect	**Correct**
January	January 23,
23, 1999	1999

Consecutive Line Divisions

3.10 Don't hyphenate more than two lines in a row.

First and Last Lines of a Paragraph

3.11 Don't hyphenate the first line of a paragraph or the last full line of a paragraph.

Last Word on a Page

3.12 Don't divide the last word on the page.

Three-Line Paragraph

3.13 Don't divide a three-line paragraph between two pages.

Single Line of a Paragraph on a Page (Widow or Orphan Line)

3.14 When splitting a paragraph from one page to another, always leave at least two lines of the paragraph on each page. Leaving a single line of a paragraph on either page results in a widow or orphan line.

EXERCISE 3–D

Directions: Mark the division points of the typed words with a slash (/) in colored ink. Do not consult a dictionary. If a word cannot be divided, indicate this by writing *NO* in the blank beside the word. Then look up the words in a word-division book. If you have divided the words correctly, put a check mark on the blank next to the word. If you have an error, write the words with hyphens inserted where the word should be divided.

preferred	________	transgress	________
stopped	________	should	________
revenue	________	selfish	________
emigrate	________	overdue	________
hazard	________	morgue	________
ahead	________	attached	________
product	________	bookkeeper	________
benefit	________	column	________
strength	________	reference	________
called	________	referral	________
minute (small)	________	scarcity	________
conspicuous	________	inaugurate	________
employment	________	platinum	________
stopping	________	debtor	________
transcribe	________	certificate	________

EXERCISE 3–E

Directions: Proofread the following letter. Using standard proofreaders' marks, indicate any changes needed in the letter. This exercise is a text review.

August 16, 1999

Ms. Sharlottia Ambrose
9556 Wilmer Circle
Kalispell, MT 59901

Dear Ms. Ambrose:

How does Tuesday, August 31, sound as an appropriate day to add to your family? The puppy of your dreams will be ready to be placed on that date; Champion Milady Cassandra's litter (born June 7) will be 11 weaks old by then. I know that hour puppies are a little older when placed then some breeders recommend, but we feel that Belgian sheepdog puppies fair better with more time in the litter. Socialization with litter mates seems very important for these dogs.

Cassandra's Crossing (the registered name of the puppy) is now 10 weeks old and is a lovable 9-pound bundle of black fur. The puppy is outgoing, energetic, and fearless. She has already shown indications of the certified herding instinct evident in previous litters by the same sire and dam. We have enjoyed watching her establish her place in the litter. Although she is the smallest female, she appears to have assumed the position of alpha female. I'm sure she will do the same in your household!

She will be current with all of her vaccinations. The title transfer papers will be mailed to you after 3 weeks. When you receive the papers, you will send them to the American Kennel Club. All you need to do is take Cassandra's Crossing home and love her. We recommend that you begin obedience puppy traning as soon as possible.

You can plan to arrive anytime in the morning of August 31. We will be home all morning since all nine pups remaining in the litter will be placed that day. We look forward to seeing you on the 31st. I'm sure you are anxious to have Cassandra's Crossing join your family.

Sincerely,

Ms. Mindy Steinbrenner

jg

EXERCISE 3-F *Directions:* Proofread the following letter. Indicate any changes with standard proofreaders' marks. This exercise is a text review.

April 1, 1999

Mr. Bill Bernoulli
437 Covered Cove
Ruston, LA 71270

Dear Mr. Bernoulli:

We hear at the Sherlock Detective Agency are confidant that we can discover the whereabouts of your pare of missing llamas, Daisy and Tulip. We understand the importance of locating family pets before they fall pray to any unscrupulous characters. Our agency will guaranty the return of Daisy and Tulip within to weeks. Weather you persecute the culprit(s) is up to you. If we due not crack this case, your elligible for a complete refund.

Its always been our policy at the Sherlock Agency to keep our clients fully informed as to hour procedures and findings in a currant invesitgation. To date, we have involved our top too detectives on this project. Smith and Weston have made a through investigation of the original cite of the disappearance and have found some evidence to suggest foul play at the seen. We have implied from our initial interview with you that you wish to keep this a quite investigation, so our two detectives have been discrete in there questions to the neighbors. They past out a lot of photographs of the llamas between an amount of patrons at the local establishments latter that day. As Smith and Weston suspected, many off these individuals no the pain of missing a pet and wish to lend a helping hand. Smith will be organizing several search parties to farther this investigation.

Unfortunately, we have heard that the infamous Moriarity has been released from prison. His criminal record shows that he was arrested for a passed incidence involving the intrastate transportation of exotic animals. Sense it makes since to keep track of Moriarity's activities, we have assigned another detective to the case in order not to waist any time. This way we will not loose site of his

Mr. Bill Bernouli
Page 2
April 1, 1999

possible involvement in this case.

The Sheerlock Agency would like to assure you that we are preceding with the investigation as quickly as humanely possible. Accept for our newest detective, our hole agency is completely involved in order to insure your satisfaction. In edition, we would like to advice you not to be under the delusion that these types of cases are impossible to crack. We have all ready uncovered pertinent evidence.

Sincerely,

John Watson

ds

CHAPTER

4

Basic Sentence Structure and Punctuation

CHAPTER OUTLINE	RULES
Parts of Speech	Ending Punctuation
Sentence Structure	**4.1–4.2** Using the Period
Phrases	**4.3** Using the Question Mark
Clauses	**4.4** Using the Exclamation Point
Complete Sentences and Fragments	Comma (Compound Sentences)
Basic Sentence Patterns	**4.5** Using the Comma in Compound Sentences
Comma Splices and Run-Ons	
Compound Sentences	

As a language develops and grows, it follows patterns and rules, and these rules help to standardize verbal and written communications. When we formally study English in school, we often complain about all the rules and the exceptions to those rules. But considering the flexibility of our language and the wonderful things words can accomplish, we can easily see the value of being in command of this powerful tool.

The more rules we know, the faster and more accurate proofreaders we can become. If we develop an accurate eye for sentence patterns and apply basic principles for sentence structure and punctuation, we won't have to spend precious time looking up rules. Our proofreading skills will reflect our accuracy and attention to detail, and the reader will notice these qualities.

As you already know from English courses, the words in sentences are used as different parts of speech that serve different functions within the sentence. By recognizing the patterns that these word groups produce, you will be able to insert the correct punctuation more easily. (An added benefit of sentence-pattern recognition is increased reading comprehension.)

This text offers only a quick review of the basics to refresh your memory. If your answers to the first few exercises in this chapter are not accurate or if you do not feel comfortable about your knowledge of basic grammar, you may need to do some extra work. An English handbook or a computerized grammar tutorial is an excellent place to start working on building your basic grammar skills.

Parts of Speech

You may remember that there are eight basic parts of speech. Each of these basic parts has two or more types, which will be reviewed here only briefly. The following is a general overview:

Noun A noun names a person, place, thing, or idea.

➤ *Washington* fought for *freedom* from the *British* at *Valley Forge.*

Pronoun A pronoun takes the place of a noun.

➤ *She* saw Washington in *his* boat.

Verb Basically, a verb expresses an action or a state of being. There are three types of verbs: action, linking, and helping.

➤ Washington *crossed* the Delaware. (action)

➤ Washington *was* President. (linking)

➤ Washington *was seen* at Valley Forge. (helping)

Adjective An adjective modifies nouns or pronouns and frequently answers these questions: "How many?" "Which one?" and "What kind?" The words *a, an,* and *the* also are adjectives and sometimes are referred to as *articles.*

➤ Washington had *a blue* coat with *eighteen silver* buttons.

Adverb An adverb modifies verbs, adjectives, other adverbs, and even entire sentences. Adverbs frequently answer these questions: "How?" "When?" and "Where?"

➤ *Tragically,* the *bitterly* harsh winter at Valley Forge *quickly* took many lives and *seriously* damaged the troops' morale.

Preposition A preposition functions with a group of words by beginning a prepositional phrase. As Chart 4.1 indicates, there are over seventy common prepositions, some of which are *above, around, behind, between, by, during, in addition to, in spite of, in, of, on, over, since, to, under, until,* and *with.*

➤ Washington ran *around* the troops, *behind* the troops, and *through* the troops before he charged *up* the hill.

Conjunction Conjunctions join words. There are two types of conjunctions: Coordinate and subordinate. By looking at the prefixes of these two words, you can figure out how they join words. The prefix *co-* means "together" or "equal," as in *co-worker,* and a coordinate conjunction joins words, phrases, or clauses on an equal basis. The prefix *sub-* means "below" or "under," as in *submarine;* a subordinate conjunction joins clauses on an unequal or lesser basis. In other words, a subordinate conjunction sends a signal to the reader that one group of words is of lesser importance than the other.

➤ Washington *and* Lafayette were both generals. (coordinate)

➤ Washington was an exceptionally tall *but* not extremely handsome man. (coordinate)

➤ *If* Washington had not been the commander of the troops, he probably would not have been the first President. (subordinate)

➤ Washington became the first President *because* he was the commander of the troops. (subordinate)

Interjection An interjection conveys surprise or strong emotions.

➤ *Wow!* Washington had a great pitching arm!

CHART 4.1 COMMON PREPOSITIONS

about	as	but (except)	from	like	over	unlike
above	as for	by	in	near	past	until
according to	at	by means of	in addition to	next	regarding	up
across	because of	concerning	in back of	of	since	upon
after	before	despite	in case of	off	through	up to
against	behind	down	in front of	on	throughout	with
along	below	during	in place of	onto	till	within
along with	beneath	except	inside	on top of	to	without
among	beside	except for	in spite of	out	toward	
apart from	between	excepting	instead of	out of	under	
around	beyond	for	into	outside	underneath	

EXERCISE 4–A

Directions: For each word in the following sentences, enter the part of speech in the appropriate blank.

1. Maple is a common name for trees in the genus by the name of *Acer,* and it is found in the Northern Hemisphere.

Maple	______________	name	______________
is	______________	of	______________
a	______________	*Acer*	______________
common	______________	and	______________
name	______________	it	______________
for	______________	is	______________
trees	______________	found	______________
in	______________	in	______________
the	______________	the	______________
genus	______________	Northern	______________
by	______________	Hemisphere	______________
the	______________		

2. Since maple wood is an extremely hard wood, it is frequently used in the furniture business.

Since	______________	it	______________
maple	______________	is	______________
wood	______________	frequently	______________
is	______________	used	______________
an	______________	in	______________
extremely	______________	the	______________
hard	______________	furniture	______________
wood	______________	business	______________

Sentence Structure

Each part of speech can be used many different ways within a sentence. The way that these parts function inside their sentence patterns mandates the rules of punctuation. If you can locate these sentence patterns, punctuation becomes quite manageable. Think of it as working a jigsaw puzzle; you are looking for certain patterns and shapes.

To start this pattern-fitting process, we need to be familiar with some of the more general parts of a sentence. Then we can take a look at some of the basic patterns and see how correct punctuation relies on seeing these patterns.

Subject Subjects can be either nouns or pronouns. The simple subject is who or what is doing the action.

➤ *Washington* led the troops.

(Who or what led the troops? Washington)

Verb The verb is actually called the *predicate,* and it is the second major part of any sentence. The complete predicate includes the simple verb and its modifiers as well as any objects or complements and their modifiers. A quick recognition of the simple verb is usually possible by asking what is happening in the sentence.

➤ Washington *crossed* the Delaware.

(What did Washington do? crossed the Delaware)

Direct Object

The direct object receives the action of the verb. After you identify the subject and the verb, ask "Whom?" or "What?" after the verb.

➤ Washington gave the British his wooden *teeth.*

(Washington gave what? his teeth)

Indirect Object

The indirect object receives the action of the direct object. After you discover the direct object, ask, "To whom?" "For whom?" To what?" or "For what?"

➤ Washington gave the *British* his wooden teeth.

(Washington gave his teeth to whom? the British)

Prepositional Phrase

A prepositional phrase starts with a preposition and ends with an object, which is a noun or pronoun.

➤ Washington went *to school.*

(This is a very simple prepositional phrase—a preposition and an object of the preposition.)

➤ Washington went *to the one-room, brick schoolhouse and the large, gray stone church.*

(This prepositional phrase has one preposition and a compound object—*schoolhouse* and *church*—each of which has its own modifiers.)

Complement

Complements are very similar to direct objects, but they can occur only with linking verbs. Think of what that means in terms of patterns. A linking verb actually links the subject to the complement, or the complement completes the subject. Complements can be nouns, pronouns, or adjectives.

Some common linking verbs are

am	sound	is	appear
are	seem	was	become
were	grow	feel	turn
taste	remain	smell	prove

In a sentence with a linking verb, you usually can locate the complement by asking "Who?" or "What?" after the linking verb.

➤ Washington was *President.*

(Washington was what? the President)

(The complement and subject often can be reversed: the President was Washington.)

Washington was *tall.*

(Washington was what? tall)

Modifiers Don't forget the many adjectives and adverbs that gather around nouns, pronouns, and verbs.

➤ *The tall* general *slowly* marched *the tired* troops along *the muddy* road on *a cold, drizzly* morning.

(Can you pick out the subject, verb, and direct object in the previous sentence? *general, marched, troops*)

EXERCISE 4–B

Directions: Underline the simple subject once and the verb twice. Put prepositional phrases in parentheses, drawing an arrow from the preposition to the object of the preposition. Label each modifier by writing *m* above it. Write the letters *do* above any direct object, *io* above any indirect object, and *c* above any complement. Circle all conjunctions.

1. The foliage of some maples is a brilliant orange or a fiery red in the fall.
2. The North American sugar maple is tapped for its sap.
3. Flowering maples produce funnel-shaped, droopy flowers and are often grown as house plants.
4. Some people give their friends flowering maples for anniversaries and birthdays.
5. These plants should be kept in moist soil and in a sunny spot during the winter months.

Please remember, if you had the slightest difficulty in completing Exercises 4–A and 4–B, you need to do extra work to build your grammar skills. Ask your instructor for the best way to get started.

Phrases

Phrases are groups of words that lack either a subject or a verb or both. There are many types of phrases, but prepositional phrases are probably the most common. Some examples are:

Prepositional Phrases	**Other Types of Phrases**
after seeing the movie	have been seen
behind the barn	an extremely tall woman
in the morning	locating many different roses

Clauses

Clauses are groups of words that contain at least one subject and one verb. There are two types of clauses: independent and dependent. Those words describe exactly what is happening in the clause. An independent clause contains a subject and a verb and expresses a complete thought, thus making this group of words independent in structure—a sentence. A dependent clause contains a subject and a verb but does not express a complete thought; it *depends* on another clause to complete the thought.

When I went to the store	(dependent clause)
I spent every dime	(independent clause)
that I had	(dependent clause)

Complete Sentences and Fragments

A complete sentence is formed when words are grouped together to contain a subject and a verb and to express a complete thought. Two words can be a complete thought: the shortest sentence in the Bible is "Jesus wept." Be careful of subjects and verbs that are preceded by some conjunctions. "When I go to the fair" is not a complete sentence. It has a subject and a verb but does not express a complete thought because of the conjunction *when.* (What happens when I go to the fair? We are not told.) In deciding whether groups of words are complete sentences, we may assume information in order to identify pronouns, but care should be taken not to assume information beyond them. "He saw it" is still a complete sentence, even though we don't know exactly who did the seeing and what this individual saw. "After he saw it" is not a complete sentence; we do not know what he did after he saw it.

An incomplete sentence is often referred to as a fragment. As the word *fragment* suggests, this group of words is only part of a sentence. It may contain a subject but not a verb; it may contain a verb phrase; it may contain both a subject and a verb but not express a complete thought. Fragments may have a variety of reasons for not reaching the status of a sentence. These examples are fragments:

the large brown dog
gulping his food and slurping the water
since I went to the store

There is a type of sentence, however, that is complete but does not visually have a subject. This sentence is a command that has an "understood" subject: the understood *you.* In the sentences "Give the dog his dinner" and "Make three copies before tomorrow," the subject is an understood *you.* You are to give the dog its dinner, and you are to make three copies.

Basic Sentence Patterns

PROOFREADING POINTER

Sentence Patterns
Sentence-pattern recognition will help you with many other proofreading tasks, including those involving usage and punctuation. Mastering this skill will make your work easier.

So far we have reviewed the parts of speech and how they function in sentences. We have also discussed phrases, clauses, complete sentences, and fragments. We can maneuver sentence parts, like pieces in a building block set, to build many different types of sentences. From this, we can pictorially illustrate basic sentence patterns. The benefit from being able to see these patterns occurs when we have to add internal punctuation. Most punctuation follows reasonably consistent rules.

Let's look at some of the sentence patterns we have reviewed. First, complete sentences have at least one subject and one verb. We can represent this pattern with letters, like this: **S V.** Of course the sentence probably would contain an assortment of modifiers (adjectives and adverbs), prepositional phrases, and perhaps direct and indirect objects, to say nothing of several other grammatical possibilities. For the most part, though, the only things we need to be concerned about are subjects and verbs and their conjunctions. Keeping that in mind, let's look at several sentences and the patterns they produce. A capital **S** or **V** indicates that the subject or verb is part of the independent clause; a lowercase **s** or **v** indicates that the subject or verb is part of a subordinate clause.

- The CEO (**S**) called (**V**) the cabinet meeting of his vice presidents. (**S V.**)
- Ethel Batiste (**S**), Bob Jones (**S**), Louis Valdez (**S**), and Sandra Waterman (**S**) went (**V**) to the meeting and objected (**V**) to the new policies. (**S, S, S,** and **S V** and **V.**)
- Walter Hupman (**S**), the CEO, listened (**V**) intently and them calmly announced (**V**) the continuation of the current policies. (**S V** and **V.**)
- The vice presidents (**S**) left (**V**) disgruntled but with their jobs still intact. (**S V.**)
- The CEO (**S**) sighed (**V**), shook (**V**) his head, and continued (**V**) with his day's plans. (**S V, V,** and **V.**)
- The vice presidents (**S**), who (**s**) knew (**v**) about the plans, were (**V**) uncomfortable during the meeting. (**S, s v, V.**)

Obviously the possibilities are endless, but this procedure does let us begin to find basic sentence patterns that will, in turn, help us to apply internal punctuation rules correctly. Internal punctuation is covered in later chapters of this text.

ENDING PUNCTUATION

At the end of a sentence, three punctuation marks may be used: period, question mark, and exclamation point. All sentences require ending punctuation.

Using the Period

4.1 Use a period after a statement or a mild command. (Space twice after a period ending a sentence.)

- José received a degree in computer science.
- Tell her what you saw.
- Please send two copies to Elaine Brookes.

4.2 Use a period after a courteous request. (The test for a courteous request: You expect the person to do something rather than answer with a yes or no.)

- Will you send two copies to Elaine Brookes. (You expect the person to send two copies.)

Using the Question Mark

4.3 Use a question mark after a direct question. (Space twice after a question mark ending a sentence.)

- ➤ Have you seen Elaine Brookes?
- ➤ Which job will you be accepting after graduation?

Using the Exclamation Point

4.4 Use an exclamation point to show strong emotion, enthusiasm, astonishment, shock, grief, outrage, or great irony. Exclamation points are used sparingly in writing. (Space twice after an exclamation mark ending a sentence.)

- ➤ Stop that!
- ➤ You have to be kidding!

EXERCISE 4–C

Directions: Label each of the following items with a *C* if it is a complete sentence or an *F* if it is a fragment. Also, insert any necessary ending punctuation.

1. ____ Mother, have you seen my socks
2. ____ I'm afraid I've lost them
3. ____ While I gathered up the laundry
4. ____ Will you help me look for them
5. ____ Seeing the laundry reminded me that I'll need them tonight
6. ____ The washing machine which always eats socks
7. ____ How can this be
8. ____ Look out
9. ____ The jar falling off the shelf
10. ____ Please take this nightmare away

EXERCISE 4–D

Directions: Read the following paragraph and then fill in the blanks, labeling each group of words with a *C* if it is a complete sentence or an *F* if it is a fragment.

(1) Maple syrup produced from the North American sugar maple. (2) The syrup actually comes from the sap of the tree. (3) Taking about fifty quarts of sap to make one quart of syrup. (4) As the sap is concentrated through boiling. (5) The coloring and flavor are imparted.

1. ____ 2. ____ 3. ____ 4. ____ 5. ____

Remember, if any of your answers to Exercises 4–C or 4–D were incorrect, you need to do extra work immediately on these basics.

Comma Splices and Run-Ons

Comma splices occur when two or more complete sentences are incorrectly joined by a comma. The simplest way to correct comma splices is to make them into two separate sentences. You can also correct comma splices by adding a coordinating conjunction **(co)** after the comma (see compound sentences) or by replacing the comma with a semicolon under certain conditions (see semicolons).

Run-ons occur when two or more complete sentences are run together with no punctuation at all between them. The correction methods are almost the same: make the two sentences separate by adding a period and the appropriate capitalization, put a comma and a coordinating conjunction between the two sentences, or add a semicolon between the two sentences.

Let's convert this information into the basic sentence patterns, including internal punctuation. The pattern for comma splices is **S V, S V.** The pattern for run-ons is **S V S V.** Both of these errors would be corrected to **S V. S V.** or **S V, co S V.** or **S V; S V.**

Study the examples below and see if you can locate the errors and the corrections.

Comma Splice Sarah Rajias wrote the proposal in four days, Sam Lazer took only one hour to veto it. **(S V, S V.)**

Run-on Sarah Rajias wrote the proposal in four days Sam Lazer took only one hour to veto it. **(S V S V.)**

Corrections Sarah Rajias wrote the proposal in four days. Sam Lazer took only one hour to veto it. **(S V. S V.)**

Sarah Rajias wrote the proposal in four days, but Sam Lazer took only one hour to veto it. **(S V, co S V.)**

Sarah Rajias wrote the proposal in four days; Sam Lazer took only one hour to veto it. **(S V; S V.)**

EXERCISE 4–E

Directions: In the spaces following the paragraph, indicate the type of error by entering *CS* for comma splices and *RO* for run-ons. If the sentence is correct, write *OK* in the appropriate space.

(1) Natural rubber is commercially obtained from the *Hevea brasiliensis* tree, although it may be obtained from many other plants. (2) This tree originally was found in South America, now it is also cultivated in West Africa and Southeast Asia. (3) Latex, the milky fluid located in the inner bark, is tapped off through a cut in the outer bark. (4) The latex is coagulated with dilute acid then it is processed. (5) The process includes the fluid's being creped or sheeted as well as smoked. (6) Natural rubber is a chain polymer of isoprene, these chains are randomly coiled but straighten when stretched. (7) The Aztecs first used rubber as early as the sixth century A.D., but Europe did not know of its existence until the sixteenth century. (8) Rubber really wasn't of any practical use until after Goodyear invented vulcanization. (9) Most of the collected latex is vulcanized some is still used as an adhesive. (10) In addition, latex is used for making rubber coating, rubber thread, and foam rubber. (11) Synthetic rubbers have been manufactured since the First World War, the Second World War is credited for extensively furthering their use.

1. ____ 4. ____ 7. ____ 10. ____

2. ____ 5. ____ 8. ____ 11. ____

3. ____ 6. ____ 9. ____

Compound Sentences

Compound sentences are two complete (independent) sentences joined by a comma and a coordinating conjunction. Remember that coordinating conjunctions act as equal *(co-)* connectors; these conjunctions tell the reader that the words, phrases, or sentences on both sides are of equal importance. Subordinate conjunctions don't say the same thing about construction; subordinate conjunctions show inequality.

There are only seven coordinate conjunctions, and you can easily memorize them as an acronym—FAN BOYS.

F	for	**B**	but
A	and	**O**	or
N	nor	**Y**	yet
		S	so

It is important to understand that coordinate conjunctions create several compound "things" or word groupings, such as compound verbs, compound subjects, compound objects, compound sentences, and so on.

Now see the FAN BOYS (marked as **co**) in action within basic sentence patterns.

PROOFREADING POINTER

Remember that a coordinate conjunction makes the word groups on both sides of it equal in importance and that there are only seven coordinate conjunctions (FAN BOYS).

S V , co S V.
Hester screamed, and Roy fainted. (**S V, co S V.**—compound sentence)

S co S V.
Hester and Roy screamed. (**S co S V.**—compound subject)

S V co V.
Hester screamed and fainted. (**S V co V.**—compound verb)

S co S V co V.
Hester and Roy screamed and fainted. (**S co S V co V.**—compound subject and compound verb)

COMMA (COMPOUND SENTENCES)

Using the Comma in Compound Sentences

4.5 Use a comma before the coordinating conjunction that unites two independent clauses.

➤ The new computer arrived on Tuesday, and Mrs. Bronson installed the software on Wednesday.

➤ On Wednesday afternoon Mr. Bronson accidentally erased the hard drive, so Mrs. Bronson prohibited his using the computer.

EXERCISE 4–F

Directions: In the independent clauses, underline any subjects once and any verbs twice. On the line preceding each sentence, write *OK* if the sentence is correct. If it is not correct, indicate the type of error by using these abbreviations: *RO* (run-on), *CS* (comma splice), or *IPCS* (incorrect punctuation for a compound sentence). Make any necessary corrections by using standard proofreaders' marks.

1. _____ Corn, originally called *maize,* is a major world crop plant and it is second in terms of acres planted when compared with wheat.

2. _____ Depending on the variety, the corn plant will grow between 3 and 15 feet high and will develop 1 to 3 ears.

3. _____ Pollination occurs when the wind causes the pollen from the male tassels at the top of the stalk to fall on the corn silks.

4. _____ These silks protrude from the top of the ear of corn and each silk is attached to a female ovary.

5. _____ These female ovaries are arranged in rows and are attached to the cob.

6. _____ Growing corn can be problematic because there are many diseases that attack corn.

7. _____ Leaf wilting is caused by bacteria wilting also occurs when the corn is not stored correctly.

8. _____ Fungi will ruin young plants, moreover, rust, virus, and smut also will damage the crop.

9. _____ The insect causing the most problems is the corn borer but locusts also have been known to ravage corn fields.

10. _____ Deer, raccoons, and other wild animals can consume a portion of the crop then there are birds that delight in taking a share.

11. _____ Even neighboring cows sometimes break out of their pasture for a healthy lunch in the corn field and can cause hundreds of dollars of damage in an afternoon.

EXERCISE 4–G

Directions: In the independent clauses, underline any subjects once and any verbs twice. On the line preceding each sentence, write *OK* if the sentence is correct. If it is not correct, indicate the type of error by using these abbreviations: *RO* (run-on), *CS* (comma splice), or *IPCS* (incorrect punctuation for a compound sentence). Make any necessary corrections by using standard proofreaders' marks.

1. _____ Five main types of corn have been developed.
2. _____ In the United States most of the corn is dent corn and is used for feed, it received its name from the small dent characteristically found on top of each kernel.
3. _____ Because of its cold climate, Canada produces flint corn but Ecuador, Peru, and Bolivia produce flour corn to make flour and cornmeal from the soft kernels.
4. _____ Of course everyone in the United States is familiar with sweet corn, which is enjoyed on the cob in the late summer or cut off for freezing or canning.
5. _____ Popcorn has a hard shell that keeps the moisture inside, when the kernel is heated, the steam expands internally and causes the kernel to explode.
6. _____ Corn is used as food for animals and for humans, it is used in baked products as well as in breakfast cereals.
7. _____ Corn is used industrially as well; paper and wallboard manufacturers use the stalk and the starch from the corn plant.
8. _____ Alcohol, oil, and syrup use processed corn moreover, the plastic industry purchases corn.
9. _____ The name *corn* is used generically in some parts of the United Kingdom to represent any type of cereal crop, this could be wheat or oats.
10. _____ Any way you slice it, cut it, serve it, or process it, corn is a vital crop to the people of the world. Have you had your share today?

EXERCISE 4-H

Directions: Using standard proofreaders' marks, make any necessary corrections in this text review.

July 9, 1992

Mr. Adam Barclay
450 Witner Place Road
Egypt Lake, FL 33614

Dear Mr. Barclay

Barclay Enterprises is definitely making a name for itself in the state of Florida. I was pleased to see your company named to the **100 and Solid in Florida** list. I know Barclay Enterprises must be delighted with the honor, you've certainly earned the recognition it brings.

I know you are interesed in adding a financial statement to your publications list. The following suggestions will help make an eye-catching publication for your company.

1. Barclay Enterprises has made a name for itself by developing unusual promotions for civic events in the state of Florida. The financial statement should also be an unusual type of promotion in line with company policy. I envision a 12-page publication.

2. While furthering the image of the company, the information contained in the financial statement. The infomation must, of course, be solid.

3. Testimonials from satisfied clients in your financial statement. We can write as much copy as we like, but the success of promotions like the Egypt Lake Junior Regatta will impress clients more than anything we can write. I know we can locate some delightful pictures of the toy sailboat races at the downtown fountain square

4. Use color in the financial statement because color enhances the feeling of spontaneity and creativity. The type in the brochure should probably done in navy.

5. Include pictures of your staff in the statement. You are a family-owned and family-operated business, clients like to know that. Loyalty to the family translates into loyalty to clients.

Mr. Adam Barclay
Page 2
July 8, 1999

7. Inclose the statement in a colorful, picture-covered folder suitable for use elsewhere. Once the financial statement has been removed from the envelope, the envelopes can be used for other purposes. Your name should be printed in small type on the envelope, but what a great form of advertising. I'd aso suggest that you print 2000 extra envelopes for organizations to use in putting together promotional material. Having the envelope represent the company.

8 Finally, the entire publication, while unusual, must be done with elegance. You may be an enterprise specializing in the unusal but the unusual is always classy.

Let's meet for lunch on Firday, July 19, to discuss the project.

Sincerely,

Ms. Cindy Dupler, Designer
Clever Creations, Inc.

ss

EXERCISE 4-1

Directions: Using standard proofreaders' marks make corrections in the editorial Andrew Raines is submitting to *Business World.* It is formatted with full justification; the lines end evenly on both sides. Don't be concerned about spacing between words unless the spacing is not consistent. This exercise is a text review.

DELEGATION: A LOST ART

by Andrew Raines
Management Consultant

When I went on job interviews, I was always prepared for that typical question, "What are you're strengths and weeknesses?" I knew the *perfect* answer or so I thought! I would look at the interviewer, think carefully, and then answer, "It is sometimes difficult for me to delegate, I find it easier just to do it myself."

Although my answer was truthful, I've learned that it was not a good answer. Delegation is an art that a wise manager needs to learn. If learning it is not easy, than the rewards need to be great. Believe me, they are. Many jobs can not even be completed if you don't delegate; noone individual can do the work of three people.

Over the years, I have developed some principles to follow for effective delegation.

1. Take an objective look at what part of the job you can do and what part you should have others do. Make a list of the tasks you need to do yourself and another list of those you can delegate.

2. Double-check to be sure the jobs you have been planning to delegate are jobs you *should* delegate. Don't delegate a controversial or unpleasant job. That's what you are being paid to do.

3. Look at your list of jobs to delegate and decide what employees can best handle the jobs. Make sure your employees have enough resources and the needed authority to complete the job.

4. Meet with the employee to review the tasks you are delegating. Goals and dead lines for the project should be clearly specified.

5. Meet periodically with the employee to review progress on the project. The employee should

always be included in the evaluation. Sometimes what looks like no progress may indeed be majer progress.

6. When the project is completed, meet with the employee to review the data.

Sometimes a project will not come out the way you had envisioned. Remember, you must accept you share of the responsibility. If the project has succeeded, be generous with your praise Make it known that the employee had the major responsibility for the project, the employee should be the one receiving the credit.

Nowadays, I find myself in the position of interviewer, not interviewee. I listen carefully to the answers to my questions and the candidate who mentions being able to delegate effectively makes a few bonus points. You can too.

CHAPTER

5

Subject-Verb Agreement, Pronouns, and Parallelism

CHAPTER OUTLINE	RULES
Subject-Verb Agreement	Subject-Verb Agreement Rules
Agreement Errors Caused by Intervening Material	**5.1** Subject-Verb Agreement
Pronoun-Antecedent Agreement	**5.2** Compound Subjects
Pronoun Case	**5.3** *There*
The Pronouns *Who* and *Whom*	**5.4** *Or, nor, Either . . . or,* and *Neither . . . nor*
Pronoun Gender	**5.5** Tense Shifts
Parallelism	**5.6–5.7** Subjunctive Mood
	5.8–5.9 Collective Nouns
	5.10–5.12 Indefinite Pronouns
	5.13 *The* Number and *a* Number
	5.14 Organizational Titles
	5.15 Portions and Fractions
	5.16 Time, Quantity, and Money
	Pronoun Rules
	5.17–5.18 Pronoun-Antecedent Agreement
	5.19 Pronoun Case

RULES (CONTINUED)

Some of the most basic rules of our language have to do with subjects and predicates. After all, these cornerstones, which we began to master as toddlers, provide the foundation for all sentences. These words helped us identify people and things we wanted; they let us describe actions we saw. As we listened and practiced our language skills, we learned that we could shape present actions into the past and future and that we could make a single object become plural. Along with this newfound power of expression, we discovered there were rules in getting these pieces of the language puzzle to fit. We built on these rules by listening, speaking, and experimenting. We even polished them through several years of formal schooling.

Today, as we communicate, we rely on that early training, for we have developed an "ear" for what sounds right. Most of the time, our ear holds us on course, but if we have become careless with our formal communications, we may need to pinpoint and fine-tune a few problem areas. If we develop a system to "red flag" these weak spots, we can train ourselves to slow down at problem areas and catch mistakes before they happen.

In Chapter 4, we reviewed the basic parts of speech, their functions within a sentence, and some basic sentence patterns. With that basic terminology in place, we can look at some specific problems that face anyone who is proofreading written material.

Subject-Verb Agreement

Subjects and verbs must agree in number. Translated, this means that if the subject of the sentence is plural, the verb must also be plural. If the subject is singular, the verb must also be singular. This seems simple enough, but there are a few little hitches. Sometimes we have to work with irregular verbs, and sometimes subjects and verbs are so far removed from each other that our ears don't hear the agreement, and we become accidentally influenced by another word, which causes an error.

We all remember learning to conjugate verbs, probably by saying, "Today I walked, yesterday I walked, right now I am walking, and I have walked before." We learned that most verbs change their forms by simply adding *-ed* or *-ing*. Then we formally learned what we instinctively knew—this rule has many exceptions. Most English handbooks contain extensive lists of these irregular verbs; Chart 5.1 is a short list of the most common ones.

CHART 5.1 IRREGULAR VERBS

Present Tense	Past Tense	Past Participle (must be used with a helping verb)
be	was, were	been
become	became	become
begin	began	begun
blow	blew	blown
break	broke	broken
bring	brought	brought
build	built	built
buy	bought	bought
catch	caught	caught
choose	chose	chosen
come	came	come
dive	dived (dove)	dived
do	did	done
draw	drew	drawn
drink	drank	drunk
drive	drove	driven
eat	ate	eaten
fall	fell	fallen
feel	felt	felt
find	found	found
fly	flew	flown
forget	forgot	forgotten
forgive	forgave	forgiven
get	got	gotten
give	gave	given
go	went	gone
grow	grew	grown
hang	hung	hung
have	had	had
hear	heard	heard
hide	hid	hidden
hold	held	held
know	knew	known
lay	laid	laid
lead	led	led
leave	left	left
lie	lay	lain
meet	met	met
pay	paid	paid
quit	quit	quit
read	read	read
ride	rode	ridden

CHART 5.1 IRREGULAR VERBS

Present Tense	Past Tense	Past Participle (must be used with a helping verb)
rise	rose	risen
run	ran	run
say	said	said
see	saw	seen
seek	sought	sought
sell	sold	sold
send	sent	sent
set	set	set
shake	shook	shaken
shine	shone (shined)	shone (shined)
shrink	shrank (shrunk)	shrunk (shrunken)
sing	sang	sung
sit	sat	sat
sleep	slept	slept
speak	spoke	spoken
spend	spent	spent
spring	sprang	sprung
stand	stood	stood
steal	stole	stolen
swim	swam	swum
take	took	taken
teach	taught	taught
tear	tore	torn
tell	told	told
think	thought	thought
throw	threw	thrown
understand	understood	understood
wake	woke (waked)	waked (woken)
wear	wore	worn
win	won	won
write	wrote	written

Which ones cause you the most problems? Make a promise to yourself to try to develop a sensitive ear to these verbs so that when you use them, you will be able to use them correctly.

Probably the verbs that are misused the most often are *sit/set, rise/raise,* and *lie/lay,* with *lie/lay* causing the most errors. All three of these verb sets share a basic principle: The first word in the pair occurs only when people or things are doing the action of their own free will, and the second word in the pair is used when the people or things are doing this action to another person or thing. For example, you *sit* in a chair by your own choosing; you *set* a book down when you act on the book by placing it somewhere. You *rise* out of the chair by your own direction; you *raise* the book over your head when you physically act on that book. You *lie* in bed on your own accord; you *lay* the book down when you physically place that book.

If you miss any of the sentences in the next exercise, you will need to do some review work on irregular verbs.

EXERCISE 5–A

Directions: Draw one line under each simple subject and two lines under each verb. Then, using standard proofreaders' marks, make any necessary corrections. Write *OK* to the left of any sentences that are correct.

1. Recently I visited an aviary and seen many different sights.
2. My experience begun when I took the early-bird walk.
3. I must have sleeped through the 15-minute lecture because I remember being awakened by the unearthly screech of a blue-and-yellow macaw.
4. The creature became quiet only after being offered a choice morsel of food.
5. A crimson-backed tanager sung with a light trill while his mate drank from a pebbled stream.
6. A blue-throated barbet set quietly underneath a shrub, but her mate sprung up and was in a flurry of activity.
7. A Nubian carmine bee eater laid quietly watching his mate then raised to help her search for food.
8. She raised a twig and held it in her beak; she scratched impatiently with one foot.
9. She lay the twig down, and then as the twig laid there, the bird slowly began to chip at the bark.
10. Her mate, who was no longer laying there but was scratching diligently as well, payed no attention to the bark-chipping procedure.
11. He had lain a fine layer of pine needles down for his next bed.
12. After carefully checking the construction of his nest, he settled down and quietly laid there.
13. The Nubian carmine bee eater must have laid there for nearly ten minutes when a Gouldian finch begun to demand the newly made bed of needles.

14. Feathers flew, and voices were risen as the two battled it out.

15. Eventually they become tired and had to rest; they drunk from the little stream and then dove into the refreshing water.

16. None of these tropical birds sung much; they mostly screeched and sprung about looking for worms and choosing other insect delicacies.

17. As the sun busted out from behind the clouds, a lilac-breasted roller began to warble.

18. I lay down my binoculars and smiled at the sound of his song.

19. My binoculars had not lain there more than three minutes, when a small child asked to borrow them.

20. The child sought to see a red-rumped paradise tanager that was laying under a shrub. Suddenly the bird rose and took flight.

Agreement Errors Caused by Intervening Material

Another subject-verb error can occur when intervening material (usually prepositional phrases or other modifiers) separates the simple subject and verb. When this happens, we may spontaneously match another closer word with the verb, causing an error. Take a look at the following sentences and see if you can spot the intervening material that might confuse a proofreader.

> One of the large leather briefcases was badly scratched. (Not all the briefcases were scratched; just one was scratched.)
>
> Sam, as well as Sue and her children, wants a vacation in May. (We are concerned only with what Sam wants.)
>
> One of the Morrison children appears to be accident-prone. (Only one child is accident-prone.)

EXERCISE 5–B

Directions: Underline each simple subject once and each verb twice. Put each prepositional phrase in parentheses. Using standard proofreaders' marks, make any needed corrections. Write *OK* to the left of the sentence if everything is correct. This exercise is basically a review. Again, if you have any difficulty with it, you need to work on supplemental exercises.

1. Many of the homes that are located in an old suburb needs to be remodeled.

2. Five homes, out of the twenty that are there, need replacement windows.

3. One of the houses appears to date back to the turn of the century.

4. Another is a wonderful reproduction of the architecture of Victorian homes but need extensive renovation.

5. One of the two-year college students want to start a housecleaning and odd-job business.

6. The idea, which is one of this student's better schemes, are to use college students when they are not in class.

7. A master schedule of everyone's class times are entered into a spreadsheet program on a computer.

8. As work requests by a potential customer is phoned into the home office, the manager checks the requests against the master schedule.

9. Students who have free time and the required ability is given a form that contain the necessary job information and location.

SUBJECT-VERB AGREEMENT RULES

Subject-Verb Agreement

5.1 Subjects and verbs must agree in number.

- An industry has to show a profit to continue to stay in business.
- Industries have to show a profit to continue to stay in business.

Compound Subjects

5.2 When two or more subjects are added together, use a plural verb.

- Sarah jogs every other morning. (**S V** single subject=single verb)
- Joe and Sarah jog every other morning. (**S S V** compound subject=plural verb)
- On the other hand, Martha, Herb, and I shop three times a week. (**S S S V** compound subject=plural verb)

There

5.3 The word *there* (or *here*) is rarely the subject of a sentence; therefore be sure to find the actual subject or subjects before writing *there is* or *there are*.

- There is one dog.
- There are two dogs.

Or, nor, Either . . . or, and *Neither . . . nor*

5.4 If the compound subject is joined by *or, nor, either . . . or,* or *neither . . . nor,* match the verb to its closest subject.

- ➤ *Either* Ms. Thomas *or* *Mr. Midas* *wants* to chair the meeting.
- ➤ *Neither* the two boxes *nor* the *crate* *is* large enough to hold the decorations.
- ➤ *Neither* the crate *nor* the two *boxes* *are* large enough to hold the decorations.

Tense Shifts

5.5 Avoid needless shifts in verb tense.

Incorrect	The board of directors acknowledges the problems with the labor unions but seemed unconcerned with finding solutions.
Correct	The board of directors acknowledges the problems with the labor unions but seems unconcerned with finding solutions.

Subjunctive Mood

5.6 Use the subjunctive mood in clauses that begin with *if* and refer to untrue or doubtful situations.

- ➤ *If* I *were* rich, I would buy you a Mercedes. (I probably will not be rich.)
- ➤ *If* Mr. Perkins *were* to become the president of Acme, many of the employees would go on strike. (Mr. Perkins probably will not become the president.)

5.7 Use the subjunctive mood in clauses that begin with *that* and express wishes, recommendations, and demands.

- ➤ I wish *that* I were able to attend the conference. (not *was able*)
- ➤ The board demands *that* he finish the project. (not *finishes*)
- ➤ Mr. Rodrigues suggested *that* he be given a second chance. (not *is given*)

EXERCISE 5-C

Directions: This exercise covers rules 5.1 through 5.7. Underline each simple subject once and each verb twice. Using standard proofreaders' marks, make any needed corrections. Write *OK* to the left of any sentences that are correct.

1. There is preventable shock hazards in most homes.
2. Removed outlet face plates and an unused outlet have the potential to be hazardous.

3. Removed outlet face plates or an unused outlet has the potential to be hazardous.
4. An unused outlet or removed outlet face plates has the potential to be hazardous.
5. An unused outlet and removed outlet face plates has the potential to be hazardous.
6. Unused outlets leave extra holes in which toddlers may stick objects.
7. Covering these with plastic protectors add to household safety.
8. There are bare wires that are exposed when the face plate was removed.
9. Ground plugs serve a purpose and should never be removed.
10. If I was building a home, I would install ground-fault-interrupt outlets near sinks and bathtubs.
11. Safety codes written by any company strongly suggests that frayed wires on appliances are replaced.
12. Aluminum ladders and a pool-cleaning pole has the potential to be hazardous as well.
13. Ladders or a pole become an excellent conductor when in contact with a power line.
14. Power companies demand that an individual calls to find out where the buried lines are.
15. I wish that a driver was able to remember to stay in the car when downed power lines are nearby.

EXERCISE 5-D *Directions*: Using standard proofreaders' marks, make any necessary corrections in this text review.

MEMORANDUM

TO: All Employees

FROM: Sally Nearhoff, Personal Director

DATE: January 8, 1999

SUBJECT: Presidents' Day Celebration

As you know, we at Grace Brothers really go "all out" in celebration of Precedents' Day and this year the management want to create a media event by having all sales personnel dress as a favorite president or first lady. Some employees may even wish to coordinate specific time periods within their own departments. There are prizes in several categories for the winners. Mr. Grace has promised a wonderful grand prize: an extra week of paid vacation! I know everyone will want to start thinking about this event now.

Mr. Grace suggests that you are given ample time to prepare. With that in mind, the Costume Department in the basement will be open for your convenience three weeks prior to this event, however, your requested not to visit their during your regular work hours. Please note that neither President Washington nor President Lincoln are to be portrayed by the staff. Only the floor managers and the department store CEO is to wear period costumes to represent these two distinctive presidents.

The sale items will be even better then last year's so we anticipate even more customers. Sense Grace Brothers is a team-oriented store, I know everyone will partipate to make this the best year ever.

mp

SUBJECT-VERB AGREEMENT RULES (continued)

Collective Nouns

5.8 Collective (or group) nouns take a singular verb when these nouns represent a single group acting as a single unit.

- ➤ The Sun Business wants to open its doors on the first day of February.
- ➤ The basketball team always makes a good showing in the playoffs.
- ➤ The committee refuses to meet on Fridays.

5.9 Collective (or group) nouns take a plural verb only when the individuals within the group unit engage in individually separate acts. (Although this rule is technically correct, the sentence generally sounds smoother when rewritten to include "the members of . . . " or " . . . members.")

- ➤ The team always scatter to their cars within thirty minutes of the ending buzzer.
- ➤ (The team members always scatter to their cars within thirty minutes of the ending buzzer.)
- ➤ The committee are in disagreement over the new contracts.
- ➤ (The members of the committee are in disagreement over the new contracts.)

PROOFREADING POINTER

Anyone* and *Everyone *Anyone* and *everyone* can be written as one word or two words.

any one	anyone
every one	everyone

When faced with the dilemma of one word or two, look for the word *of* immediately following. If you find an *of,* then use two words. If you don't find an *of,* then use one word.

Indefinite Pronouns

5.10 Use a singular verb when using any of these pronouns:

anybody	everybody	nobody	somebody
anyone	everyone	nothing	someone
anything	everything		something

- ➤ Everybody loves a puppy.
- ➤ Has anyone seen my umbrella?

5.11 Words such as *all, any, half, more, most, the rest,* and *some* take singular verbs if they refer to something that cannot be counted.

➤ Half *of the milk* is gone.

➤ Some *of the applesauce* is spoiled.

5.12 Words such as *all, any, half, more, most, the rest,* and *some* take plural verbs if they refer to something that can be counted.

➤ Most *of the students* forget to bring a reference manual.

➤ All *of the apples* are covered with blight.

PROOFREADING POINTER

None The indefinite pronoun *none* is generally viewed as singular, meaning *not one.*

➤ None of us has any ideas.

None may also agree with the object of the preposition.

➤ None of the secretaries agree with you.

EXERCISE 5–E

Directions: This exercise covers rules 5.8 through 5.12. Using standard proofreaders' marks, make all necessary corrections.

1. Everybody in both schools want to take an extra two days to study before the final exams.
2. Most of the student body agree that the time could be used wisely.
3. Some of the students agree that there would be a terrible temptation to party on the first of those two days.
4. Anyone knows that constant study is practically impossible for most students.
5. The academic committee don't agree on the availability of extra study time.
6. The committee agrees that extra study time is good but aren't able to agree on a collegewide schedule.
7. Many of the students feel that the economics exam is considered to be the hardest final exam.
8. Most of the questions on the final exam is multiple choice.
9. Some of the test questions are straight from the book, but some of the questions come from the lectures.
10. Some students at one college want to vote to have no exams at all!

EXERCISE 5–F

Directions: Using standard proofreaders' marks, correct any errors. This is a text-review exercise.

TO: Basil Holmes, District Attorney

FROM: John Watson, County Coroner

DATE: May 18, 1999

SUBJECT: Death by Drowning

When we talked last week in the courthouse hallway, you mentioned that you're next case had to do with a drowning. In our discussion you seem uncertain as to the exact physical reactions an individual would undergo when drowning, I thought this description would answer your questions.

In a drowning, an individual dies from asphyxia. Immediately after being submerged, one's reflex reaction for holding one's breath takes over, however, water eventually enters the lungs. The larynx will begun to spasm, this causes further asphyxia. There is abnormal heart rhythms. Generally, red blood cell damage occur due to water absorption changing the mineral concentration of the blood. The stomach may distend and lung edema may occur if the victim has not died yet. If artificial respiration, cardiac massage, and blood-disorder corrections are quickly applied, it is possible for the victim to survive and recover completely.

If you need further clarification on this or any other medical diagnosis, please do not hesitate to contact me. As you know, the morgue was located in the subbasement of the west wing of the courthouse. I would be glad to arrange a tour of hour facilities for you or your associates.

ss

SUBJECT-VERB AGREEMENT RULES (continued)

The Number and *a* Number

5.13 Use a singular verb when the word *number* is preceded by *the.* Use a plural verb when the word *number* is preceded by *a.*

➤ *The* number of violent crimes occurring in Samsonville is increasing.

➤ *A* number of gangs have been formed.

Organizational Titles

5.14 Use either a singular or a plural verb with the name of an organization that contains two or more names. The singular form emphasizes the unity of the organization, whereas the plural form emphasizes the individuals. Be consistent in the use of singular or plural verbs within the document.

➤ Becker, Robbins, and Robbins is a law firm that has its offices on Third Avenue.

➤ Stamford and Sons are having disputes over the change of the company's name.

Portions and Fractions

5.15 Use either a singular or a plural verb with a subject indicating a portion or a fraction. The number of the subject is determined by examining the prepositional phrase that modifies the subject. Use a singular verb if the object of the preposition *of* is singular or is implied. Use a plural verb if the object of the preposition *of* is plural or is implied.

➤ Two-thirds *of the student body* passes the state proficiency exams each year.

➤ Two-thirds *of the students* pass the state proficiency exams each year.

➤ A majority *of votes* is needed to pass the bill. (A group of votes is implied.)

➤ A majority *of employees* have contributed to the scholarship fund. (Several individual contributions have been made.)

> **PROOFREADING POINTER**
>
> **Subject-Verb Agreement**
> When using foreign words, be sure to check whether they are plural or singular.

Time, Quantity, and Money

5.16 Use a singular verb with a subject that represents a total amount of time, quantity, or money. Use a plural verb with a subject that represents a number of units of time, quantity, or money.

➤ *Fourteen* gallons is all that my gas tank will hold. (The subject describes the total quantity.)

➤ *Fourteen* gallons are pumped every thirty seconds with this new device. (Each gallon is counted.)

➤ *Two weeks* is a reasonable amount of time between visits. (The subject represents the total amount of time.)

➤ *Two weeks* have passed since the fair was in town. (Each week has been counted.)

PROOFREADING POINTER

Subject-Verb Agreement The verb form of *to use* is often misused. The past tense is *used* and is frequently followed by an infinitive phrase. "I *used to walk* to school" is a typical example. When we say this out loud, we have a tendency to run the *-ed* and the *to* together. As a result of our not hearing the two separate sounds, we sometimes write that sentence incorrectly as "I *use to* walk to school." Just think about what is being said: The time frame is indeed in the past tense, so don't forget the final *-ed.*

EXERCISE 5–G

Directions: This exercise covers rules 5.13 through 5.16. Using standard proofreaders' marks, correct any errors. If the sentence is correct, write *OK* to the left of the number.

1. Forty acres is the size of the farm.
2. Allston, Grady, and Burroughs is having its offices renovated.
3. Allston, Grady, and Burroughs is responsible for remodeling their individual offices.
4. A number of new retail stores have opened in the downtown area.
5. The number of new retail stores in the downtown area have grown.
6. One-fourth of the student population is anticipated.
7. One-fourth of the student population has voted.
8. A majority of the student population vote is needed.
9. The number of students who do not speak English is growing.
10. A number of students who do not speak English is signed up for this course.
11. Huxley, Buxley, and Sons is having a labor dispute.
12. Huxley, Buxley, and Sons is a continual pollutant to our environment.
13. Seven pies is the record for the ten-minute eating marathon.
14. Seven pies is a lot of food to consume in ten minutes.
15. Four working days is enough time to complete the project.

EXERCISE 5–H

Directions: Using standard proofreaders' marks, make any necessary corrections in this text-review exercise.

THE ORIGIN OF BILLIARDS

No one is quite sure of the origin of billiards. Some of the references to the game has come from writers. For example, Shakespeare suggested Cleopatra knew of the game. One historian suggested second-century Ireland was when and where it started. Some French researchers suggest England was responsible, although the French made the game extremely popular. English researchers suggest that billiards must have originated in France, the name *billiards* are derived from a Fench word meaning "stick."

As far as historians can determine, billiards probably started in fourteenth-century England, it seems logical that the game was a winterized adaptation of the popular bowling on the green (something like our bowling). Of course, on a much smaller scale. The balls were no longer rolled, but were pushed by a heavy stick called a *mace*.

Eventually the game was adapted too play on a large table. According to the accounts, the table resembled a miniature croquet field. There were a number of arches on the table through which the ball had to be knocked. Later, pockets were built into the table ends. Eventually, the arches were removed and more pockets were added. The beginning of modern pocket billiards. The mace was changed to a crooked stick, and eventually too a straight one. Pieces of a good grade of leather was attached to the ends of the sticks to keep the end of the cue from chipping.

A Frenchman did much to advance the game in the eighteenth century. Captain Mingaud become a skilled player during his political imprisonment. After his release, he toured the country, and amazed the citizenry with his brilliant billiard shots. In the nineteenth century, an Englishman by the name of Jack Carr was credited for being the first individual to apply chalk to the end of the stick. Today skilled players continued to make the game popular.

How is you're billiard playing? Rack 'em!

Pronoun-Antecedent Agreement

Pronouns must agree with their antecedents (the words they represent). This doesn't sound like a hard task, but in reality pronouns must agree in three areas: number (singular or plural), person (first, second, or third), and gender (feminine or masculine). Therefore, when we see the sentence, *One of the Macinaw Elementary School children has her poem published in today's paper,* we know from the pronoun *her* that there is one person (number), that she is a female (gender), and that the sentence was written in third person. (Remember from your writing classes how first person "I" and second person "you" were practically banned from formal report writing?) As proofreaders and as writers, we have to be careful to make sure that the pronoun *her* in our example is a correct match with One of the Macinaw Elementary School children, especially when there is intervening material.

Pronoun Case

A far more complicated problem is pronoun case. A pronoun's case has to do with that pronoun's grammatical position within a sentence. Fortunately, we seem to absorb these rules almost automatically during our language-acquisition years. If we did not learn them correctly, however, or if we have forgotten or misused these rules, our "ear" for correctness becomes a little tone deaf. For example, are you ever confused about whether to use *who* or *whom*? Would you say *between you and I,* or would you say *between you and me*? You would never say *Me went to the mall,* but on occasion you might hear someone say *Me, Sam, and Martha went to the mall.* Is it ever correct to say *them things*? These dilemmas can be solved through an investigation of pronoun case.

Pronouns have several cases, but the three we use most frequently are subjective case, objective case, and possessive case. Now this is where the grammatical position of the pronoun fits into the picture. If we are trying to show possession or ownership, we use **possessive case** (*your* coat, *his* picture, or *their* car) to show who owns or possesses that object. The possessive case pronoun always functions as a modifier, and the possessive case probably causes the least confusion. However, the subjective and objective cases are not difficult once we have refreshed our memory. What word do you see in *subjective* and *objective*? That's right—*subject* and *object*—and that's the key to pronoun case. We use **subjective case** when the pronoun is used as the subject or complement of the sentence, and we use **objective case** when the pronoun is used as the direct object, indirect object, object of the preposition, or one of the other types of objects.

To see how this works, let's take a look at a simple sentence: *Lynn gave Lynn's car to Bob.* (This sentence is a prime example of why we use pronouns—it gets a bit ridiculous to keep repeating the antecedent.) The first thing we automatically would do is to use possessive case and change *Lynn's* to *her.* Then if we had been in an extensive communication about Lynn, we might not even feel the need to keep repeating her name. We might substitute the subjective case pronoun, saying, *She gave her car to Bob,* since this pronoun is the subject of the sentence. We might not wish to keep repeating Bob's name, either; so we might add a pronoun here too. But this time we need to use the objective case since *Bob* in this sentence is the object of the preposition *to.* Thank goodness, we don't have to go through all this convoluted thinking; we can just blurt out *She gave her car to him.* This automatic fill-in-the-blank construction is true most of the time, but occasional snags may trip us if we aren't careful. Chart 5.2 lists the pronoun cases.

CHART 5.2 PRONOUN CASE

	SUBJECTIVE CASE		OBJECTIVE CASE		POSSESSIVE CASE	
	Singular	**Plural**	**Singular**	**Plural**	**Singular**	**Plural**
First	I	we	me	us	my, mine	our, ours
Second	you	you	you	you	your, yours	your, yours
Third	he she it	they	him her it	them	his her, hers its	their, theirs
	who	who	whom	whom	whose	whose
	whoever	whoever	whomever	whomever		

One easy way to put pronouns into cases is to fill in a very simple sentence. Your ear will let you automatically fill in the blank _____ *gave* _____ *to* _____. (I gave it, you gave it, he gave it, and so on. I gave it to you, to him, to her, and so on.)

Intervening Material Just as intervening material has the potential to mislead us in subject-verb agreement, it can mislead us in forming pronoun cases. The best solution is to remove the material mentally in order to "hear" any mistakes. Here's an example: *Sarah went to the mall with Jim, Sue, Tierza, George, Betty, and I.* Now take out the intervening list of names: *Sarah went to the mall with I.* Whoa! We know that's not right; it doesn't sound right. Our "ear" is hearing a violation of the rule that the preposition *with* must be followed by a pronoun in the objective case.

Courtesy Another helpful hint when tackling pronoun case has to do with courtesy. When using first person in a list of other names in the subject position, we should put the other people first and put ourselves last. Some people might say, "Me, Jim, Sue, Tierza, George, and Betty went to the mall." Did you notice the error? Did you check the grammatical structure? The pronoun is functioning as a subject in this sentence, so we need to use the subjective case *I* instead of *me.* If we follow the courtesy suggestion and refer to ourselves at the end of the list, we notice the correct combination of *I went* more easily. *Jim, Sue, Tierza, George, Betty, and I went to the mall.*

Complements We also need to be careful when pronouns function as complements in sentences. Remember that a linking verb creates a complement (although it reminds us of a direct object). Consider the sentence *Sarah was the dancer.* We know the subject is *Sarah,* the verb is *was,* and the complement is *dancer.* We also see how easy it would be to reverse the wording and still have the same meaning: *The dancer was Sarah.* Keep this in mind when you read these sentence pairs, which use pronouns. *She was the dancer. The dancer was she. He was the person on TV. The person on TV was he.* Remember, pronouns that are complements must be in subjective case. Be patient if this sounds a little strange to your "grammar ear." With a little concentration, this, too, will sound perfectly comfortable after awhile.

Now see how you do in this next exercise on pronoun case. If you miss any, you will want to do some extra reviewing on your own.

EXERCISE 5-1

Directions: Using standard proofreaders' marks, make any necessary pronoun corrections. Be ready to explain why you used the case you did.

1. Just between you and I, Henry split the reward with Mary, Janeen, Bill, Terri, and I.
2. I haven't seen Mr. Knowles and him for years. Was it them in the restaurant?
3. Him and Mr. Knowles tried to convince Ms. Smith and myself to go to the party.
4. This month Ms. Wynski said him and I could take a special correspondence course.
5. Interest rates were at their lowest, which should encourage the home-construction industry to try to regain some of their earlier losses.

The Pronouns *Who* and *Whom*

Probably the pronoun question that gets to all of us at one time or another is whether to use *who* or *whom.* When we use these words rapidly, the distinction between them blurs, and for many of us, that distinction has been lost for a long time. However, we can sort it out by checking the grammatical structure of the sentence in which they appear. *Who* is subjective case; *whom* is objective case. There's an easy way to remember this. Study the pronoun cases in Chart 5.2 again. Look at the objective case side. Do you see the words *me, him, them*? Notice the letter *m* in each of these words. *Whom* also has the letter *m,* and it is also objective case.

A fast and safe way to answer the who-whom question is to find the subject to each verb. Every verb (or compound verb) must have its own subject (or compound subject). If your verb is missing a subject, then *who* is usually the answer. Once you pair your subjects and verbs, consider them welded together! To see how this works, check out the following sentence:

> The woman who is wearing the green sweater and the man in the tan coat are the people with whom he shared his lottery ticket.

Now pair all the verbs with their subjects.

> The woman (S) who (s) is wearing (V) the green sweater and the man (S) in the tan coat are (V) the people with whom he (s) shared (V) his lottery ticket.

woman/man are	(compound subject and verb of the independent clause)
who is wearing	(dependent clause that describes woman: *Who* is the pronoun representing woman.)
he shared	(part of the dependent clause that describes people)

Remember that the subjective case *who* can be used as a pronoun only in the subject positions or the complement positions. In the example sentence, *are, is wearing,* and *shared* are all verbs that must have partners. Once you have paired them and checked the possibility of complements, anything that is left will have to be used in the objective case.

In fighting the who-whom battle, some books suggest that you test the structure by substituting the pronouns *she* or *her* to decide what case sounds right. There's only one problem—are you absolutely sure you can trust your ear? By taking a second to think of the grammatical structure, you will know you're right. The good news is that the more you practice, the more quickly you will be able to correct any errors, almost without thinking!

See how you do in the next exercise, which covers only *who* and *whom.* Remember to pair subjects and verbs to help determine the case.

EXERCISE 5–J

Directions: This exercise covers *who* and *whom* only. Using standard proofreaders' marks, make any necessary changes. (Remember to pair subjects and verbs to help determine the proper case.)

1. Mr. and Mrs. Branzell, who we know as good friends, will be watching our home while we are on vacation.
2. Choose whoever you wish to go to the party.
3. I'm sure that whoever it is will be fine.
4. Their home was full of people, some of who I had never met.
5. That is Ms. Donnelly who I thought had already left the party.
6. Do you know who the man was who bought the winning ticket?
7. Never ask for who the bell tolls.
8. There was no one in my graduating class who did not expect to be a success in the future.
9. The directions for building the town square will be given by whoever wins the architectural bid.
10. Do your best for whoever offers you the job.

Pronoun Gender

In today's society, we realize the impact of gender in the language we use. Each of us has an obligation to avoid using sexist language. Part of the gender-language dilemma is reflected in singular pronouns. Obviously, there is no problem when an antecedent-and-pronoun combination clearly represents a gender—*the woman . . . she; the boy . . . he,* and so on. Nor is there a problem when plural pronouns, such as *we* or *they* are used, since they do not represent a specific gender. The dilemma arises with the use of indefinite pronouns, as in this sentence: *Each of the children must bring _____ lunch. Each,* the antecedent, must be matched to a *singular* possessive case pronoun in third person. If we say *her* lunch, we are saying that all the children are girls; if we say *his* lunch, we are saying all the children are boys. We cannot say *their* lunch because that would be matching a plural pronoun with a singular antecedent. (Unfortunately, this maneuver is the one most frequently used to combat the problem, but it is incorrect.) Until several years ago, the singular masculine-gender pronoun was used to represent all of humankind, all individuals, regardless of gender. Textbooks of that era would have said *his lunch* without a second thought. Today, using the singular masculine gender is not grammatically incorrect, but trying to remedy this situation certainly shows a greater sensitivity to the impact of language.

Solutions There are actually four solutions to this problem. The first, is to **use the combination approach—*he or she.*** Our example would then read *his or her* lunch. This approach works well if the wording is used only a time or two, but the writing style becomes increasingly awkward as this combination is repeated within any given paragraph. The second solution is to **change the original antecedent to the plural form.** We could rewrite *each of the children* as *the children* and then use a plural pronoun—*their.* The third option is to **rewrite the sentence** so that no pronoun is used—*Each of the children must bring* a *lunch.* There is a fourth course of action that is to be considered only in desperation. When none of these three solutions works, we can **arbitrarily pick a singular pronoun** that would reflect gender—*his lunch* or *her lunch.*

Gender can cause the proofreader to do some creative maneuvering, but the results will no doubt be worthwhile, considering the far-reaching impact language has on each of us.

The pronoun rules follow. After you study the rules and the examples accompanying them, try your hand at the exercise. Remember, this section still contains some basic review. If you are not comfortable with this material, you will need to do some outside work on pronouns.

PRONOUN RULES

Pronoun-Antecedent Agreement

5.17 Pronouns must agree with their antecedents (the nouns they represent) in number (singular or plural), person (first, second, or third), and gender (feminine or masculine). Check to see that the pronoun clearly points to the intended antecedent. (Rewriting may be required.)

➤ **Samson** was known for *his* strength.

➤ The **children** ran to tell *their* neighbor the news.

➤ The **school board** announced *its* decision to award **Iyako Suko** the **scholarship.** *She* will receive *it* at the award banquet.

➤ The **girls** reported the **boys'** soccer meet in the school paper. *They* enjoyed the article. (Who enjoyed the article, the girls or the boys? The pronoun does not clearly point to the antecedent. In this case it would be clearer to repeat the noun: The *boys* enjoyed the article.)

5.18 Use a pronoun that agrees with the antecedent closest to the verb when a compound subject is joined by any of the following: *or, nor, either . . . or, neither . . . nor.*

➤ *Either* Tom *or* the **boys** will want *their* pictures taken.

➤ *Either* the boys *or* **Tom** will want *his* picture taken.

Pronoun Case

5.19 The case of the pronoun is determined by the pronoun's grammatical use in the sentence.

➤ *She* gave Mr. Henderhoff the briefcase. (A subject uses subjective case.)

➤ Ms. Radowsky gave *him* the briefcase. (An indirect object uses objective case.)

➤ Ms. Radowsky gave Mr. Henderhoff *her* briefcase. (A modifying pronoun showing ownership uses possessive case.)

Possessive Pronoun Before a Gerund

5.20 Use the possessive case of the pronoun before a gerund.

➤ I can't stand *your* **whining.** (It's your whining, not you, that I can't stand.)

Who, Which, and *That*

5.21 Both *who* and *that* are used to refer to people; *which* and *that* are used to refer to animals, objects, and places. Use *who* when referring to an individual person or the individuality of a group. Use *that* when referring to a class, species, or type. Technically, *which* is used to introduce nonessential clauses, and *that* is used for essential clauses. (See Chapter 8 for a discussion of these clauses.) Many writers use the pronouns *which* or *that* incorrectly.

➤ Mr. LaRocca is the only **one** *who* makes us turn in our homework.

➤ Morticia is the **kind** of person *that* always makes you feel welcome.

➤ Mad Dog's **car,** *which* had just been repainted, was a thing to behold.

➤ I felt *that* **I needed more time for myself.** (essential clause)

Who and *Whom*

5.22 Use *who* when the grammatical structure of the sentence reflects a subject or a complement. Use *whom* when the grammatical structure of the sentence reflects an object, indirect object, object of the preposition, or any other type of object.

- *Who* was the speaker? (*Who* is the subject.)
- The speaker was *who*? (*Who* is the complement.)
- The speaker was a politician *who* was well known. (*Who* is the subject of the verb *was.*)
- To *whom* did you wish to speak? (*Whom* is the object of the preposition *to.*)
- The young senator will vote for a Supreme Court justice *whom* others have approved. (*Whom* is the direct object in the clause *whom others have approved.*)
- Donna is the woman for *whom I* made the wedding cake. (*Whom* is the object of the preposition *for,* and *I* is the subject of the verb *made.*)

Pronouns Following *Than* or *as* in a Comparison

5.23 Use subjective case when the pronoun follows *than* or *as* in a sentence when a comparison is being made unless the pronoun is an object of an implied verb.

- Sarah is *as tall as he.* (Sarah is *as tall as he is tall.*)
- He likes Sarah better *than me.* (He likes Sarah better *than he likes me.)*

Pronouns With Common Gender Antecedents

5.24 Avoid using either a masculine or feminine pronoun when the antecedent could be either gender.

Solution Use *he or she, him or her,* or *his or hers* unless the writing becomes awkward.

- Each child should bring *his or her* own lunch.

Solution Change the singular antecedent to a plural.

- The children should bring *their* own lunches.

Solution Reword the sentence to avoid using pronouns.

- Each child should bring *a* lunch.

Solution If none of the above solutions works, use *he* or *she* (but only in desperation!).

- Each child should bring *his* own lunch.

PROOFREADING POINTER

Pronouns

- Don't let your reader be confused! Be sure to use the antecedent (noun) before using the pronoun.
- Foreign words cause difficulties with those of us who don't know their meanings, to say nothing of their genders. Be sure the pronoun's gender agrees with the foreign word's gender.

-Self Forms of Pronouns

5.25 *-Self* forms of pronouns (also known as *reflexive* and *intensive* pronouns) are used to reflect or intensify other words. Do not use *-self* forms as substitutes for subjects or objects. These pronouns may also be used to emphasize another word.

- The engineer wanted *me* to solve the problem. (not *myself*)
- I gave *myself* a present.
- I felt that the bouquet *itself* was an adequate thank-you.

EXERCISE 5-K

Directions: This exercise contains pronoun-usage errors only. Using standard proofreaders' marks, correct any errors. Assume that the pronoun antecedent is correct. If you find it necessary to change the pronoun subject of the sentence, you may also need to change the verb in order to have the proper subject-verb agreement.

1622 N. HAMPTON ROAD COON RAPIDS, MN 55433

July 22, 1999

Mrs. Sarah Morton
7599 Midstreet Avenue
Hermantown, MN 55811

Dear Mrs. Morton:

We at Clawtrack Tires are sorry to hear of your recent inconvenience. We appreciate you telling us about the problem you have had with our radials. We feel we have a superior line of radial tires, and we are concerned with the quality of each tire. Furthermore, Clawtrack Tires wants you to know they are committed to total customer satisfaction.

As you know, we will pay for four new tires and have your local Clawtrack dealer, George Sampson, install it. He is the person with who you will be able to trust your tire care. Your dealer will inspect each tire for flaws, accurately inflate them to the proper poundage, and then balance them before they replace the tire. For the past inconvenience, we would also like to offer a free front-wheel alignment at the time of her tire replacement.

In order to encourage proper tire care, we are offering our customers the following tips. Inspect your tires once a month for any uneven wear. Uneven wear patterns may be caused by improper inflation pressure, misalignment, improper balance, or suspension neglect. While checking your tires, look for stones and bits of other foreign objects that have lodged in the treads. It can cause problems if they work deeper into the tire. Also, if your tire continually needs more air, one should have them checked to see if the wheel or valve may be the problem.

Mrs. Sarah Morton
Page 2
July 22, 1999

Again, we are sorry for the inconvenience but appreciate you having a continued interest in our radial tires. We know that Hermantown's local dealer, George Sampson, will personally attend to your needs. Clawtrack Tires is confident in their dealers, who will always offer a customer quality service.

Please let us know how you enjoy your new tires.

Sincerely,

CLAWTRACK TIRES, INC.

Samuel DeCoco, Vice President
Consumer Affairs

fj

EXERCISE 5–L *Directions:* This exercise is a text review. Using standard proofreaders' marks, correct any errors.

TO: Vernon's Video Chain

FROM: Visual Futures, Inc.

DATE: March 5, 1999

SUBJECT: VCR Cleaning

As you know, over the past year we have been experiencing some customer dissatisfaction with our line of VCRs. After some research we found that 70 percent of all VCR owners fail to follow the manufacturer's instructions to keep the product in good running order by cleaning the heads regularly. Most of the repairs are necessary simply because the machine is to dirty to work properly. How frequently the owner plays rental tapes and the quality of the tapes they use is the two most important factors in determining how often the machine should be cleaned.

Caution your customers to buy a good head cleaner. The number of cleaners that are to abrasive is appalling. If an abrasive cleaner is used constantly, the heads will simply wear out. It is important is to follow the manufacturer's instructions carefully. A number of companies suggests applying a good head cleaner after every 30 to 40 hours of use, some suggest a weekly cleaning.

Please advice your customers that head cleaning does not take the place of an annual professional cleaning, lubrication, and adjustment.

Warn owners to return rental tapes if he or she sees dropouts on the screen or hears noise. The rental tape should not even be played or rewound. These tapes should be returned for clean ones. If the rental company will not let you run a cassette for a minute or too to check for dropouts, then the consumer needs to make sure he can return the cassette without a charge if the tape is dirty.

Remember, clean heads means a better-running machine, this translates into fewer warranty returns and happier customers.

vt

PROOFREADING POINTER

Parallelism

- Whenever you check a list, be sure it is parallel in construction.
- Whenever you notice compound verbs, objects, phrases, or other compound constructions, quickly review the words for parallelism.

Parallelism

As strange as this may sound, well-written material has a balance and a rhythm all its own. How we arrange words in a sentence is as important as which words we use. When we express two or more ideas, we should balance them grammatically by using parallel construction. Consider this sentence: *The management course is fun, interesting, and challenging; and it is not very expensive.* Notice there are four descriptors of this course. Three are adjectives, and the last is a complete clause. Now listen to the more balanced rhythm of this sentence when we correct for parallelism: *The management course is fun, interesting, challenging, and inexpensive.*

Proofreading is the final place to check the balance and flow of words—to make sure that the construction is parallel.

Parallel Construction

5.26 Use parallel construction within sentences or among elements in closely related material by expressing parallel ideas in parallel form.

Incorrect My first-grade teacher had soft eyes, a warm heart, and a voice that was musical.

Correct My first-grade teacher had soft eyes, a warm heart, and a musical voice.

Incorrect Ms. Lawrence likes playing tennis and to jog.

Correct Ms. Lawrence likes playing tennis and jogging.

Incorrect The committee will listen and abide by the director's decision.

Correct The committee will listen to and abide by the director's decision.

EXERCISE 5–M

Directions: Using standard proofreaders' marks, correct these sentences for faulty parallelism. If no corrections are necessary, write *OK* to the left of the sentence.

1. Those women have imagination and are thoughtful.
2. The Cub Scouts will want to play and sing after dinner.
3. Money is more easily spent than to save.
4. If a wellness or physical fitness program is implemented, the company usually receives several benefits: increased productivity, less absenteeism, deaths are fewer, and health insurance rates are reduced.
5. After implementing a health program, employees report improved stamina, sounder sleep, losing weight, visiting the doctor less, and a reduction in smoking.

6. Thomas Jefferson, the third U.S. President, encouraged learning and helping to start the Library of Congress by selling 6000 of his own books.

7. Every morning John Quincy Adams, the sixth U.S. President, read his Bible and swimming in the nude to start his day.

8. The ninth U.S. President, William Henry Harrison, gave the longest inaugural speech on record; it contained 8500 words and lasting two hours.

9. John Tyler, the tenth President, was the father of 15 children; he had 8 children by his first marriage and his second wife bore 7 more.

10. James Garfield, the twentieth President, entertained his guests by writing Latin with one hand and wrote Greek with the other at the same time.

EXERCISE 5-N

Directions: This is a text-review exercise. Using standard proofreaders' marks, correct any errors.

Federal Duck Stamp Office
1849 C Street, N.W., Suite 2058
Washington, DC 20240
February 18, 1999

Dear Postal Patron:

We want to remind you of two truly effective ways all Americans can contribute to preserving our treasured wildlife. By purchasing the Duck Stamp and subscribe to the Duck Stamp Collection, you receive stamps that depict waterfowl in their natural habitats. You will also have the satisfaction of knowing that you have contributed to safeguarding key wintering and breeding habitats.

This stamp program is one of the most successful conservation programs ever initiated by the government. They started in 1934, Congress passed the Migratory Bird Hunting Stamp Act. All of the waterfowl hunters had to purchase annually and carry a Federal Duck Stamp.

Early explorers and settlers took only a little over 400 years to deplete the great flocks and heards of birds that once flourished in North America. Eager hunters killed thousands upon thousands, marshlands were drained to grow crops. Then the Great Dust Bowl years occurred, it became apparent that something had to be done. The Migratory Bird Conservation Act of 1929 was only a stop-gap measure but it was a significant step in the right direction.

Anyone for who a stamp is purchased should know that over 98 cents of every Duck Stamp dollar goes directly toward the purchase of wetlands for North American Waterfowl. These lands become a part of the National Wildlife Refuge System and benefits many other species of plants and animals. One-third of the nation's endangered or threatened species finds food and shelter in these wetlands. Wetlands along the coast also provides habitats for fish. Lastly, it helps to maintain groundwater supplies and water quality and protects

Postal Patron
Page 2
February 10, 1999

shorelines from erosionand pollution.

You may purchase a variety of Federal Migratory Bird Hunting and Conservation Stamps (Duck Stamp) through the U.S. Fish and Wildlife Service. It makes a wonderful collector's item. Just think, if you had bought the first stamp in 1934, it would have cost you only one dollar. Then if you annually purchased a stamp for your collection, by 1992 all 59 stamps would have cost you only $242, however, the value of this collection would now be worth over $4,000.
Nice investment!

You may also wish to purchase the Duck Stamp Collection. They include a data sheet on each duck stamp issued since the first one in 1934. Each sheet includes a photograph of the stamp and the original art, short biography of the artist, names of the designers and engravers, inscription, first date of sale, and the number of stamps sold. This collection may be purchased through the Government Printing Office.

Purchasing the annual Duck Stamp or a subscription to the Duck Stamp Collection is one weigh you can make a difference. Isn't our natural heritage worth saving?

Sincerely,

U.S. FISH AND WILDLIFE SERVICE

Ms. Carlotta Jenkins
Superintendent of Documents

jk

CHAPTER

6

Introductory Commas

RULES

Commas Following Introductory Material

- **6.1** Five or More Words or a Verb Form
- **6.2** Subordinate Clauses
- **6.3** Conjunctive Adverbs and Transitional Expressions
- **6.4** Transitional Expressions Following a Conjunction in Compound Sentences
- **6.5** Interjections
- **6.6** Confusing Material

Well-written material is easy to follow because it contains clues for the reader. These clues come in many forms, and they reflect the logic and organization within the written material. Such clues are often found at the beginning of sentences. This introductory material may be transitional words that connect previous materials, phrases that modify the beginning words of the next sentence, or even entire clauses that show conditions or reasons that influence the rest of the idea. No matter what purpose is being served, all introductory material must be identified and analyzed for appropriate punctuation.

The general rule is to add a comma after introductory material (sometimes referred to as *introductory elements* in many English handbooks); however, specific rules will help clarify introductory comma usage.

COMMAS FOLLOWING INTRODUCTORY MATERIAL

Five or More Words or a Verb Form

6.1 Use a comma to separate introductory material that contains five or more words or that contains any form of a verb (also known as a *verbal*).

- *In a far and distant country,* a frustrated writer works on a horror movie script. (There is no verb form but the phrase contains more than five words.)
- *Screaming,* Susan ran out of the theater. (*Screaming* is a verb form called a *present participle.* Without the comma, this introductory word would read like a title to her name—Screaming Susan.)
- *To satisfy a need for safe thrills,* most adolescents will beg to attend a movie that drips with blood and gore. (*To satisfy* is a verb form called an *infinitive.*)
- *Gathered in huddled groups,* these preteens will sit through horror movie after horror movie. (*Gathered* is a verb form called a *past participle.*)
- *Sitting stiffly,* the moviegoers barely show signs of breathing. (*Sitting* is a verb form called a *present participle.*)
- *During a horror movie* the preteens will scream at anything that moves in the next scene. (The comma is not needed when the introductory material contains fewer than five words and no verb form.)
- In 1973 *The Exorcist* was released. (The comma is not needed when the introductory material contains fewer than five words and no verb form.)

Subordinate Clauses

6.2 Use a comma to separate any subordinate clause that precedes an independent clause. These clauses are easily recognized because they start with a subordinate conjunction. Commonly used subordinate conjunctions are

after	in case	when
although	in order that	whenever
as	no matter what (why, when, etc.)	where
as if	once	whereas
as long as	provided that	wherever
as soon as	since	whether
as though	so that	which
because	than	while
before	that	who
even if	though	whom
even though	unless	whose
if	until	

- *After Myra Santelli chaired the meeting,* the committee became more cooperative.
- *When the director noticed the team's progress,* he sent his congratulations.

➤ *Because the band made a local commercial,* their popularity and visibility continued to grow.

Subordinate Conjunction A subordinate or dependent clause is always introduced by a subordinate conjunction. (Remember that a conjunction "joins" and that *subordinate* means the group of words is not as important as the main subject and verb.) In fact, if we place a subordinate conjunction in front of an independent clause, that clause automatically becomes dependent (subordinate). For example, *I saw Ms. Jones* is a complete sentence (independent clause). *When I saw Ms. Jones* is not a complete sentence and is called a dependent clause or subordinate clause. Now let's put this into a complete sentence and look at the pattern it produces. *When I saw Ms. Jones, I ran for cover.* If we use the sentence pattern method and write **sub** above the subordinate conjunction, the sentence would look like this:

sub s v , SV.
When I saw Ms. Jones, I ran for cover. **sub s v , S V.**

A subordinate clause (**sub s v**) that comes before an independent clause (**S V**) is *always* followed by a comma.

When one of these subordinate conjunctions is at the beginning of a sentence, it should serve as a red flag to remind us of the needed comma at the end of the introductory material. (Some texts refer to these subordinate conjunctions as *subordinate clause markers.*) Occasionally, some subordinate conjunctions serve as prepositions when they introduce a phrase instead of a clause, as in this example: *After Tuesday I will no longer need your services.* Most of the time, however, the subordinate conjunctions make it easy to spot the introductory material.

PROOFREADING POINTER

Red-Flag Words If the first word of a sentence is

Although

After

As

Because

If

Since

Unless

When

While

you will need a comma 99 percent of the time.

EXERCISE 6–A

Directions: Using standard proofreaders' marks, make any needed corrections. This exercise is based on Rules 6.1 and 6.2.

1. Student absences from class, cause many problems for both the teacher and the student.
2. From the teacher's perspective, handouts from each class will have to be set aside and then will have to be taken back to class each time until the missing student is matched to the papers and matched to the exact missed days.
3. Although the syllabus clearly states that quizzes may not be made up, students always ask for a make-up.
4. If a student cuts several classes his or her grade will begin to reflect the amount of material covered in the usual class discussion but missed by that student.
5. From the student's perspective, the gaps caused by missed material are extremely frustrating.

6. Coming back to class, may also embarrass the student who does not wish to be questioned or noticed.
7. Although students with honest faces give a variety of reasons for their absences these next few excuses seem rather creative.
8. After a particularly rainy spring quarter one student suggested it was unreasonable to assume anyone would be in class on the day of the downpour.
9. After missing a test another student insisted his absence was unavoidable.
10. While he was shaving, he accidentally dropped his electric razor into the toilet.
11. Being only half-shaven and having no safety razor, the student did not feel his vanity could undergo the other students' scrutiny.
12. During some quarters, an unusual number of third cousins having toe operations require students to participate in hospital vigils.
13. If the dog ate the term paper there seems to be no need for the student to come to class empty handed; it is best to stay at home and watch the dog.
14. Going to a funeral, always seems to be an acceptable excuse unless the funeral is held repeatedly over several quarters and for the same individual.
15. According to many secretly amused teachers there is no end to the variety, quality, and imagination displayed in the art of reporting absenteeism.

EXERCISE 6–B *Directions:* Using standard proofreaders' marks, make any needed corrections. This exercise is based on Rules 6.1 and 6.2.

ETYMOLOGY

Etymology is that branch of linguistics which studies the origin of individual words. Although the Greeks were the first to formally study word histories we continue with this type of research even today. What true etymological research should be, is clearly reflected in the Greek word itself. Meaning "the science of the truth," the word *etymology* shows us today that the Greeks wanted to understand each word fully and completely in order to use it properly. In the nineteenth century, the linguistic philosophy changed. The science was reduced to a mere cataloging of words. After finding the beginning language and translation, the etymologist's work was done. In the twentieth century, the idealistic researcher does more. Acting as an ethnographer this individual tries to reconstruct the true meaning of the word based on the culture of the people who first used it. By establishing the literary and social value of the word, the researcher can begin to see the relationship between the culture and philosophy of those people. The history of the word is put into an entire cultural framework.

Anyone might find it amusing to wonder why the origin of the word *botulism* meant "sausage poisoning" to the Germans. *Alligator* originally meant "worm of the pebbles." Other words originated from their inventors. The cardigan sweater derived its name from the seventh Earl of Cardigan. The verb *to lynch,* owes its origin to a Western judge by the same name. In helping to settle the Old West, Judge Lynch seemed to hang the accused first and ask questions later. What other words come to mind?

EXERCISE 6–C

Directions: Using standard proofreaders' marks, make any necessary corrections. This is a text-review exercise.

MEMORANDUM

TO: Auto Examiners Service Managers

FROM: Eugene Axletree

DATE: April 1, 1999

SUBJECT: "Spring Into Spring" Special

Spring is upon us and that means it is time for our annual service special for the Auto Examiners chain of service stations. Since this winter has been an unusually harsh one for our area we want to promote the summer-readiness checkup with an additional twist—winter damage inspection.

Besides the usual check list for this annual event I want each one of you to be sure your personal do the following:

√ check all belts
√ change air filter
√ check for cracks in distributor cap
√ inspect brakes, brake fluid, and brake lines
√ tires should be checked for proper inflation
√ look for indicators of tire-tread wear
√ windshield wipers should be inspected
√ check air-conditioning system
√ exhaust system inspection
√ test battery strength
√ check fluid levels
√ changing oil
√ inspect electrical system and wires
√ test for front-end alignment

Remember that customer satisfaction is our goal, therefore, take a little extra time to talk to each customer about his vehicle. As an extra bonus this year please include a free car wash and underchassis scrub with every spring special.

The "Spring Into Spring" special starts Monday, April 4. Let's make this year's special better then last year's. Please remember to file your sales figures with the main office by May 21. Thank you for helping Auto Examiners to be tops in service and customer satisfaction.

dr

Conjunctive Adverbs and Transitional Expressions

6.3 Use a comma to separate conjunctive adverbs and transitional expressions when these are used as introductory materials. *The comma is not needed after one-syllable conjunctive adverbs.*

Conjunctive Adverbs		Transitional Expressions	
accordingly	nonetheless	afterward	in conclusion
also	otherwise	also	in contrast
besides	similarly	as a result	in short
consequently	still	at the same time	in the distance
finally	subsequently	before	meanwhile
furthermore	then	besides	moreover
hence	therefore	certainly	nevertheless
indeed	thus	finally	next
instead	as a result	first, second, etc.	of course
likewise	at the same time	for example	on the other hand
meanwhile	on the contrary	for instance	similarly
moreover	on the other hand	further	soon
nevertheless		furthermore	still
		here	then
		in addition	there
		in comparison	too

➤ *Furthermore,* I don't want to hear from you ever again. (conjunctive adverb)

➤ *Therefore,* Erma Smith will have to handle the case. (conjunctive adverb)

➤ *On the other hand,* I find it hard to resist a good mystery. (transitional expression)

➤ *In comparison,* I rarely will touch a romance novel. (transitional expression)

➤ *Then* I will read nonstop for days. (one-syllable conjunctive adverb and transitional expression)

Transitional Expressions Following a Conjunction in Compound Sentences

6.4 When a transitional expression follows a conjunction in a compound sentence, use one comma after the transitional expression. If the transitional expression is a simple adverb like *therefore* or *moreover,* the comma following it is omitted.

➤ He made a strong presentation for adopting the new procedures for handling insurance claims, and as a result, the plan was accepted.

➤ I went to the store, and therefore I was not home when the auditor arrived.

Interjections

6.5 Use a comma to separate an interjection from the rest of the sentence. (Interjections are words that express strong emotions or surprise: *wow, ouch, no, goodness, stop.*)

➤ *Wow,* I certainly did have trouble with that test!

➤ *Well,* I can tell you that Mr. Blane will never believe her alibi.

Confusing Material

6.6 Use a comma to separate introductory material that may confuse the reader.

➤ *After a while,* longer apprenticeships will be required for technicians. (Notice what might happen if the comma is removed: *after a while longer . . .*)

The following chart summarizes conjunctions and transitional expressions.

CONJUNCTIONS AND TRANSITIONAL EXPRESSIONS

Coordinate Conjunctions	Subordinate Conjunctions	Conjunctive Adverbs	Transitional Expressions
and	after	accordingly	afterward
but	although	also	also
for	as	besides	as a result
nor	as if	consequently	at the same time
or	as long as	finally	before
so	as soon as	furthermore	besides
yet	as though	hence	certainly
	because	however	finally
	before	indeed	first, second, etc.
	even	instead	for example
	even if	likewise	for instance
	even though	meanwhile	further, furthermore
	if	moreover	in addition
	in case	nevertheless	in comparison
	in order that	nonetheless	in conclusion
	no matter what (why, when, etc.)	otherwise	in contrast
		similarly	in short
	once	still	in the distance
	provided that	subsequently	meanwhile
	since	then	moreover
	so that	therefore	nevertheless
	than	thus	next
	that	as a result	of course
	though	at the same time	on the other hand
	unless	on the contrary	similarly
	until	on the other hand	still
	when		then
	whenever		
	where		
	whereas		
	wherever		
	whether		
	which		
	while		
	who		
	whom		
	whose		

EXERCISE 6-D *Directions:* Using standard proofreaders' marks, make any needed corrections on this promotional letter. This exercise is based on Rules 6.3, 6.4, and 6.5.

FARMER'S PHARMACY

4028 Sycamore Street • West Carrollton, OH 45449

October 19, 1999

Dear Neighbor:

We're sure you've noticed the changes on the corner of Vine and Sycamore Streets. In fact, we're now ready to open our doors to you, our neighbors. Moreover we at **Farmer's Pharmacy** want to take this opportunity to announce our grand opening. Check out the enclosed flier. Great specials, aren't they?

We value you as a neighbor and a customer, as well as a concerned and alert consumer. Furthermore we wanted to discuss with you the precautions that any consumer should take when purchasing over-the-counter (OTC) medicines. OTC medicines are among the most safely packaged consumer products in the world. By law most are sealed in tamper*evident* packaging for your protection. However this does not make these packages tamper*proof*.

As a result **Farmer's** is taking this opportunity to offer you five easy pointers to help protect you and your loved ones against the possibility of tampered packaged medicines. First read the label. All OTC medicines will have labels describing which tamper-proof techniques have been used. Second carefully look at the outer packaging. Next look at the medicine itself after you open the package. If it looks suspicious, be suspicious. Fourth look especially for capsules or tablets that are identical. Finally don't use any medicine from a package that shows cuts, slices, tears, or other imperfections.

Farmer's Pharmacy wants to encourage you to be a wise consumer. No, one can prevent tampering altogether. On the other hand we are constantly on the alert for our customers. Likewise, we are encouraging you to be equally careful. If you ever suspect tampering, please call it to the attention of the manager. Together we want to make this world a safer place for all of us.

Don't forget to visit us on the corner of Vine and Sycamore Streets. We want to meet our new neighbors! At the same time we look forward to being of service to you—7 days a week, 24 hours a day!

Warmly,

Ed Farmer
Farmer's Pharmacy

cc

Enclosure

EXERCISE 6–E

Directions: Using standard proofreaders' marks, make any needed corrections on this memorandum. This exercise is based on Rules 6.3, 6.4, and 6.5.

TO: All Store Managers of Terrific Tapes Unlimited

FROM: Martha Platter

DATE: November 17, 1999

SUBJECT: Consumer Information During Audiocassette Tape Sale

The Central Office of Terrific Tapes Unlimited feels that it would enhance customer relations if all employees would offer the following four tips to anyone purchasing audiocassette tapes. First, keep cassettes in their cases, away from heat and the elements, when not in use. Similarly, avoid storing cassettes on top of the speakers or a TV where magnetic fields may erase higher-frequency sounds. Third eject the tape after playing. Finally use a head cleaner after every 20 to 30 hours of playing time. Of course we recommend our in-store brand of cleaner.

In the past TTU has experienced an expected after-Christmas slump in sales. Subsequently there will be a mid- to late-January sale, which we are calling Inventory Invitation. The Art Department is already hard at work on our advertising campaign.

We feel sure that this Christmas season will bring the projected sales. No I predict record-making sales. Moreover we wish each employee a warm and wonderful holiday.

mc

EXERCISE 6–F

Directions: This is a text-review exercise. Using standard proofreaders' marks, correct all errors.

THE COMMON COLD

Although we have been plagued by the common cold for centuries no one seems to be able to do anything about it, but persevere through it. Hacking and wheezing we make our way through the worst of it. There seems to be no proven treatment accept to let it run it's course. Wait; don't we know anything about this pest?

Well we do know that it is characterized by the familiar symptoms of sneezes, coughing, sore throat, and nasal discomfort. Colds seem too be more common in the winter months, however, the influence of whether is secondary to the more serious reality that the common cold is an infectious disease.

Curing the common cold is important for two reasons. First it has a decided nuisance value. It is the leading cause of absenteism in industry and in education. Since it is so contagious, the cold can literally infect and reinfect people who are in close contact with each other. In some cases, it seem epidemic in proportion. Secondly, a cold can be serious because of it's potential to lead to complications. Middle ear infections and sinusitis are two ailments that can occur after a cold. They're also may be a a connection between the common cold and bacterial pneumonia.

There is no specific cure for the common cold and there appears to be no direct proof that nutrition and vitamins significantly altar susceptibility. Although many of us swear by the vitamin C method and the chicken soup remedy the scientist isn't staking his reputation on any announcements. Some bacterial vaccines are recommended as a method to increase resistence against secondary infection.

The medical community recommends frequent hand washing. The spewed bacteria are often present on surfaces, such as doorknobs and telephones. The well individual will touch these surfaces and then later will touch his or her own face. Bingo! If hand washing became more frequent many of those germs would go down the drain instead of inside our systems. Of course frequent spraying of those surfaces with an anti-bacterial spray would be beneficial as well.

The common cold seems to be with us. If scientists can successfully send men into space then, they surely should cure the common cold. Don't you think so?

EXERCISE 6–G *Directions:* This is a text-review exercise. Using standard proofreaders' marks, correct the errors.

BOWLING

When do you think the game of bowling got started—during the nineteenth century? During the Renaissance? During Biblical times? Believe it or not archaeologists have found artifacts and cave-wall drawings that date back to the Stone Age. These findings indicates that primitive Europeans rolled large pebbles at stones or animal bones.

Egyptians enjoyed bowling as far back as 5200 A.D. Since the Egyptian tombs contained articles for the deceased one's afterlife it has been relatively easy to identify the daily activities and pastimes of the occupants. These tomb findings of food, articles of clothing, tools, and weapons indicate that the Egyptians rolled stone balls at marble bars.

As the ages went by bowling found another use. Sometime during the Middle Ages, possibly around 1300 A.D., an individual would roll a stone at a wooden club standing in a corner. If he could successfully knock the club down then he was found innocent of his offense, and would not be required to attend church as often as the fellow who could not knock down the club.

America was introduced to bowling in the 1620s when the Dutch settlers brought the game of ninepins, as it was than called, to Manhattan. The influence of the Puritans did not contribute to the sport's popularity. In fact some Puritan leaders had the activity outlawed in certain areas for its sinfulness and frivolity. Nevertheless the sport of ninepins continues to grow. In the late 1840s an extra pen was added to get around the old laws. It was at this time that the name changed to tenpins. In 1895, the founding of the American Bowling Congress (ABC) helped to standardize the game.

Today over 17 million men, women, and children bowl in leagues or on a regular basis. Even many small communities have at least one bowling establishment. Strike!

CHAPTER

7

Review

The underlying principle used in learning to proofread is practice, practice, practice. In addition to the cumulative exercises that appear throughout this text, Chapters 7, 12, 16, and 20 are devoted entirely to a review of material presented in earlier chapters. This is the first of the four review chapters.

As you complete the exercises in this chapter, be alert for all the kinds of errors covered earlier in the text. The topics reviewed in these exercises include the following:

- Comma splices
- Divisions
- Introductory commas
- Parallelism
- Pronoun agreement
- Reading for meaning
- Run-on sentences
- Sentence fragments
- Spelling
- Subject-verb agreement
- Troublesome words

Mark all exercises with standard proofreaders' marks.

PROOFREADING POINTER

When in doubt, check it out!

EXERCISE 7–A

Directions: Compare the memorandum on this page with the memorandum on the next page. Some errors may not be marked on the first copy. Using standard proofreaders' marks, indicate any errors on the comparison copy.

MEMORANDUM

TO: All Employees

FROM: Angela Tracey
Office Manager

DATE: March 8, 1999

SUBJECT: Voice Mail Is Here

On Monday, March 14, you'll find the long-awaited voice mail system has been installed on our phone system. Even though there has been some resistance to the installation of the system, there are several reasons we will benefit from the system.

1. It will save our employees time and money. According to research surveys, we can reduce the number of unsuccessful calls from 75 percent to only 30 percent.

2. The voice mail system will help our customers. They won't have to wait as long on hold and they won't end up in a game of telephone tag.

3. We'll be able to call our offices in California and leave messages, rather than having to call between 12 and 4 or wait until the next day. We can leave a message one evening and the answer will be waiting for us the next morning.

Of course, the key to the successful use of any voice mail system is making sure that you and all the other employees are properly trained in the use of the system. We'll begin the training session at 8 a.m. on Monday in the conference room of Everett Hall. We're so excited about this program that we're providing breakfast at 8—coffee, juice, and rolls! If you're in a good mood to begin the training, than the training can't help but be a success.

COMPARISON COPY 7-A

MEMORANDUM

TO: All Employees

FROM: Angela Tracy
Office Manager

DATE: March 8, 1999

SUBJECT: Voice Mail Is Hear

On Monday, March 14, you'll find the long awaited voice mail system has been installed on our phone system. Even though there has been some resistance to the installation of the system, their are several reasons we will benefit from voice mail.

1. It will save our employees time and money. According to research surveys we can reduce the number of unsuccessful calls from 75 percent to only 30 percent.

2. The voice mail system will help our customers. Employees won't have to wait as long on hold and they won't end up in a game of telephone tag.

3. We'll be able to call our offices in California and leave messages, rather than having to call between 12 and 4 or wait untill the next day. We can leave a message and the answer will be waiting for us the next morning.

Of course, the key to the successful use of a voice mail system is making sure that you and all the other employees are properly trained in the use of the system. We'll begin the training session at 8 a.m. on Monday in the conference room of Everett Hall. We're so excited about this program that we're providing breakfast at 8—coffee, juice, and rolls! If you're in a good mood to begin the training, than the training can't help but be a success

EXERCISE 7–B

Directions: The address labels on this page were typed from the mailing list on the next page. Using standard proofreaders' marks, indicate any corrections needed on the labels. Also correct any errors that may not be marked on the mailing list. The labels do not have to be in alphabetical order.

<table>
<tr><td>Mrs. Mary Maierson
1245 Milwaukee Place
Portales, NM 88130</td><td>Mr. Keith Wartenbee
8945 Brighton Boulevard
Cohoes, New York 12047</td><td>Mr. Emanual Perinone
2023 Marion Avenue
Fridley, MN 55432</td></tr>
<tr><td>Ms. Maria Filippo
2 Fourth Street
Hopkinton, MA 01748</td><td>Mr. Keith Kennerson
56 Winton Place
Easton, MD 21601</td><td>Mr. Michael Morrison
1673 Old US 35, NW
Clewiston, FL 33440</td></tr>
<tr><td>Dr. Andrew Anderson
92010 Blairhouse Circle
Hartselle, Alabama 35640</td><td>Dr, Esther Patton
One Ellerbee Boulevard
Chowchilla, CA 93160</td><td>Mr. Mortimer Montague
56 Inverness Road
Helena, AR 72342</td></tr>
<tr><td>Mr. Jonathan Davinski
1789 EastView Drive
Adel, GA 31620</td><td>Kimberly Ellis
109 West Fortune Road
Moscow, ID 83843</td><td>Mr. Dzle Merry
90 Allerton Drive, SW
Urbana, IL 63801</td></tr>
<tr><td>Mr. Allan L. Drury
378 Huntington Drive
Madisonville, KY 42431</td><td>Mrs. Donna Kay Shaad
789 Swing-a-Long Lane
Dearborn, MI 48120</td><td>Ms. Marla Minature
78 Chevington Circle
Covington, LA 70433</td></tr>
<tr><td>Mr. Jerald Drew
804 Luck Avenue
Laurel, MT 59404</td><td>Ms. Monica Whiteside
45 Pine Place
Norfolk, NB 68701</td><td>Mr. Arthur Chan
9909 Nevena Place
Laurel, MS 39440</td></tr>
<tr><td>Mrs.Gerrie Jones
89 Winterton Plaza
Troutdale, OR 97060</td><td>Ms. Dawnetta Lucas
40 Phoenix Point Drive
Bend, OR 97701</td><td>Mr. Richard Bartlett
1012 Wilshire Drive
Laurel, MT 59404</td></tr>
</table>

Mailing List

Mr. Keith Wartenbee
8945 Brighton Boulevard
Cohoes, New York 12047

Mr. Keith Kennerson
56 Winton Place
Easton, MD 21601

Mr. Michael Morrison
1673 Old US 35, NW
Clewiston, FL 33440

Mr. Andrew Anderson
92010 Blairhouse Circle
Hartselle, Alabama 35640

Dr Esther Patton
One Ellerbee Boulevard
Chowchilla, CA 93610

Mr. Mortimer Montague
56 Inverness Road
Helena, AR 72342

Ms. Maria Filippo
2 Fourth Street
Hopkinton, MA 01748

Miss Dawnetta Lucas
40 Phoenix Point Drive
Bend, OR 97701

Dr. Richard Bartlett
1012 Wilshire Drive
Laurel, MT 59404

Mrs. Mary Maierson
1245 Milwaukee Place
Portales, NM 88130

Mr. Jonathan Davinski
1789 EastView Drive
Adel, GA 31620

Mrs. Janice Severence
90 Mollycoddle Drive
Wheeling, WV 26003

Ms. Kimberly Ellis
109 West Fortune Drive
Moscow, ID 83843

Dale Merry
90 Allerton Drive, SE
Urbana, IL 63801

Mr. Emanual Perinone
2023 Marion Avenue
Fridley, MN 55432

Mr. Allan L. Drury
378 Huntington Drive
Madisonville, KY 42431

Mrs. Donna Kay Shaad
789 Swing-a-long Lane
Dearborn, MI 48120

Ms. Marla Minature
78 Chevington Circle
Covington, LA 70433

Mr. Jerald Drew
804 Luck Avenue
Laurel, MT 59404

Ms. Monica Whiteside
45 Pine Place
Norfolk, NB 68701

Mr. Arthur Chan
99909 Nevena Place
Laurel, MS 39440

Ms. Gerrie Jones
89 Winterton Plaza
Troutdale, OR 97060

EXERCISE 7–C *Directions:* Using standard proofreaders' marks, indicate any errors in the following copy.

JOHNSTON SCHOOL OF SMILES
148 Spring Road, Laurel, MT 59404

March 16, 1999

Ms Lurrinda Lavin
908 Kentucky Place
Laurel, MT59404

Dear Ms. Lavin

The Johnston School of Smiles is pleased to accept you a member of the fall class for 1999. Classes begin on September 21 at 8 a.m. at the downtown branch located at 234 Maryland Boulevard. We'll put on our best smile as we wait for you to arrive.

I'm sure you know that the Johnson School of Smiles is one of the oldest marketing training programs in the southern United States. We have trained sales personnel from all 50 states in the United States. We even have students from Canada.

Our classes are small and friendly. Our faculty members are the best we could find in the United States; the faculty are all recognized leaders in the sales promotion field. We know both you and your employer will be pleased with the increased sales you'll be making when you complete the course.

Just for the record, we do teach you the correct way to smile and that lesson is so important in the sales field that it is the first lesson we teach you. We'll look forward to seeing you on Monday be sure you're ready to smile.

Sincerely

Mrs. Megan Christine Raymond
Admissions Director

nn

EXERCISE 7–D *Directions:* Using standard proofreaders' marks, indicate any errors in the following newsletter.

Calcyon High School Band Notes

CB members attend BOA camp

Four members of the Calycon Varsity Band will be attending the Bands of America Summer Band Institute at Normal, Illinois, on June 19 to 27. Student participants will be learing marching fundamentals, marching music basics, and leadership skills. In addition, each student will select a taraget skill for additional practice during the week-long camp.

Marvin Westfeld and Eric Jamison will be attending the marching perfection sessions. Allison Dwayer will be working with the field commander division, and Lynn K. Sauder will be attending the color guard division. All for of the students will also be attending the advanced leadership workshop for the two days prior the the opening of the formal BOA camp.

Its a date--for a picture!

The official band picture will be taken on August 21 at 3 p.m. at the White Memorial Stadiem. The formal gray uniform will be worn. Inspection will be at 2 p.m.

FROM THE DIRECTOR

Summer band camp is over but the marching season is just beginning for the 245 members of the Calcyon Marching Band. This year the band is made up of 27 color guard members, 10 rifle corps members, 3 field commanders, and 215 musicians.

The first football game of the season will be against rival Newark High School. The band's half-time show will be an extravaganza of sound and motion featuring popular show tunes.

This fall the band will be performing at all home and away games, four band contests, the Veterans Day parade, and the traditional Octoberfest celebration.

Rehersal schedule

Monday	*3–5:30 p.m.*
Tuesday	*3–5:30 p.m.*
Wednesday	*6–6 p.m.*
Friday	*Inspection at 6 p.m.* *Game time is 7:30 p.m.*

EXERCISE 7–E *Directions:* Using standard proofreaders' marks, indicate any errors in the following report.

IS MEMORIZATION OUT OF VOGUE?

In early American schools, students were subjected to the dubious pleasure of memorizing lists of just about everything. Today's teachers do require students to memorize such things as math facts, short poems, and spelling words; but the concept of learning by rote memorization is not popular. Education in today's society strives to teach problem-solving skills, critical thinking, and higher-order thinking. Rote memorization is not considered a method to achieve any of the higher order skills, but is that a valid conclusion?

A few schools have been going against the grain and adopting the principles of rote memorization, drilling, recitation, and repeated practice as a mainstay in the fight to educate children in the basics. What they have found is that these same principles also help prepare the children for the more difficult task of applying what they learn in school to everyday life.

Rodolfo Bernardo, principal of the Allen Classical/Traditional Academy (a magnet elementary school), believes in using memorization to teach the basics. "You've got to start with the basics to move to more complex things." Mastering the basics gives students a sense of achievement. Bernardo's teachers send their students to the principal's office as a reward; most other teachers send their students to the princpal's office as a punishment. The students sent to the princpal's office are given candy and plenty of praise for their very real accomplishments.

In the Allen Classical/Traditional Academy, test scores on national achievement tests have increased 17.5 points, a gain that is considered significant by any method of calculation.

Test scores in another school, Kreole Elementary in Moss Point, Mississippi, have also increased as a result of the use of memorization. Students were not getting the basics; of course they had trouble with the higher-order skills.

2

The school superintendent introduced his teachers to Kumon math, which is a drill-and-practice approach to learing math. Drills must be completed within a given time limit with 100 percent accuracy. The self-esteem of the students grew right along with the mastery of the material. Encouraged by the success of the highly structured Kumon math approach, The Moss Point principal, Carl Davis, and his teachers looked for other highly structured programs. What they found was the Direct Instruction Model. The program uses lots of cumulative review and practice, including both individual and choral responses. It worked! Once students mastered the basics, they were able to move on to the hgher-order skills.

Still another success story is the Wesley School in Houston, Texas. In a school where most of the students are considered "at-risk," testing found 90 percent of the students reading above grade level. A visitor to Wesley will find the use of drills and recitation, both choral and individual, a common occurrence. Principal Thaddeus Lott believes that mastering the basics gives them "the confidence to attack and be decoders of almost any word."

Maybe it is time for memorization, recitation, and drill to come back "in vogue." Memorization, recitation, and drill—these three principles that have helped students in at-risk schools become winners. These same principles have even helped students develop the critical-thinking skills desperately needed today.

EXERCISE 7–F *Directions:* Using standard proofreaders' marks, indicate any errors in this text-review exercise.

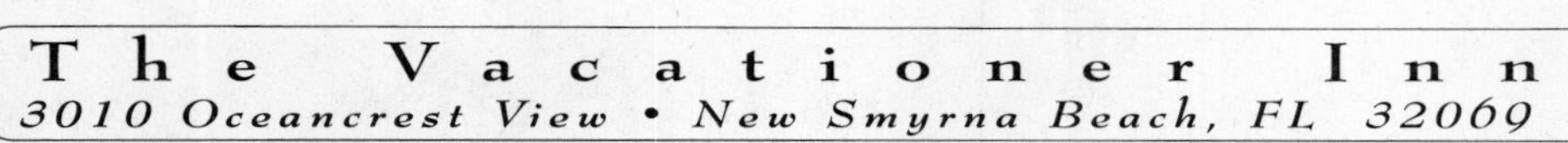

January 17, 1999

Ms. Daniella Boyton
8903 Allenreed Avenue
Jackson, MI 49201

Dear Ms. Boyton:

When you look out the window of your home there in Jackson, the 6 feet of snow you see may make it difficult for you to visualise the sunny beaches of Florida. But never fear; they still exist.

Last summer you spent the weak of June 5 with us at the Vacationer Inn in New Smyrna Beach, Florida. Remember how nice it was last year, its even better this year. We have renovated every room at the Vacationer. Each room contains a refrigerator, a small kitchette, and a jacuzzi.

The rooms aren't the only improvements we've made. The pool area has been enlarged with the addition of a second pool (for adults only). And yes, we are allowing rafts in the adult pool; we're even supplying them. Both pools will feature country/Western and easy listening music. A poolside cash bar will be open from 1 a.m. to 10 p.m. Carbonated beverages will also be available. Located adjacent to the adult pool is an adults-only game room. We still have the regular game room for youngsters, but this one is just for the adults. We're featuring the old-fashioned pinball machines, Japanese pachenko machines, and just a few of the video games.

Ms. Danella Boyton
Page 2
January 17, 1999

If that's not enough, we're offering a special package rate for the first two weeks in June. Join us for the week of June 7 at regular rates and we'll let you join us for free the week of June 16. The rates include a continentel breakfast and one beverage daily at the poolside cash bar, as well as all the usual features of the Vacationer.

Call us at 555-Pool. We'll take your reservation by phone, and send you a confirmation. Join us for sum fun in the sun!

Sincerely,

THE VACATION INN

Mrs. Martha Mahan, Owner

ss

EXERCISE 7–G *Directions:* Using standard proofreaders' marks, indicate any errors in the following letter.

Hapeville Animal Shelter

477 Endicott Drive
Hapeville, GA 30354

December 1, 1999

Ms. Rebecca Anderson
6704 Elberon Avenue
Hapeville, GA 30354

Dear Friend of HAS:

The year 2000 will be a milestone in our history, it will be the beginning of a new year and a new century. The Hapeville Animal Shelter would like to thank you for all the support you have given our four-legged friends during 1999. We hope we can count on you again as we start our last project of the current century.

And what is this new project. It's really quite simple. We want to start out the new year with no orphaned animals. That means we need good homes for the 11 dogs and 7 cats in our shelter. The animals adapted from our shelter will be neutered, and will be current on all required shots. What makes this project special is the $10 fee; it will be reduced from our regular $55 fee.

We do need your help, however. As a Friend of HAS, you can help in two ways. First, we need donations to cover the $45 loss in fees charged as we try to place the animals in homes. At $45 an animal, we'll need a total of $820 for the fees. If every member of Friends of HAS contributed only $8 we'll be able to cover the entire fee reduction. And think of the joy the animals and the owners will share as they start out the new century as a family.

The second way you can help is to read the enclosed poster and see if you can find a home for any of the animals featured. They are all special, we just need to find the special family that needs each of them. We'll look forward to hearing from you and, hopefully, from families wanting to adopt our animals.

Sincerely,

Ms. Abigail Van Wert, Adoption Coordinator

ss

Enclosure

EXERCISE 7–H

Directions: Using standard proofreaders' marks, indicate any errors in the following flier, which is the poster referred to in Exercise 7–G.

Adopt a New Family Member for Christmas

Ambrose Ambrose is a field-trained English setter that loves to babysit children and perform obedience routines. He hates baths but loves the attention he gets.	**Wrinkles** An adorable mixed 5-month-old puppy. Wrinkles looks and acts like the adolescent he is. His coat looks as though he just got a permanent.	**Permanent Press** This 6-month-old litter mate of Wrinkles is the opposite of his brother in every way. He is quiet and dignified and would love to sit quietly by the fire.
Mollie McGee This full-groan cat had to be left behind when her family moved to Alaska. She's a fastidious groomer. Mollie loves to sleep and watching sleeping children	**Rover** A full-grown Old English sheepdog, Rover needs plently of room. He comes from a family who relocated to an apartment. His repertore of skills include answering the phone with a *Whuff!* He hasn't learned to hang the phone up yet!	**McGuffey** A gray-stripped male, approximately 2 years old. McGuffey has wonderful house manners and never claws the furniture. He likes hunting mice,eating blueberry bagels, and to take and afternoon nap. He naps with Bessie the dog.
Chelois A 9-year-old Belgian sheepdog, Chelois has one ear that folds over. She likes affection and food. She's crate trained and obedience trained. She likes to sing in the evening.	**Haloween** Born on Haloween, this black-and-orange tortoiseshell kitten likes to be handled. She even tolerates being dressed in doll clothes.	**Bessie** A black-and-white dog of mixed breed, Bessie is good with children and other animals. Her best friend at the shelter is McGuffey. (They'd like to be placed together)

Cachet
Cash (as he is commonly called) is a large Belgian sheepdog. He is crate trained, house broken, and very affectionate. He likes to watch the television at the kennel. He's a great couch potato.

Kitten
This mixed breed pup is fond of playing, energetic, and an insatiable eater. She needs a family home with plenty of room for her to run. Her coat feels more like a cat's fur than like the coat of an 8-week-old pup.

Rudy
Rudy is a cocker spaniel puppy who comes to us from an abusive home. She is affectionate with adults but she doesn't like very young children. She'd love to be placed in an adult home.

Socks
A beagle mix, Socks is an enthusiastic food inhaler. Small enough to live in an apartment, Socks would be a good companion to an adult. Her name's from the white color on her paws. Socks also loves to sit on your lap.

Taffy
Taffy is a spitz mix and she is a spitfire. An engaging personality, an energetic activity level, and small size make Taffy an ideal house pet for a family with older children.

Anonymous Amos
A beautiful male cat, Amos loves to sit on the widow sill and watch the outside. He is trained to go outside, he'll even let you know he needs out by jumping up and down at the door. Amos also plays in paper bags for hours each day.

Elizabeth
Elizabeth is a ten-week-old border collie mix who likes to cuddle, take walks, and chasing sticks. She's on the small side and would be ideal for a small home.

Oscar Meyer
Oscar is a large gray cat who's most distinguishing feature is his appetite. He even steels dog food from the other animals. We estimate he is about three years old.

Spot
Spot is a white cat with one black spot. Her favorite pasttime is chasing string around the kennel. She likes to be held, but only for a few minutes. She's too inquisitive to sit still for long.

As a special Christmas gift to you and our four-legged friends, any of these animals can be taken home for the reduced fee of only $15.

Bring some love into your home!

Contact Abagail VanWert, Adoption COordinator
Hapeville Animal Shelter
555-7111

CHAPTER

8

Essential and Nonessential Commas

RULES

Comma Rules for Nonessential Elements

8.1 Nonessential Elements

8.2 Appositives

A pair of commas can indicate a great deal to a reader. Consider this: A large grocery chain sent an urgent letter requesting all its managers to oversee carefully the recall and removal of a certain brand of tuna. "All Terrific Tuna, which was processed between March and May of 1993 in the water-packed cans, should be immediately destroyed." The placement of the commas in this sentence caused the company to waste thousands of dollars of uncontaminated tuna. Why? In this case, the commas indicated that *all* Terrific Tuna cans had to be destroyed, not just a three month's supply of the water-packed tuna. The sentence should have been written without any commas to indicate which tuna was to be destroyed.

The previous situation is an example of how commas mark off essential and nonessential material within a sentence. (Some grammar handbooks discuss this topic under the term *restrictive and nonrestrictive elements.*) The key to the comma dilemma is to determine whether the material is necessary to the meaning of the sentence. Yes, you will have to make some judgment calls, but they are made fairly easily in most everyday writing situations.

Let's begin by looking at two examples. The italicized words in the next two sentences are dependent clauses that help identify (modify) their preceding nouns.

> The woman *who is wearing the red jacket* is the new vice president.
>
> Jane Suko, *who is wearing the red jacket,* is the new vice president.

PROOFREADING POINTER

Essential or Nonessential? Remember the old adage "When in doubt, leave it out"? It's a good rule to follow when deciding whether material is essential or nonessential. If you have carefully analyzed a sentence and still cannot make the judgment call, leave out the commas.

PROOFREADING POINTER

If a dependent clause or a phrase modifies a proper noun (specific name of a person, place, or thing), the material will almost always be nonessential and will need commas to set it off.

In the first sentence the dependent clause is necessary because it identifies the woman who is the vice president. Because this material is essential, it should not be set off by commas. In the second sentence, however, the commas set off nonessential material—it is very unlikely that another Jane Suko would be in the conversation.

The next three sentences show another frequent arrangement of essential and nonessential material; the italicized words are the dependent (or subordinate) clauses.

I went window shopping *after I finished the lawn.*

I went window shopping *because I had no money to spend.*

I went window shopping, *although I had no money to spend.*

All these clauses are dependent because they are introduced by a subordinate conjunction (a word used to introduce dependent clauses). Generally speaking, the majority of dependent clauses that follow the main idea of the sentence will contain essential information and will not need to be set off by a comma. The basic sentence pattern would look like this: **S V sub co s v** (the independent clause followed by the subordinate conjunction and its dependent clause). The subordinate conjunctions *although, though,* and *even though* are exceptions to this rule of thumb. These subordinate-clause markers are *always* nonessential and therefore always need a comma. However, do not be misled; quite a few subordinate conjunctions can cause the phrase or clause to be either essential or nonessential, depending on the context. A list of these and other subordinate-clause markers appears in Chart 8.1.

CHART 8.1 SUBORDINATE-CLAUSE MARKERS

Nonessential	Essential	Nonessential or Essential	
all of which	as . . . as	after	in which
although	not so . . . as	as	since
even though	so . . . that	as if	so that
though	than	as soon as	to which
for	that	as though	unless
no matter how	until	at which	when
no matter what		because	where
no matter why		before	which
none of which		by which	while
none of whom		for which	who
some of whom		if	whom
whereas		in order that	whose

Another group of words that may be classified as essential or nonessential is the appositive. Appositives are relatively easy to spot since they are minidefinitions.

The shortstop, *Jason Rickett,* owns a blue Porsche.

Because an appositive renames or defines a noun that immediately precedes it, the appositive is almost always nonessential and is set off by commas. One-word appositives are exceptions to this rule.

My neighbor *Thuy* just moved here from Vietnam.

COMMA RULES FOR NONESSENTIAL ELEMENTS

Nonessential Elements

8.1 Use commas to set off nonessential (unnecessary) words, phrases, and clauses.

Nonessential

- I saw the survivors from the shipwreck, none of whom looked well. (*None of whom* always indicates nonessential material.)
- My oldest brother, who is an exercise freak, broke his ankle while jogging. (There can be only one oldest brother.)
- Samantha and John's baby, who was born on Christmas Day, received a red-and-white blanket from the hospital. (The baby has already been identified.)

Essential

- I saw the horse that took first place at the Kentucky Derby. (Only one horse won the Derby.)
- All the babies who were born on Christmas Day received red-and-white blankets. (Not all babies received blankets.)
- Much of the corn that is grown in the Midwest is used for animal feed. ("That" clauses are always essential; this one identifies which corn.)
- Mr. Ochoa will make the presentation as soon as the guest speaker stops talking. (*As . . . as* always indicates essential information—in this case, when the presentation will be made.)

Appositives

8.2 Use commas to set off nonessential appositives (words, phrases, or clauses that rename a preceding noun or pronoun). The commas may be omitted if the appositive is only one word and is closely related to the preceding word.

- Annie Wedge's dog, Carboncrest Cachet, took best of show.
- Annie Wedge's dog Cash took best of show.
- The cranky child, a little boy with a runny nose, finally fell asleep.
- The first prize went to an unknown artist, a man who appeared not to have bathed or shaved in a week.

EXERCISE 8–A

Directions: Using standard proofreaders' marks, make all necessary changes. This exercise covers only this chapter's material.

1. The four-lane bridge that was finished yesterday cost $3.2 million.
2. Mr. Weston my next-door neighbor saw my son Jack at the game that was televised last Sunday.
3. Jack and his friend Larry Tate are roommates at the University of Iowa.
4. They reside in one of the oldest dormitories Dorsey Hall which is in East Quad.
5. Jack tells me that Larry is always late to his morning class no matter how many alarms have been set.
6. Grace Jones my neighbor on the west side of the street has a daughter who is planning to go to the university although I have serious reservations about the girl's ability to be accepted.
7. All employees who have worked more than five years are eligible for additional vacation time because of the new stress-reduction program.
8. Only the employees whom the vice president put on the list are eligible for a promotion when the new production line is installed.
9. Under the guidance of Suzanne Edmond vice president of production Widget International the top-selling gadget company for 1993 celebrated its fortieth anniversary last month.
10. Stories that have a happy ending and that show the good guys always winning are fun to read because we can feel secure in the belief that good triumphs over evil.

EXERCISE 8–B *Directions:* Using standard proofreaders' marks, indicate any necessary changes in this report. This exercise covers only this chapter's material.

OBSESSIVE-COMPULSIVE DISORDER

In the mental illness called *obsessive-compulsive disorder* (OCD), a person becomes trapped in a pattern of repetitive thoughts and behaviors, that are senseless and distressing. Usually, people, who have this disorder, which is estimated to affect 2 percent of the population, cannot stop themselves from being compulsive in their actions although they know that their behaviors are unwarranted. If OCD is left untreated, it may become serious enough that people, who have this disease, may not be able to function at work or at home.

People with obsessions unwanted ideas or impulses that consume the mind, find themselves in a state of constant anxiety. To deal with this anxiety, an individual may perform any number of repetitive behaviors, which are known as *compulsions*. Hand washing and repetitive checking the most common compulsive behaviors can be done so frequently and in such identical and repetitive detail that the acts are referred to as *rituals*.

A person is not considered to have OCD unless the obsessive and compulsive behaviors are extreme enough to interfere with everyday life. Just being meticulous in one's work or activities does not mean an individual has OCD although in kidding he or she may be referred to that way.

OCD generally starts in the teenage or young adult years, and both males and females of all ethnic groups are susceptible. Many people struggle for years to try to keep this disorder a secret although it will eventually show itself. The illness eventually leads to dysfunction if left untreated. An unfortunate consequence of this secrecy is that people with OCD usually do not receive professional help until years after the onset of their disease. By that time, obsessive-compulsive habits may be deeply ingrained and very difficult to change. However, treatment is available.

EXERCISE 8–C *Directions:* Using standard proofreaders' marks, indicate any necessary changes on this continued report. This exercise covers only this chapter's material.

OBSESSIVE-COMPULSIVE DISORDER
(continued)

Two treatments the use of medications and behavior therapy are available to individuals suffering from obsessive-compulsive disorder. The medication clomipramine can relieve the symptoms in many people. Fluvoxamine and fluoxetine two other medications may also be effective, because they enhance the brain's ability to use the naturally occurring brain chemical, serotonin. Just getting patients to recognize their behaviors is not effective since most patients are acutely aware of their behaviors. However, a behavior therapy approach known as *exposure and response prevention* has been found to be effective for many people. In this therapy the patient is exposed to the feared object or idea and then is discouraged or prohibited from carrying out the usual ritualistic behavior for several hours. In a study done at Temple University, three-fourths of the patients, who enrolled in this course, showed improvement.

Causes of obsessive-compulsive disorder are unknown. It used to be thought, that the offending attitudes and obsessions were somehow learned in childhood. However, the positive response to medication suggests a neurobiological basis. The search for causes now focuses on the interaction of two forces neurobiological factors and environmental influences. It is believed that people who develop OCD have a biological predisposition to react strongly to stress, that this reaction takes the form of intrusive and distressing thoughts, and that these thoughts lead to more anxiety and stress, eventually creating a vicious circle the person cannot escape without help. Brain-imaging studies, positron emission tomography show that these patients have a different pattern of brain activity.

Whatever the causes, science is beginning to offer relief to people, who suffer the paralyzing effects of obsessive-compulsive disorder.

EXERCISE 8-D

Directions: Using standard proofreaders' marks, indicate any changes in the following letter from the city parks director. These letters may contain errors from previous chapters.

October 10, 1999

Mr. Andrew Jasper
9088 Drew Plaza
Canandaigua, NY 14424

Dear Mr. Jaspar:

It was a pleasure to meet with you last week too discuss the details of the Y-Bridge Park project. Your ideas for an art project representing the history of the Y-Bridge seams right on target for what we had in mine.

We weren't sure of the submission deadline at the time of our meeting. In order to dedicate the work at the same time that we dedicate the new park next July 4, we need to have the project designs turned in to Anton Cruise, assistant parks director in the Office of City Parks and Planning by Febuary 1. The committee will then meet to select the art project we want to place in the park. The artist selected will be notified by April 2, and will then have approximately two months to complete the project.

Project designs need to be submitted in triplicate; only one mock-up of the project needs to be turned in with the plan. If the plan is selected, the mock-up becomes the property of the city of Zanesville. If your plan is not selected, Andrew, we will return two copies of the design specifications and the mock-up.

Good luck with your project. We look forward to seeing you design for are park.

Sincerely,

Ms. Thessalonia Bunton
Parks Director

kl

EXERCISE 8–E

Direction: Using standard proofreaders' marks, indicate any changes in the following letter from the city parks director. These letters may contain errors from previous chapters.

April 1, 1999

Mr. Andrew Jasper
9088 Drew Plaza
Canandaigua, NY 14424

Dear Mr. Jasper:

It is a pleasure to inform you that your project "Traveling the Y: A Time of Decision" has been selected for our park. We are pleased to request the project as submitted in the design. At the time of completion a commission of $22,000 will be paid to you. All expenses will be paid in accordance with the itemized expense list submited with the project design. We'll purchase from the suppliers you specified the materials you requested, and have the materials delivered directly to your studio. They should arrive within two weeks. The large pottery and wood design will cover the fountains in the park as you specified.

We were delighted with your idea for a 24-foot walk-on replica of the bridge. The ceramic tile echings will bring to life the history of the bridge. The smaller versions of the structure of the earlier bridges will be placed over other park fountains as suggested.

YB Pottery will be handling the wood and ceramic designs. They will be contacting you directly to discuss the design of the project, and to make arrangements to meet with you. All travel for the project will be arranged with this office.

We look forward to seeing the completed project at the Fourth of July dedication. Congradulations on your creative design.

Sincerely,

Ms. Thesselonia Bunton
Parks Director

hh

CHAPTER 9

Other Commas

RULES

More Comma Rules

9.1 Parenthetical Expressions

9.2 Abbreviations Following Names

9.3 Company Connections

9.4 Direct Address

9.5–9.6 Dates

9.7–9.8 Geographic Locations and Addresses

9.9–9.10 Series

9.11 *And* Omitted

9.12 Commas With Closing Quotation Marks

9.13 Contrasting Material

9.14–9.15 *Too*

Punctuation marks are the street and road signs for the written word, and commas are perhaps the most frequently used (hence, most often abused) marks. Commas help to guide the word traveler to a clearer, more precise meaning. At a glance, the reader can see that introductory material is divided from the main idea, or that a sentence contains a series of items, or that a sentence has two major and equal parts. All this is indicated by commas.

However, commas should not be overused. There are quite specific rules and observable patterns for inserting commas. Unfortunately, some people have been taught a shortcut that creates poor punctuation: Place a comma whenever you pause or need a breath within the sentence. To see how this shortcut can get you into trouble, read the following sentence out loud and notice any slight pauses: *Martha, Jane, Juanita, and Sally left the mall an hour ago but haven't returned home yet.*

Did you pause between *Sally* and *left* and between *ago* and *but*? Putting a comma in either of those places would be incorrect. Moreover, you probably didn't take a breath anywhere within the first five words, but the three commas found there are all necessary.

Some people who follow this false shortcut insert so many commas that their punctuation looks as though they were hyperventilating. In short, your breathing pattern is not a good guide for comma placement. Instead, follow the comma rules in this chapter and in earlier chapters in this text. Please remember that you may have to refresh parts of your grammar terminology if some of the terms used in this chapter have escaped from their grammar file in your brain.

MORE COMMA RULES

Parenthetical Expressions

9.1 Use one or more commas to set off parenthetical expressions (transitional expressions and editorial comments found within a sentence). Parenthetical expressions are unnecessary to the meaning of a sentence. The following list includes some common parenthetical expressions.

- That particular CEO, *generally speaking,* gives her employees a second chance.
- I knew one employee, *for example,* who used office equipment for a personal project but was allowed to remain in her job.
- She lost her job when the government contracts were discontinued, *sad to say.*
- That was the coldest day of the year, *wasn't it*?
- Sit still, *please.*

Common Parenthetical Expressions

according to her
according to our records
accordingly
actually
after all
afterward
ah
alas
all in all
all things considered
also
anyway
apparently
as a matter of fact
as a result
as a rule
as I see it
as it happens
as usual
as you know
at any rate
at first
at the same time
be that as it may
believe it or not
besides
between you and me
briefly
by all means
by and large
by contrast
by the by

by the same token
by the way
certainly
clearly
consequently
conversely
doubtless
even so
finally
first
first of all
for example
for instance
for now
for one thing
for the most part
for the time being
fortunately
frankly
furthermore
generally
generally speaking
happily
hence
however
ideally
if necessary
if possible
in addition
in any case
in any event
in brief
in conclusion
in effect
in essence
in fact
in general
in my opinion
in other words
in reality
in short
in summary
in the final analysis
in the first place
in the long run
in the meantime
in time
in turn
incidentally
indeed
instead
later
likewise
literally
meanwhile
moreover
namely
naturally
needless to say
nevertheless
next
no
no doubt
obviously
of course
on balance
on the contrary
on the one hand
on the other hand
on the whole
ordinarily
otherwise
perhaps
periodically
personally
presumably
rather
second
secondly
similarly
so
still
strictly speaking
that is
that is to say
then
theoretically
therefore
this fact notwithstanding
thus
to begin with
to be honest
to say the least
to sum up
to tell the truth
too
under the circumstances
unfortunately
usually
what is more
without a doubt
without doubt
yes
yet

Abbreviations Following Names

9.2 Use commas to set off abbreviations for academic titles and religious orders, but do not use commas to set off *Jr., Sr.,* roman numerals, *Inc.,* or *Ltd.* The only time commas may be used before these expressions is when the preference of the company or individual is to include the commas.

- ➤ Susan Cleary, *Ph.D.,* and Harry Hopkins *III* will be married in July.
- ➤ The Reverend Simon LaTour, *D.D.,* filed a grievance against Wonderful Wines *Inc.*

Company Connections

9.3 Use commas to set off a long phrase (six or more words) beginning with *of* when the phrase immediately follows a person's name or a company's name and describes a geographic location or business affiliation.

- ➤ José Felicia, *of the Preservation of Historic Buildings Society,* filed an injunction today.
- ➤ José Felicia *of the Historic Buildings Society* filed an injunction today. (fewer than six words)

Direct Address

9.4 Use commas to set off the name of the person or group being addressed.

- ➤ I want you, *Mr. Wattkins,* to work on the Billings project.
- ➤ I want to speak to you, *my friends,* about the candidate for city council.

Dates

9.5 In the date line of a letter, use a comma to separate the date and the year.

June 5, 1999 December 18, 1999

9.6 Within a sentence, use commas to set off the year when it follows the date; use commas to set off the date when it follows the day of the week. Do not use commas when only the month and the year are used.

- ➤ Ralph Sanchos saw the old Towers Building on Thursday, *October 22, 1982,* before the remodeling started.
- ➤ I was born on Sunday, *June 5,* in the early morning.
- ➤ Sarah Klein flew to Paris in *June 1991* to visit her aunt.

Geographic Locations and Addresses

9.7 In the inside address of a letter, use a comma to separate the city and the two-letter state abbreviation. Do not use a comma between the state and the ZIP Code.

Mr. Ralph Hamlin
124 Broad Avenue
Rockland, ME 04841

9.8 Within a sentence, use commas following each item of an address, including the ZIP Code. Do not, however, place a comma between the state and ZIP Code. The state name is not abbreviated within a sentence.

➤ If you wish to write Leah a letter, you will need to know that she is visiting her uncle at *124 Broad Avenue, Rockland, Maine 04841,* all this summer.

EXERCISE 9–A

Directions: Using standard proofreaders' marks, make all necessary corrections in this dialogue at a trial. This exercise covers Rules 9.1 through 9.8.

1. I am asking you, Mr. Beekman to tell me clearly about the events that occurred on Friday, March 26, 1999 in Tulane, Ohio on that fateful night.
2. Mr. Masen it was like this; actually I am positive it was like this.
3. Sam Waters of the Department of Building and Safety Codes and Laws of Racine went to 9010 West Sycamore Street, Tulane OH, around 5:30 p.m.
4. I know this because I had been in Ethel's Clip Joint—that's a barber shop by the way, before anyone questions my reputation.
5. Anyway at Ethel's you can clearly see the whole front of 9010 West Sycamore; furthermore there's an enormous picture window that's always lit up.
6. Mr. Beekman tell us who or what is located at 9010 West Sycamore Tulane before you go further into the events of the evening.
7. It's the offices of Whooey, Doolittle, and Lou, Inc.; these guys are attorneys for the Megabucks Construction Company.
8. Between you and me brother it's also a front for a bookie joint that's out of Nowhere Kentucky.
9. Anyway Whooey and Doolittle were yelling and shaking their fists at Sam just as they had done two nights earlier, Wednesday March 24 around 8 p.m. What a sight!
10. On Friday March 26 1999 there were two more people—Wylie Fox, III, and Wilma Wigg, CPS of Secretaries Unlimited, which is located at 1234 West LaFayette Racine OH.
11. The four of them were really yelling at Sam, but then something really unusual Mr. Masen, happened—the power went off inside 9010 West Sycamore.
12. The next thing I knew, we in the Clip Joint saw those characters running out the door; Wylie Fox, III, was leading the way.
13. Sam Waters's body was discovered two hours later, when his cousin, Sarah Nightingale R.N., went looking for him since he was so late and all.
14. That's all I know strictly speaking Mr. Masen.

EXERCISE 9–B *Directions:* In the following letter, make all necessary corrections by using standard proofreaders' marks. This exercise covers Rules 9.1 through 9.8.

April 18 1999

Dear Citizens:

We all have been following no doubt the plans proposed by the city council to beautify the downtown area in the hope of increasing business. A great deal of organizing has been done by Frieda Willmer Ph.D., of the Downtown Historic Preservation, Planning, and Beautification Committee and Joe Green, of Treeman Architectural Firm. A great deal of work has gone into these plans, and those of us who have visited the main library have seen the model that is on display. Still much is to be done, and we citizens must be farsighted enough to pull together and shoulder this responsibility if we want the downtown area ever to have any hope of fiscally coming alive once more.

On April 13, 1999 John Fisher, III, of Maxwell Savings and Loan Inc. spoke to the Gardening Club about this plan. Mr. Fisher requested that this organization donate its energies and resources to planting red geraniums in the flower boxes that line the city blocks from 102 Main Street to 502 Court Street. The community should also remember that the flower boxes were suggested by Mabel Whittier and donated by Tom Harris, Jr., of Harris Lumber and Supply. The Gardening Club has agreed to do this next month.

The next planning meeting is scheduled for April 27 in the town hall. This community needs to have its citizens dedicated to the many projects that we have planned. I would like to see everyone at the meeting. Bring a positive and willing attitude. No contribution is too small.

Sincerely,

Ralph Wyneski

EXERCISE 9–C

Directions: In the following letter, make all necessary corrections by using standard proofreaders' marks. .

September 7, 1999

Mr. Benjamin Masters, Jr.
16604 Federated Way
Meriden CT 06450

Dear Mr. Masters:

Ms. Gayle Sims has asked me for a letter of recommendation; I gladly accepted. Ms. Simms has worked for Maria Sanchez—of Beekman, Bender, Heurzler, Nachez, Terrence, Whitefeather, and Associates—for the passed four summers. Ms. Sims has been MS. Sanchez's secretary as well as a assistant to our accounts department. We will be sorry to see her leave, but will be eager to see her take her place in the business world since she has recently completed her master's degree.

I enthusiastically recommend Ms. Sims to you Mr. Master, for a variety of reasons. First she exhibits effective interpersonal skills. On several occasions our firm needed someone to help clients fill out questionaires or to assist in conducting interviews. Mrs. Sims proved quite capable of putting our clients at ease and of being accurate and detailed when gathering information. When our firm moved in June, 1993, Ms. Sims cheerfully provided extra assistance in packing, unpacking, and reorganizing. Additionally she has excellent communication and math skills. Ms. Sanchez has reported that Ms. Sims's correspondence was always grammatically written and neatly typed. Our accounts department remembers several times when she stayed after work in order to accommodate special needs.

If we had a permanent full-time position available we would hire Ms. Sims in an instant. Unfortunately, we do not, however, we do wish the best for her and feel confident in her ability to be a success. It has been a pleasure to watch this girl mature in a professional setting. One can not expect to hire a better employee then Ms. Gayle Sims.

Sincerely,

Walter Huerzler
Senior Associate

rb

Series

9.9 Use a comma after each item of a series that contains three or more words, phrases, or clauses. Do not use a comma before the first item or after the last item of the series. A comma is required before the conjunction separating the last two items. (For information on punctuating items in a series when the items contain internal commas, see Chapter 13.)

➤ Jason has *three dogs, one cat, and a snake.*

➤ Lisa *made two copies of the report, filed several papers, and wrote one memo.*

➤ *He pushed past the stranger, then he ran past the officer, and then he was tripped by a little old lady.*

➤ Before he ran *over the hill, through the woods, and to Grandma's house,* he stopped at the convenience store to drink a quart of milk. (The comma following *house* is there to separate the introductory clause from the rest of the sentence.)

9.10 Do not use commas between items of a series when all items are separated by conjunctions.

➤ Mr. Grant bought one apple *and* two oranges *and* one grapefruit for his lunch.

And Omitted

9.11 Use a comma to separate two or more adjectives that modify the same noun. Two simple tests can help you to decide whether the comma is necessary. The first test is to try to insert the word *and* between the adjectives. If *and* can comfortably be used, an *and* has been omitted and a comma is necessary. The second test is to reverse the order of the adjectives and see if they still sound appropriate.

➤ A *cold, stormy* night was the opening scene of the horror movie. (Try the tests: a cold and stormy night; a stormy, cold night.)

➤ Hutchins and Son Inc. won the contract to demolish the *dilapidated, uninhabited* building. (Try the tests: the dilapidated and uninhabited building; the uninhabited, dilapidated building.)

Commas With Closing Quotation Marks

9.12 Commas (and periods) go inside closing quotations marks.

➤ "You are a maniac," Mary screamed at Paul. "I will never marry you."

Contrasting Material

9.13 Use commas to set off contrasting material when the material interrupts the flow of the sentence or reverses the meaning of the sentence. The words *but, not,* and *rather than* are often used to introduce these expressions.

➤ Juanita chose Larry, *not Sam,* as her escort.

➤ Preserving the world's ecological balance should be a daily task, *rather than an occasional activity.*

➤ He played volleyball instead of golf. (*Instead of golf* doesn't interrupt the flow of the sentence.)

Too

9.14 When the word *too* is used as an adverb (meaning "also") within a sentence, use commas to separate *too* from the rest of the sentence.

➤ I, *too,* saw the UFO.

9.15 Do not use a comma when the adverb *too* falls at the end of a sentence or means "excessively."

➤ We saw the UFO *too.*

➤ We were only *too* happy to leave work an hour early.

EXERCISE 9–D

Directions: Make all necessary corrections by using standard proofreaders' marks. This exercise covers Rules 9.9 through 9.15.

1. "Stop that complaining" snapped Mark. "It was Ralph not I, who turned in the report."
2. "Please send copies to Ms. Finley, Mr. Hansome and Mr. Lathe" said Ms. Lomas, "and I suppose we had better send a copy to Ms. Kelsey, too."
3. "That was an incredibly, boring lecture." reported Mary. "Don't you think so too?"
4. "Well, I actually thought the information about the unused cast-off enzymes was completely fascinating", Sarah reflected thoughtfully.
5. "I can't believe that you too, were held spellbound," sniffed Mary. "I was only too happy to be out of that dark dank basement they call a lecture hall."
6. "Next week I have a term paper, and a midterm, and a book report due" John moaned.
7. "Then that will make you too busy to attend Sam's party," Mary replied. "I wouldn't let anything, but a small avalanche, keep me from it."
8. "It would have to be an awfully large avalanche before it kept you from going to a party, a dance or even a movie," replied John.
9. "It would have to be a huge, enormous avalanche to keep you away", retorted Sarah.
10. Mary snipped back, "You people are just too good to me. I'd rather be in the dentist's chair, or Mr. Taylor's lecture class than here. Furthermore, I'm going to get Sam not you to help me with my homework."

EXERCISE 9–E *Directions:* Make all necessary corrections by using standard proofreaders' marks. This exercise covers Rules 9.9 through 9.15.

MEMORANDUM

TO: All Freshman English Faculty

FROM: Dr. Maria Barry, Department Chair

DATE: September 6, 1999

SUBJECT: Mandatory Freshman English Assessment Test

As you know, we too have been in the process of developing an assessment package for each academic program. As part of this comprehensive assessment process, we have chosen to administer an English writing-skills test. This assessment tool is a test that has been developed by a five-member committee from the English Department rather than a nationally normed test constructed by individuals who are not familiar with our institutional goals. We feel it is a sound reasonable instrument that will measure our incoming students' abilities.

Please inform your students in English 101 that they must take this assessment instrument before they complete the fifth week of this quarter. We have reserved the lecture auditorium in McGuffey Hall for this purpose. The test will be offered over a three-week span at ten different times. Students will need to register to ensure getting a seat. Registration sheets have been posted in the basement of the administration building. Students will need to take the following to the examination: two soft-leaded pencils, an eraser, a dictionary and a student card or driver's license for identification.

The test will last approximately two hours. The clearly written easily followed instructions will make the test easy to administer. We will need faculty to help proctor the test. We will need graders, too. The college is allowing us to offer a small, but equitable, per diem. Please notify the departmental secretary if you are interested in assisting.

Results of this assessment will be calculated and distributed by midterm of the following quarter. I know that you too will be eager to see the results.

Thank you.

EXERCISE 9-F

Directions: Make all necessary corrections by using standard proofreaders' marks. This exercise covers the rules from this chapter.

TO BREATHE OR NOT TO BREATHE . . . RADON

In the past few years, we have become increasingly concerned about the air we breathe. Issues range from pollen to second-hand tobacco smoke from mold in air-conditioning vents to office supply fumes and from asbestos to radon. Some of these pollutants occur naturally rather than being made by humans. Radon is one of these natural but dangerous pollutants.

Radon is an odorless tasteless gas that is a natural by-product of decaying uranium and can be found in the atmosphere and soil in varying quantities. When it is present in well water or in surrounding soil, it enters the home through small spaces and openings, such as cracks in concrete, floor drains, sump-pump openings, wall and floor joints in basements and the pores in hollow-block walls. It can seep into ground water, too.

Outdoors, radon harmlessly diffuses into the atmosphere. Indoors, however, radon may become trapped, causing serious risk to the inhabitants. Radon gas breaks down into radioactive particles that become trapped in our lungs when we breathe. The trapped particles continue to disintegrate, giving off small bursts of radiation that may damage the lung tissue. In turn lung cancer may develop.

The only way to know whether a home has a radon problem is to test for it. Test kits may be purchased over the counter at most hardware, grocery and convenience stores. Be sure the kit has been approved by federal or state health, environmental protection, or consumer protection agencies. Follow the directions carefully. Although short-term testing is the most common method, long-term testing offers the most accurate results.

The concentration of radon in the air is measured in units of picocuries per liter of air (pCi/L). The average home probably contains 1 or 2 pCi/L. If the level tests above 4 pCi/L, a follow-up test is administered. A level of 4 pCi/L is comparable to smoking ten cigarettes a day or having 200 chest X rays a year.

The level of radon may be reduced in a number of ways, but these ways vary according to the source of the gas, and the ways in which it enters the home, and the kind of construction used in the home. Specially designed filter systems can be installed to eliminate radon from water. Costs for radon reduction vary according to the method used, and the severity of the problem. It is advisable to seek qualified professional help to reduce radon levels in the home or workplace. Local state or national government agencies are usually prepared to make these recommendations.

The federal government has undertaken an extensive public outreach effort to encourage individuals to test their homes. This effort includes the establishment of a national hotline, 1-800-SOS-RADON. Pamphlets and additional information are available by writing to the U.S. Environmental Protection Agency, Public Information Center, 401 M Street, SW, Wash. D.C., 20460.

Check your radon today so that you can breathe deeply tomorrow.

EXERCISE 9-G *Directions:* Make all necessary corrections by using standard proofreaders' marks. This exercise is a review of material previously covered in this text.

DIETER, BEWARE!

Eat all you want and still lose all you want! It's easy and fun! You don't even know your on a diet! It's a new discovery that brings miraculous results! This secret blend of exotic ingredients is a magical breakthrough! Have you ever read any of these claims like these and found yourself wanting to believe them? It would be nice wouldn't it to have all these claims come true? If you answered in the affirmative your not alone, over 50 million Americans this year will spend an estimated $30 billion on all types of diet programs and products. Because of the strength and variety of advertisements and the overwhelming desire to be thin, we the consumers can be a little to gullible when we read those diet ads. The Federal Trade Commission (FTC) and the Food and Drug Administration (FDA) wants you dear reader to be wary of certain products.

Because diet patches have not been shown to be safe or effective; the FDA have already seized millions of patches from manufacturers and promoters. The FTC has brought legal action against several marketers that claimed they had a "magnet" diet pill that allegedly "flush fat out of the body." The use of special "starch blockers" may even cause diarrhea, nausea and stomach pains. Spirulina a species of blue-green algae have not been proven effective for losing weight. Some bulk producers or fillers may reduce hunger, because they absorb liquid and swell in the stomach. One such filler, made of guar gum, is harmful because it caused obstructions in the intestines, stomach or esophagus.

The FDA have banned 111 ingredients once found in over-the-counter diet products.

Substances include alcohol, caffeine, dextrose and guar gum. None of these substances have been effective in weight loss or appetite suppression. The FTC and a number of state attorneys general have successfully brought cases against marketers of pills claiming to absorb or burn fat. Therefore remember the maxim *Buyer, beware*!

There are a variety of phony weight-loss devices, too. "Appetite-suppressing eyeglasses" are everyday eyeglasses that have colored lenses. The lenses supposedly causing the retina to project an image that lessons the desire to eat. Although electrical muscle stimulators are legitimately used in physical therapy treatments; improper use can cause electrical shocks and burns. "Magic wait-loss earrings" are suppose to stimulate acupuncture points controlling hunger.

Its better to be safe not sorry when entering a diet program. Remember the old movies in which the con artist stands on the back of the wagon and coaxes the customers, saying, "For only pennies a day, you too can partake of this magic elixir". Ask some hard questions. Get some legitimate facts. Consult your doctor.

For more information or to file a complaint, write to :

Food and Drug Administration
Consumer Affairs and Information
5600 Fishers Lane, HFC-110
Rockville, MD 20857

Federal Trade Commission
Correspondence Branch
Washington, D.C. 20580

EXERCISE 9-H *Directions:* Make all necessary corrections by using standard proofreaders' marks. This exercise is a review of material previously covered in this text.

Perfect
Plants &
Potteries, Ltd.

558 Vancover Way
Englewood, CO 80110

April 20, 1999

Dear Neighbor:

Unquestionably, moving is an exciting busy time. It offers the excitement of meeting new neighbors and the sadness of leaving old ones. It means packing and unpacking and to make decisions about keeping, selling, or to give away. Moving offers a variety of new experiences in a new home, unfortunately, not all of these experiences may be pleasant ones, particularly when it comes to moving the nonhuman members of your family—your plants. We at Perfect Plants and Potteries Ltd. wish to offer you a few extra tips, time savers and coupons that should practically guarantee a successful move with your green-leafed friends.

If you follow the "do-it-yourself plan", you will probably have better control over your plants' environment. Temperatures above 95°F or below 35oF can cause irreversible harm to your plants. Proper packing can alleviate some of this problem. Most plants can survive approximately a week without water or sunlight,be sure your plant's soil is moist before putting the plant in a carton carrier. After a prolonged period of darkness, the plant must be gradually reintroduced to sun light. Cuttings will survive several days if kept moist in a plastic bag containing vermiculite or peat moss, however, potted plants have a better chance of surviving. Some houseplants are susceptible to shock and will need time and tender loving care to recover.

Several states have laws governing the interstate travel of plants. Some states require a quarantine time, others require an authorized agriculture inspector's certification that your plant if free of disease and pests. Some states refuse entry or thru transit of any plant, and will stop vehicles at random for inspections. Be sure to check with the proper authorities.

Neighbor
Page 2
April 20, 1999

Most professional moving companies will except plants under certain provisions. For more information write American Movers Conference, 200 Mill Road, Alexandria, VA, 2314.

If your planning a move we hope these hints will help you when it comes to moving your green friends. Don't forget that you can remember your friends in the old neighborhood through our long-distance service. It's as easy as picking up your phone. If your not planning a move, we at Perfect Plants and Potteries Ltd. will be glad to continue to serve you. By the way, don't forget that plants make wonderful housewarming gifts not to mention all those other special occasions.

Think green!

Sincerely,

PERFECT PLANTS AND POTTERIES LTD.

Elliott Anderson

CHAPTER

10 Capitalization

RULES

Capitalization Rules

10.1 Proper Nouns and Common Nouns

10.2 Academic Subjects

10.3 Languages, Races, and Cultures

10.4 Geographic Locations

10.5 Geographic Nicknames and Regional Areas

10.6 Compass Directions

10.7 Days, Months, Holidays, Special Events, and Historical Events

10.8 Seasons, Decades, and Centuries

10.9 Celestial Bodies

10.10–10.11 Brand Names and Trademarks

10.12 Beginning Words

10.13–10.14 First Word After a Colon

10.15 Salutation, Complimentary Close, Addresses

10.16 Titles Before Names

10.17 Titles Used in Place of Names

10.18 Titles After Names

10.19 Titles of Executive Officers in Bylaws, Minutes, and Policies

10.20 Titles in Direct Address

10.21 Organizational Terms

10.22 Organizations

10.23 Academic Degrees (Titles)

10.24 Titles of Literary and Artistic Works

10.25 *The* in an Organization's Name

10.26–10.27 Titles of Acts, Bills, and Laws

10.28 Advertising Material

10.29 Names of Software

10.30 Abbreviations

10.31 Nouns Followed by Numbers or Letters

Imagine you are solving a mystery and the clue is the abbreviation *Cl.* Would that hint mean that you should measure something (centiliter) or that you should locate a chemical (chlorine)? If someone wanted a *BD*, would you give that person a bundle or a bank draft? If something were stamped *DD* would that mean it had been delivered or that someone had received a dishonorable discharge? Does *D* stand for day or for democrat? In all these cases, the answer depends on capitalization! (By the way, the second choice in every case is the correct answer; the first choice is the lowercase definition of the abbreviation.)

As you have just witnessed, capitalization can completely change the meaning of a word or an abbreviation. Capitalization also supplies a hint concerning the importance or specificity of the word; for example, a proper noun is always capitalized. The *Senator from Georgia* refers to a U.S. Senator; the *senator from Georgia* refers to a state senator. This chapter reviews frequently used rules regarding capitalization. Just remember, a word is not just any word when capitalization is involved.

CAPITALIZATION RULES

Proper Nouns and Common Nouns

10.1 Capitalize actual names of specific people, places, or things (proper nouns). Do not capitalize nouns that describe general classes of people, places, or things (common nouns). Adjectives derived from proper nouns are usually capitalized.

Proper Nouns or Adjectives	Common Nouns
England	country
Loch Ness	loch (lake)
Mary Smith	woman
Beadling Company	company
Lincoln Memorial	monument
Edison High School	high school

PROOFREADING POINTER

Common Noun or Proper Noun?

plaster of paris	german chocolate cake	bone china
india ink	roman numerals	venetian blinds
braille alphabet		

These terms each contain a proper noun or adjective that has been so widely used that it has become a common noun or adjective and is no longer capitalized.

Even current dictionaries disagree about whether these words should be capitalized. So consult an accepted dictionary for your field and then be consistent with your capitalization.

Academic Subjects

10.2 Capitalize names of specific academic courses that are numbered or listed in a formalized curriculum. In general, do not capitalize a course of study; proper nouns or adjectives that appear in the phrase describing the course of study are capitalized.

- ➤ I am taking *marketing* at the community college. (not a specific course)
- ➤ I am taking *Marketing 201* at the community college. (numbered course)
- ➤ Sue will be taking *world history* next fall. (a course of study, not a specific course)
- ➤ Sue will be taking *American history* this spring. (proper adjective describing a general course of study)

Languages, Races, and Cultures

10.3 Capitalize the names of races, languages, and cultures. Terms like *black* and *white* are considered generic and are not capitalized.

- ➤ According to the 1990 census, *Hispanics* made up 9 percent of the U.S. population.
- ➤ Do you speak *Spanish*?
- ➤ Southeastern Ohio's residents are a part of the *Appalachian* culture.
- ➤ Some popular films and books are portraying *Native Americans* more realistically.

Geographic Locations

10.4 Capitalize the names of specific geographic locations.

McLean, Texas
Thames River
Glacier Bay National Park
Mississippi River
Cape of Good Hope
Isle of Man

Geographic Nicknames and Regional Areas

10.5 Capitalize the nicknames of geographic locations and the names of regional areas.

Silicon Valley
Windy City
Bay Area
Right Bank
Big Apple
French Quarter

Compass Directions

10.6 Capitalize compass directions when they indicate a region but not when they indicate a direction.

- ➤ Turn right at the second light and go *south*.
- ➤ We hope to visit the *South* during our vacation this summer.
- ➤ The wind was blowing *north* by *northwest*.

Days, Months, Holidays, Special Events, and Historical Events

10.7 Capitalize days of the week, months of the year, holidays, special events, and historical events or time periods.

➤ The newspaper is published *Monday* through *Friday,* except on *Christmas* and *New Year's Day.*

➤ Historians cite the *First Battle of Bull Run* (held at Manassas Creek) as an important event of the *Civil War.*

➤ My great-grandmother was a flapper in the *Roaring Twenties.*

Seasons, Decades, and Centuries

10.8 Do not capitalize seasons, decades, and centuries.

➤ Moles forage actively for grubs in the *spring.*

➤ I wonder what computers will be able to do for us during the *twenty-first century.*

Celestial Bodies

10.9 In general, capitalize the names of celestial bodies. The words *sun, moon,* and *earth* are not capitalized unless they are used with the names of other planets in the solar system.

➤ I saw the *Big Dipper,* but I couldn't find the *North Star.*

➤ Hospital emergency rooms report an increase in unusual accidents during a *full moon.*

➤ The three planets closest to the *Sun* are *Mercury, Venus,* and *Earth.*

➤ The light of the *sun* is needed to grow plants.

Brand Names and Trademarks

10.10 Capitalize brand names and trademarks. A common noun following a brand name or trademark is not capitalized.

Jell-O™ gelatin	Hershey's™ chocolate
Kleenex™ tissues	Mustang™ convertible

10.11 Some brand names, trademarks, and proper nouns have been so widely used that they often appear as common nouns, such as *aspirin* or *penicillin.* Other words like Xerox are registered trademarks, not generic terms. These words are capitalized when they refer to a company or brand name. If you are not sure whether such words are trademarks, consult a dictionary.

I want to *photocopy* these pages.

We purchased a *Xerox* copier.

I took two *aspirins* and went home early.

PROOFREADING POINTER

Watch out for the word *fiberglass.* It's an unusual brand name that has been so widely used that it often appears as a common noun. It's spelled one way (and capitalized) when used as a brand name and another (way and lowercased) when used as a common noun.

Fiberglas—Brand name
fiberglass—product

EXERCISE 10–A

Directions: Using standard proofreaders' marks, correct any errors. Indicate the rule number for each error marked. If a sentence contains no errors, circle the number of the sentence. This exercise includes examples of Rules 10.1 through 10.11.

1. _____ Racenel electronics signed the government contract on Tuesday in the Peach room of the White house.
2. _____ Specifications in the contract included locating the manufacturing plant in the west.
3. _____ Consequently, Racenel will be using the north star as a guide as they move west.
4. _____ Aileen Aikato, who has handled our japanese accounts for the last Decade, will be joining the staff as the supervisor of government accounts.
5. _____ In preparation for the move, three members of the Racenel Staff will be required to learn Japanese in order to communicate with the major supplier of the Moranto bearing Company.
6. _____ Callie Jones, Christine King, and Mortimer Morton have been enrolled in JPC 101 (Japanese culture) and JPL 100 (Japanese as a Second Language).
7. _____ We feel the Japanese Culture course will prove helpful in our meetings with Moranto's representatives.
8. _____ Midland Electrical Company, our Parent Company, will be supplying the moving vehicles necessary to transport our office to Drusso, California.
9. _____ The movers should arrive on June 4 to pack our equipment.
10. _____ We hope to have the move completed by July 5 since the terms of the Government contract specify July 20 as the starting date for our contract with Moranto.

EXERCISE 10–B *Directions:* Using standard proofreaders' marks, correct any errors in the following memorandum. This exercise contains errors related to Rules 10.1 through 10.11.

MEMORANDUM

TO: Judy Rose

FROM: Alex Drake

DATE: April 15, 1999

SUBJECT: Skill Testing

On tuesday, June 30, we will be scheduling office skills tests. The tests will cover Typing, English, Japanese Culture, and Proofreading. The results of these tests will be added to the results of the promotion interviews to determine the top six candidates for promotion to associate administrative secretary.

These tests cover a wide variety of topics. The best way to prepare for the tests seems to be enrollment in a course at Wilderness Community college. Racenel Electronics will pay for any course you take at wilderness if you receive a grade of *C* or higher in the class.

For those of you who haven't been to Wilderness, it is located one mile west of Harpsichord Monument on Madison Street on the upper east side. Copies of the College catalog are available in the Human Resources Office. If you have any other questions, call Shelly Rubright at Ext. 334.

fg

Beginning Words

10.12 Capitalize the first word of a sentence, a quoted sentence, an item in an outline, an item in a list beginning on a separate line, and an independent expression.

➤ I said, "*He* won't become president of the company."

➤ *No!* Don't take that printer out of this building.

➤ I. *Basic* camping equipment
  A. *Sleeping* bag
  B. *Flashlight*
  C. *Bug* repellent

First Word After a Colon

10.13 Capitalize the first word after a colon if the material following the colon consists of two or more sentences or a formalized rule. Also capitalize the first word of material following a short introductory phrase like *Remember* or *Note* when it is followed by a colon.

➤ The company takeover will require several changes: *First,* the departments will be restructured to reduce their number from five to three. Next, the department heads will be given the title of vice president.

➤ This is the rule: *A* comma must be placed before the coordinate conjunction in a compound sentence.

➤ Wanted: *Summer* help

10.14 Do not capitalize the first word of an incomplete sentence following a colon or of a complete sentence that defines or explains the main idea expressed before the colon.

➤ Rhonda Williams purchased several pieces of equipment: *an* electric hole punch, two adding machines, and an answering machine.

➤ The field trip was a success: *no* one got lost, and no one got sick.

Salutation, Complimentary Close, Addresses

10.15 Capitalize the first word of a salutation or complimentary close. Capitalize titles in business correspondence in inside addresses, signature lines, or envelope addresses.

➤ *Dear* Mrs. Jones:

➤ *Sincerely* yours,

➤ Mrs. Sarah Walinsky
Associate Producer

EXERCISE 10–C

Directions: Using standard proofreaders' marks, correct any errors. Indicate the rule number for each error you mark. If a sentence contains no errors, circle the number of the sentence. This exercise includes examples of errors relating to Rules 10.12 through 10.15.

1. ______ Dear Mr. Anderson
2. ______ Dear professor Monnett
3. ______ Sincerely Yours
4. ______ Very cordially yours
5. ______ sincerely
6. ______ we hope you will be able to join us for lunch.
7. ______ Carol White hopes to sponsor three contests: Typing, word processing, and accounting.
8. ______ Wanted: kitchen help
9. ______ MALC has established a new attendance policy: All students will be penalized one letter grade for missing more than three classes.
10. ______ Remember: Lunch at noon

EXERCISE 10-D *Directions:* Using standard proofreaders' marks, correct any errors in the following letter. This exercise contains errors related to Rules 10.1 through 10.15.

June 3, 1999

Mr. Manley Koontz
2398 Linden Avenue
Loveland, OH 45124

Dear mr. Koontz:

Many people always believe people are at their worst. Our organization knows this is not true. The recent response of our Community to the financial plight of the local Feed America campaign is a classic example of the way the citizens of Loveland show their best sides.

Last march we found our usual funding for the homeless shelters across the state was almost gone. The demands of the homeless in this time of economic recession had forced shelters to spend almost 30 percent more than budgeted. The recent layoffs at several large corporations in the state contributed significantly to this problem.

The reason didn't really matter: we still had to feed the homeless. We asked if every organization in the Loveland area would have each employee donate two cans of food to the shelter. Our community responded in a way we would never have anticipated. We received an average of five cans per employee, and most companies matched contributions. Our shelter will be able to handle the increased patrons for the remainder of the year.

The next time someone mentions that people are always at their worst, we'll be sure to remind them how wrong they are. The Citizens of loveland are at their best. Thanks for your support.

sincerely,

Miss Greta Gayle, coordinator
Feed America

jl

Titles Before Names

10.16 Capitalize courtesy titles (*Mr., Ms., Rev., Dr.,* and so on) when they occur before names. Also capitalize titles representing company or military rank when they occur before a name and are used in place of more common courtesy titles.

➤ *Mr.* Smith has an appointment at 3:15 with *Professor* Carol Hoeffler.

➤ *Lieutenant* Samuel Juarez is the son of *Dean* Juanita Pasquale.

Titles Used in Place of Names

10.17 Capitalize position titles of national and international officials and high-ranking state officials when they are used in place of personal names. Do not capitalize the titles of local officials.

➤ If the *President* or the *Prime Minister* were to get a private audience with the *Pope,* it would be a sign that these elected officials had unusually high international prestige.

➤ U.S. *Senators* probably spend more than eight months of the year away from their states, but state *senators* reside year-round in their states.

➤ The *mayor* and the *representative* from Cleveland had an important meeting with the *Governor* and the *Lieutenant Governor.*

Titles After Names

10.18 In general, do not capitalize a title that follows a name or is used as an appositive. Titles of most national and international officials and high-ranking state officials are capitalized. Local official titles are not capitalized.

➤ Horatio Jones, *city council member* of Hedgeville, is a cousin to Augusta Rathbone, *a professor* at the university.

➤ Willis Geyser, *the vice president of marketing,* made the keynote speech at the fall conference.

➤ Kate Murray, *the Senator from Maine,* made a motion to amend the federal bill.

Titles of Executive Officers in Bylaws, Minutes, and Policies

10.19 Capitalize the titles of company officials used in bylaws, minutes, and company policies.

➤ The *Treasurer's* report included a profit of $2,307 from the waffle sale. (title used in minutes of a meeting)

➤ The *state representative from Idaho* and the *president of Amalgamated* met this past Thursday. (titles not in minutes, bylaws, or policies)

Titles in Direct Address

10.20 Capitalize a title when it is used in direct address. Words like *sir, miss,* or *madam* are not capitalized.

➤ I'm telling you, *Professor,* I did do that experiment.

➤ I want you, *sir,* to take a seat and be quiet.

Organizational Terms

10.21 Capitalize organizational terms (*advertising department*) when the title is preceded by the word *the* and the title refers to a division of the writer's organization. Do not capitalize these terms if they are not preceded by *the,* if they refer to a division in another organization, or if they are not the complete title.

➤ *Our company's* officers met and decided to abolish *the Complaint Department.*

➤ Our *rival company* still has its *complaint department.*

➤ Mr. Waters is a member of *the Orientation Committee* for *our firm.*

➤ Mr. Waters is a member of *an orientation committee.*

➤ Ana Perez was hired by *the department.*

Organizations

10.22 Capitalize the main words in names of organizations and businesses.

Houghton Mifflin Company	the Public Broadcasting System
the United Nations	the National Organization for Women

Academic Degrees (Titles)

10.23 Do not capitalize the names of academic degrees unless they are used in apposition after an individual's name.

➤ Cheryl Lamont will receive her *bachelor of arts degree* in June.

➤ Mike Johnson, *Doctor of Divinity,* will be the commencement speaker.

EXERCISE 10–E

Directions: Using standard proofreaders' marks, correct any errors. Indicate the rule that applies to each error you mark. If a sentence contains no errors, circle the number of the sentence. This exercise includes examples of errors relating to Rules 10.16 through 10.23.

1. ______ Tien Ng, Systems Analyst, made a recommendation to purchase a new computer network.

2. ______ The new chairman of the Reorganization committee will be Don Neumann, Marketing Director.

3. ______ The company policy states, "All accountants will be directly responsible to the treasurer."

4. ______ Three companies will be sending representatives to the meeting: Alterations Plus, Malibu markets, and Kreegers Closets.

5. ______ The keynote speaker for the conference will be president Ann Rail of Merger, Incorporated.

6. ______ I know, doctor, that I should exercise, but I hate to!

7. ______ If you would like to have any additional information about our return policy, write Sandra Weinerth in our Customer Services Department.

8. ______ The guidelines for the policy on late arrivals were developed by Virginia Boggs, our head resident.

9. ______ We hope to hire Andrew Kringer, master of education, to design the new curriculum in fashion merchandising.

10. ______ The Mayor will be present at the ground-breaking ceremony for the new building.

EXERCISE 10-F *Directions:* Using standard proofreaders' marks, correct any errors in the following memorandum. This exercise contains errors related to Rules 10.1 through 10.23.

MEMORANDUM

September 3, 1999

Edward Mentor, Chair
Wage and Benefits Committee

COMMITTEE ASSIGNMENTS FOR 1999–2000

Committees play a very important part in the organization of Eldridge electronics. during the next 12 months, we will be depending heavily on the work of three committees. The work of these committees is essential to both the morale and productivity of our Company during this time of reorganization.

The organizational meetings of the three committees will be held on September 10 in Room 234. We'll all meet as a group at the beginning with president Drinkman addressing the group at 9 a.m. Following the group meeting, the Wage and Benefits committee will meet in 234; the Acquisitions committee will meet in 233; and the Employee Activity committee will meet in 230.

Wage and Benefits	**Acquisitions**	**Employee Activity**
Edward Mentor, chair	Carol Clements, chair	Fran Brilla, chair
Lonny Claypool	Jack Butters	Evan Dalrymple
Joan Collinghouse	Bill Cover	Eileen Jones
Lee Gunnels	John Denton	Mark Spaniolo
Jenny Shaad	Sheila France	Virginia Spencer

Jim Davis, president

cs

EXERCISE 10-G *Directions:* Using standard proofreaders' marks, correct any errors in the following manuscript. Errors may cover any rules covered earlier in this text.

USO Serves in War and Peace

The gentle nature of America's men and women is seen in the kind acts done on both a large and small scale on a daily basis—from helping a neighbor shovel sno from a walk to sending aid to earthquake victims on foreign soil. But the work of the United Service Organizations (USO) shows the basic nature of the American people.

Established in 1941 the USO was formed by six civilian organizations—the Salvation Army, National Catholic Community Servics, Young Men's Christian Association, Young Women's Christian Association, National Traveler's Aid Association, and the National Jewish Welfare board—as a direct response to president Franklin Roosevelt's call for a civilian organization to "handle the on-leave recreation of our armed forces."

The organizations employs a staff of only 750 employees, which gives over 20,000 Americans the opportunity to do what we do so well—volunteers. Since the USO is not a government agency, the funding to run the organization is securred from contributions from individuals and corporations, the United Way, and the Combined Federal Campaign.

A Changing Organization

In the early days of the organization, USO branches were opened in railroad cars, churches, barns, and museums. They provided a place to meet with friends, write letters, or mend uniforms. Housing referrals and counciling were also available to service personnel and their families.

USO branches provided more than just aid through personal services. They often provided a touch of home for Americans who found themselves far from home and family. The USO in Honolulu was famous for its banana splits; they used over 250 gallons of ice cream every day.

The USO put on shows for the servicemen, with many performers volunteering time to entertain service personnel. Bob Hope is a name that comes immediately to mind when the USO shows are mentioned. Other performers who have given their time are Ray Bolger, Barbara Mandrell, Billy Joel, and Marilyn Monroe.

During the Vietnam war, there were 25 USO branches in Vietnam and Thiland. When the military forces moved from required service to an all-volunteer organization following Vietnam, the existance of the USO was questioned. But the services of a volunteer organization to provide a link with home and civilian life was to valuable to eliminate. Today's military service still requires deployment of troops to remote locations where unfamiliarity with the native language, boredom, loneliness, and inadequate housing create a continuing need for the USO.

Where ever troops are sent in service for the United States, the USO is sure to follow. That's a comforting thought.

Titles of Literary and Artistic Works

10.24 Capitalize the first and last word in titles of literary and artistic works. Capitalize all other words in the title except articles (*a, an,* and *the*) and prepositions of three or fewer letters (such as *for, of, in, out, on, to,* and *up*).

The Taming of the Shrew
The Sound of Music
Tender Is the Night

The in an Organization's Name

10.25 Capitalize *the* at the beginning of a title if it is included in the official name of the organization. If you are not sure *the* is part of the official name, do not capitalize it.

The New York Times	*the Classified Connection*
The Ohio State University	the Miami University
The Wall Street Journal	the World Trade Center

Titles of Acts, Bills, and Laws

10.26 Capitalize the official titles of legal acts, bills, and laws.

the Dred Scott Decision	the Equal Rights Amendment
the Missouri Compromise	the Pendleton Act

10.27 Capitalize only the proper nouns in names of scientific laws.

Bernoulli's principle	Newton's law

Advertising Material

10.28 Imaginative names used in advertising copy may be capitalized.

Winter Wonderland Sale	Dog Days Sale
Spring Into Spring Fling	Hot Summer Sale

Names of Software

10.29 Follow the capitalization style used by the manufacturer for names of computer software packages.

WordPerfect	PageMaker
dBASE IV	CorelDRAW!

Abbreviations

10.30 In general, capitalize abbreviations if the word or words they represent would be capitalized. Academic degrees and business expressions are often exceptions to this rule. (More information on abbreviations can be found in Chapter 19.)

10 a.m.	Ext.	FICA
CEO	M.A.	9 yds.

Nouns Followed by Numbers or Letters

10.31 In general, capitalize nouns followed by a letter or number. Do not capitalize *line, note, page, paragraph, size,* or *verse.*

Stanza 3	page 12
Chapter 5	size 14

EXERCISE 10–H

Directions: Using standard proofreaders' marks, correct any errors. Indicate the rule that applies to each error you mark. If a sentence contains no errors, circle the number of the sentence. This exercise includes examples of errors relating to Rules 10.24 through 10.31.

1. ______ We are planning to launch a new sales campaign to promote the sunglasses produced by the Reishiner Corporation.
2. ______ We plan to call the campaign "When You Don't Want to See the Light."
3. ______ We will be looking for an employee proficient in Word Perfect and PageMaker for layout for this promotion.
4. ______ If you'll look on Page 7 of the promotion brief, you'll see that we plan to use Batman for the layouts.
5. ______ We've already secured the services of a noted actor to play the part. You'll find his name in paragraph 3 of Chapter 6.
6. ______ I'm sure we don't need to remind you that all work on this project is confidential. Any violation of the Confidentiality Clause will result in immediate dismissal from the company.
7. ______ We plan to run the initial advertisements in the *Buckeye*, published by the Ohio State University.
8. ______ College students are particularly fond of Reishiners.
9. ______ The initial production order will plan for at least 10 Dz to be shipped ASAP to the campus bookstores.
10. ______ As a special promotion, Batman will make an appearance in Columbus on the same night that a local movie theater plans a Batman special featuring *The Return Of Batman.*
11. ______ In *the return of Batman,* Batman seems to defy Newton's Law.

EXERCISE 10-1 *Directions:* Using standard proofreaders' marks, correct any errors in the following letter. This exercise contains errors related to Rules 10.24 through 10.31.

PET
GROOMING
by MATT
599 West Lake Road
Huntington, WV 25701

November 24, 1999

Ms. Karen Spring
2087 Appalachian Way
Huntington, WV 25701

Dear Ms. Spring

We know that Christmas is a busy season for your family. Unfortunately, too often you can't give that adorable cat enough attention during the holidays, or maybe you just want to give him (or her) the luxury of professional grooming as a Christmas Offering. Pet Grooming by Matt is pleased to announce the **Clean cat for Christmas** special to help you repair his ruffled fur, whatever the reason!

The **Clean cat** special will run for two weeks starting December 1. The special includes grooming, bathing, a massage—they love it—and a bow tie or ribbon. We don't do nails, but most cats won't be concerned. We've read the book *Grooming for your cat* and know exactly the right way to pamper your pet. If your cat could use the CorelDraw software on our computer, he'd draw the word *Purrfect* (not the software Word Perfect)!

The price for a **Clean Cat For Christmas** is only $75. Incidentally, the package includes a poster-size Christmas portrait of you and your cat. Call now for more information on this timely special; both you and your cat will enjoy the holiday season more.

Sincerely

Matt Mortimer

dd

PS We always follow the guidelines of the 1996 Humanity to Animals act.

EXERCISE 10–J *Directions:* Using standard proofreaders' marks, correct any errors in the following memorandum. This exercise contains errors related to Rules 10.1 through 10.31.

TO: Andrew Jackson

FROM: Austin McPeak, Human Resources Manager

DATE: September 27, 1999

SUBJECT: Calling the Roll—By the Numbers

As far as we're concerned, no one should ever be known by a number. It is important for us to know your numbers—your telephone number and social security number; we need you to verify your numbers with our office. If you will call my Secretary, Susan Abele, at ext. 782, she will verify your numbers. Your social security number remains confidential with this office.

We do plan to publish an Employee Telephone Directory with home phone numbers and names of spouses listed. If you have an unlisted number and don't want your number included, be sure to tell Susan. We need to have your number on file with our office, but we will respect your wishes on whether to include it in the employee directory.

While we're on the subject of numbers, we also want to put together a listing of phone numbers for classrooms and labs. These numbers will not be published but will be listed with the Switchboard in case of emergencies. no calls will be put through to classrooms unless the call is a true emergency.

If you have classes in any of the following rooms, could you make a note of the phone numbers and give them to Susan. Thanks for your help!

room 234	room 345	room 355	room 401
room 568	room 900	room 901	room 978

ss

EXERCISE 10-K *Directions:* Using standard proofreaders' marks, correct any errors in the following letter. This exercise contains errors related to Rules 10.1 through 10.31.

July 5, 1999

Mr. David Jones
4598 Eddlington Plaza
Dock Junction, GA 31520

Dear Mr. Jones

Country classics has always felt that our customers are the most important factor in the success of our business. Our customers tell us that they feel important when they come into our showpasture.

This week we are having a **Thank You Sale** to show our appreciation to you for the loyalty and patronage you have given us over the years. The Sale will begin next monday, July 13, on the pasture at 1236 Jefferson Gulley road. The sale runs for one week; of course, we'll take Sunday off in accordance with the Sunday blue laws.

This sale will feature our usual fantastic buys on *7 Year Plus* pickup trucks. All the trucks have been thoroughly cleaned with special care. No rust spots have been repaired since we always follow our Policy of what you see is what is really there. No one is trying to make these trucks look better than they really are.

The Country Classics Guarantee goes along with every sale made on our showpasture. While we don't repair body work on the trucks, we do guarantee the trucks for one year of mechanical operation. Country Classics may not look great, but they run like the new trucks they are to our customers.

Prices on these trucks are at a record low. Stop in at Jefferson Gulley road and see why The Country Classics truck will fit right in on your farm or ranch.

Sincerely

Ms. Annie O. Pryor
Sales Manager

kl

EXERCISE 10-L

Directions: Using standard proofreaders' marks, correct any errors in the following memorandum. Errors may cover any rules covered earlier in this text.

MEMORANDUM

TO: Allison Reed

FROM: Kenneth Edgerton

DATE: July 8, 1999

SUBJECT: Uppercase and Lowercase

Allison, I understand that you and Jeff have a friendly bet going on the origin of the words *uppercase* and *lowercase*. It just happens that I can provide the definitive answer to this question.

In the early days of the printing industry, type was set by hand as the printer put together small blocks of wood, each containing a letter. To speed this process printers separated the type into fonts—one style in a specific size of type. The capital letters and the small letters also had to be kept seperate so the printer setting the type new were to reach for the letters to build the words. Over the years, the capital letters were kept in the top case (uppercase) and the small letters were kept in the bottom case (lowercase). Even though the typewriter and computer have eliminated the need for hand-set type, the use of the words uppercase and lowercase have continued, and is universally recognized today in the printing field.

How's that for trivia! I hope the answer brings a favorable outcome to your bet!

cs

CHAPTER

11

Apostrophes

RULES

If your name were Jones, would your family receive more money from a winner's notice that read, "The Joneses and the Smiths' tickets have won $1000," or from one that read, "The Joneses' and the Smiths' tickets have won $1000"? If you want the entire amount, take the second notice; the first would require you to split the prize.

As you already know, an apostrophe shows ownership or represents omitted letters in contractions. In addition, the apostrophe is used to form plurals of certain letters and numbers. The rules in this chapter will give you examples of each use.

APOSTROPHES IN CONTRACTIONS

Contractions

11.1 Use an apostrophe to indicate omitted letters or numbers in common contractions to achieve an informal style in business writing. Do not use contractions in normal or formal business writing.

➤ I *won't* [will not] be going to the meeting.

➤ Herb Smith *can't* [cannot] find the minutes from the last meeting.

➤ The Class of *'95* [1995] will hold its reunion in the year 2000.

APOSTROPHES IN SINGULAR AND PLURAL POSSESSIVES

Nouns, Compound Nouns, and Capitalized Singular Abbreviations Not Ending in *s*

11.2 If a noun, compound noun (singular and plural), or an all-capital singular abbreviation does not end in *s,* add an apostrophe and an *s* to show possession.

boy's	PTO's
John's	children's
father-in-law's	mother-in-law's

Nouns, Compound Nouns, and Capitalized Abbreviations Ending in *s* (Singular)

11.3 In general, if a singular noun, a singular compound noun, or an all-capital singular abbreviation ends in *s,* add an apostrophe and an *s* to show possession. If the resulting word is difficult to pronounce, the *s* may be omitted.

Jones's	Congress's
New Orleans'	MTS's

Nouns, Compound Nouns, and Capitalized Abbreviations Ending in *s* (Plural)

11.4 If a plural noun, plural compound noun, or all-capital plural abbreviation ends in *s,* add only an apostrophe to show possession.

Navajos'	girls'
know-it-alls'	CPSs'
students'	witnesses'

PROOFREADING POINTER

Possessive or not possessive? To determine whether a word shows possession, check two things:

1. Make sure the word following it is a noun. A possessive construction has two consecutive nouns.
2. Reverse the order of the two words and insert *of* or *of the*. If the sentence still makes sense, the noun is possessive.

The man's car is in the repair shop.
(The car of the man is in the repair shop.)

Sue's vacation starts next week.
(The vacation of Sue starts next week.)

Joint and Individual Ownership

11.5 To show individual ownership, make each name possessive. Be sure the noun following the names is plural.

➤ *Mark's* and *Nancy's cars*

➤ *Bill's* and *Jean's assistants*

11.6 To show joint ownership, make only the last name possessive.

➤ *Ed and Larry's boat* (They jointly own one boat.)

➤ *Ed and Larry's boats* (They jointly own more than one boat.)

APOSTROPHES FOR CLARITY IN FORMING PLURALS

Plurals of Lowercase Letters, Some Capital Letters, and Some Lowercase Abbreviations

11.7 Use an apostrophe to form the plural of some lowercase abbreviations, of all lowercase letters; and of the capital letters *A, I, M,* and *U*. Using an apostrophe with these capital letters avoids confusion with the words *As, Is, Ms,* and *Us*. Do not use the apostrophe to form plurals of other capital letters, numerals, and uppercase abbreviations.

c's	*r*'s	lbs.
M's	*U*'s	yds.
6s	*P*s	tsps.
bldg.'s	FYIs	nos.

PROOFREADING POINTER

Unusual Possessives Some expressions referring to time, measurement, and celestial bodies form possessives, even though time, measurement, and celestial bodies are inanimate objects. These phrases merit special attention when proofreading copy.

a day's time
two weeks' vacation
one week's vacation
an hour's work
several dollars' worth
a dollar's worth
a month's notice
this year's profit
the sun's rays

EXERCISE 11–A

Directions: Make all necessary corrections by using standard proofreaders' marks. This exercise covers the use of the apostrophe only.

1. I borrowed Sues and James' computer to do Mr. Reisler's paper.
2. After four hours' of work, I took a short break to watch my sister's favorite soap opera in their room on their TV.
3. Unfortunately, the soaps characters' were also wrestling with a writing project.
4. It seemed that a manuscript had been carelessly left in Bitsy Deltoid's handbag, which was on the front seat of her father's-in-law car, and it had been stolen.
5. After much searching, the Deltoids' detective, posing as a secretarial' agencys employee, found the manuscript in the office of a famous movie companys semiretired director'.
6. The manuscript was in an open box that had MTS's logo on it.
7. The manuscripts cover had a new title page, but the manuscript obviously belonged to the Deltoid's.
8. The plot line was the same, word for word, and so was the typing.
9. The original had been typed on an old manual typewriter that produced erratic characters: all the *e*'s and *L*'s were slightly askew.
10. At this point in the soap opera's plot, I became so confused that I lost interest.

11. I decided to have a small snack to clear out my brains' cobwebs.
12. When I felt my brain cell's reactivate, I regained my interest in tomorrows assignment.
13. "It wont be long now," I muttered. "The sooner I finish Mr. Reislers paper, the sooner I will be a graduate of the Class of 99.
14. After two hours work, Id finished my paper. "I cant believe it," I shouted.
15. When I turned in my masterpiece the next day, I noticed that Bob and Mary's individual papers were on a similar subject.

EXERCISE 11–B *Directions:* Make all necessary corrections by using standard proofreaders' marks. This exercise covers the use of the apostrophe only.

Ravelle

ELEMENTARY SCHOOL
1010 River Drive
Washington Court House, OH 43160

August 24, 1999

Dear "New" Parents:

Welcome to Ravelle Elementary School! We look forward to meeting with you and discussing your child or childrens' needs. We have a first-rate team of teachers, staff, and counselor's to help children enjoy their growth in learning.

To introduce you to our faculty and staff, we will be having our first PTA get-together at Ravelle Elementary next Thursday at 7 p.m. If you wish to see the entire facility, and we hope you do, we will have small group tours' that will start a half hour earlier from the main entrance, as well as tours immediately following the PTA meeting. We are very proud of our parent's involvement in our school system. This years president is Ramona Wideall, and we are pleased to have her enthusiasm channeled into our schools' activities and discussions.

You might also be interested in attending the citywide consolidated PTAs' organizational meeting on October 5 at 7 p.m. in the high school auditorium. Ravelle Elementary has always enjoyed an active profile in the citywide organization.

At Ravelle Elementary we feel that a childs' education includes mental development as well as physical, psychological, and social development. For that reason we offer a comprehensive program: from the beginning of the ABC's and the basic concepts' in math to discussing music and art, to practicing team sports,' to participating in our communitys recycling programs and other service projects, and finally to enjoying a variety of field trips and outings.

"New" Parents
Page 2
August 24, 1999

We believe that every child has the potential to be a success. Moreover, we also believe that education starts with the whole family and at home. Without a parents' interest and support, a child has a difficult battle to reach success. Since its important to us that your child get off to a positive start, we want to share with you some tips on how to start the education process at home. Therefore, we will be sending you information from the U.S. Department of Educations Office of Educational Research and Improvement. We feel these suggestions will allow you to take a proactive stance in your childs education.

We look forward to meeting you next Thursday. Please call us at the main office (555-1234) if you have any questions and concerns. We want to be the best at our jobs—educating minds toward the future. We need your support in developing our countrys most valuable resource.

Sincerely,

Lorena Caldwell, Ph.D.
Principal

cf

EXERCISE 11-C *Directions:* Make all necessary corrections by using standard proofreaders' marks. This exercise covers the use of the apostrophe only.

Ravelle

ELEMENTARY SCHOOL

1010 River Drive
Washington Court House, OH 43160

September 7, 1999

Dear Parent:

As we promised, we are starting a newsletter to help parent's efforts in becoming more proactive in their childrens' education. We have taken these suggestions from a pamphlet from the U.S. Department of Educations' Office of Educational Research and Improvement. We hope you find these comments helpful as you watch your childs progress up the ladder' of success.

The Office of Educational Research and Improvement offers four steps children can take to become better students. They are for children of all grades. The articles approach will sound simple because it is. However, these four steps can make a world of difference in your youngsters' lives.

You can teach your children strategies for these four steps:

Paying attention	Learning and remembering
Keeping interested in schoolwork	Studying

You can increase your child's ability to pay attention by using three techniques: using self-talk and positive images, asking questions, and setting specific study goals. Children can use self-talk to help control attention spans. You can encourage this at home by helping them control their attention spans while playing a game or working at a hobby. Make sure that "I can't do it" and "It's hopeless" are replaced with positive self-talk. Discourage negative images. Help them to imagine themselves responding correctly in class. Talk about their successes. The second technique, asking questions, helps to focus their attention while studying. Help them create questions to ask about each assignments' requirements. Lastly, encourage your childs ability to set goals. Setting small goals, such as finishing a chapter or a math problem, will be a good start.

Keeping interested in school work is the second step in becoming a better student. True, teachers' teach and parents' parent, but only the student can do a students' learning. Children must take responsibility for their own learning. They must believe that three hour's worth

Parent
Page 2
September 7, 1999

of studying may make the difference between success and failure. The next time they bring home test results, written comments, or report cards, calmly discuss the reasons why they did well or poorly. Help them relate their efforts to the results.

Learning and remembering is the third step. Understanding a subject doesnt just happen; it wont appear magically. It takes work. It requires taking the subject's material, making it interesting, and relating new information to old and familiar information. There are some strategies for doing this. Encourage your children to try to draw conclusions from the material they are studying. Show children how to build bridges by looking for similarities between the new and the familiar. By constantly looking for each chapters main idea, children concentrate on learning the material's central theme. Help children learn how to ask appropriate questions as they read. When there are many items of information to learn, students should group them in categories.

Studying is the essential fourth step. Help your children by creating schedules' for study time and by providing a quiet place to study that has a good light. Encourage children to begin an assignment by previewing the material to be studied, thereby creating a mental map. When reading the chapter, they should try to fit details into this mental map by using the learning and studying techniques. Children should take notes to help them remember the material and study for tests. Help your children to get into the habit of creating their own self-tests. Encourage them to prepare for tests by spacing studying over days or weeks rather than going into the test after a nights cramming.

The Office of Educational Research and Improvements' steps to success can help all children from elementary school through high school. We know that you will want to provide the building blocks for your child's success and that a small investment in time now may help bring on lifes rewards.

Sincerely,

Lorena Caldwell, Ph.D.
Principal

cf

EXERCISE 11-D *Directions:* Make all necessary corrections by using standard proofreaders' marks. This exercise is a review of material previously covered in this text.

Ravelle

ELEMENTARY SCHOOL
1010 River Drive
Washington Court House, OH 43160

September 26, 1999

Dear Parent:

This is this Falls second installment of our newsletter. We hope you found the first one useful. This letter covers the importance of a students ability to write well. Again, the Office of Educational Research and improvement offers suggestions for the parents part in their childrens education.

For a variety of reasons many schools are unable to give children sufficient instruction in writing. As a result, todays research shows that more and more children have difficulty with the process and liking writing less and less. When you help you're children with writing, you help your children to do well in school, enjoy self-expression and become more self-reliant.

Writing is more than putting words on paper; its a final stage in the complex process of communicating that begins with thinking. Writing well requires clear thinking, therefore, children may need to have his memories refreshed through conversation. Writing well takes time so the process may take longer than a school period allows. Writting well also requires reading good books to help stimulate childrens' creativity. Writing well requires a meaningful task, not "busy work." Writing well requires a child to be interested in what they are writing. Additionally, writing well requires practice and revision, therefore children need to be encouraged to do and redo.

In helping your children to learn to write well remember that you're goal is to make writing easier and more enjoyable. There are a few pointers that can help you achieve this goal. First provide a place to write that has good lighting and a flat hard surface. Next, provide plenty of paper, pens and pencils. Furthermore, be patient, allow thinking time. Focus your genuine attention on what your children have written. Never write or even rewrite the paper for

Parent
Page 2
September 26, 1999

him or her. Meeting a deadline and assume responsibility for ones own work are important goals for your children to achieve. And be sure to take a positive approach by saying something good about the writing.

The office of Educational Research and Improvement also make a number of other suggestions for you the parent. Encourage your children to participate in real correspondence by writing a letter rather than jotting one line on a card. Suggest taking notes on an outing or field trip. Encourage him to keep a journal of events and feelings. Have your children make lists. Encourage them to copy favorite poems or quotations. Talk with your child as much as possible about their impressions, and encourage them to describe people and events to you. Have them help you with letters so that they can see that writing is an important and useful adult activity.

We at Ravelle elementary know you will want to take the time to work with your children to encourage their writing skills. If we may be of any assistance in this matter, please call Frank DiCara who is our Language Arts Coordinator during the regular school hours at our main number (555-1234).

Please let this letter serve as a final reminder for the citywide PTA's organizational meeting on October 6 at 7 p.m. in the high school auditorium. This is the meeting where you will be able to exchange ideas with parents from other PTA's.

Finally, I want to thank each of you for making the return to school this fall such a smooth one. The children are enthused and ready to learn. We know that you as parents are responsible for this and it certainly makes our jobs as educators much easier.

Sincerely,

Lorena Caldwell, Ph.D.
Principal

cf

EXERCISE 11–E *Directions:* Make all necessary corrections by using standard proofreaders' marks. This exercise is a review of material previously covered in this text.

Ravelle

ELEMENTARY SCHOOL

1010 River Drive
Washington Court House, OH 43160

October 18, 1999

Dear Parent:

We appreciate the positive responses we have receive concerning the Office of Educational Research and Improvements' materials. Although it has been only a short time the teachers have noticed increased conversation about learning and writing among the children. Since this is our last Fall news letter we wanted to cover one more topic—testing.

We know you are aware of how important testing is. It may measure a basic skill, affect a grade or establish a child's placement in school. Moreover, the ability to do well on tests can help throughout life—from academic learning to obtaining a job.

Its good to be concerned about taking a test, its not good to get text anxiety. Unfortunately, some students suffer from test anxiety which means experiencing excessive worry until it becomes debilitating. Students who suffer from test anxiety, tend to worry about success in school and to worry especially about doing well on tests. They worry about the future, and are extremely self-critical. Instead of feeling challenged by the prospect of success they become afraid of failure. This makes them anxious about tests and there own abilities. Ultimately they become so worked up that they feel incompetent about the subject matter or the test.

Telling children to relax and not to worry won't help, but there are some constructive actions you can encourage them to take. First, space studying over days or weeks. Real learning takes time and review in order to understand the information and relate it to what you already no. Avoid "cramming" the night before, instead get a good nights sleep. Remember that

Parent
Page 2
October 18, 1999

rest, exercise and good nutrition are key ingredients to effective learning.

Hear is some helpful tips to tell your child to follow while they are taking the test. Read the directions carefully, ask the teacher to explain if you dont understand them. Glance quickly at the whole test. See what kinds of questions their are. When taking an essay exam, read all the questions first, and make notes in the margins. In any test pace yourself. If you dont know the answer to a question skip it, and go on. Dont waist time worrying about it. Do the best you can, then let it go emotionally.

The office of educational research and improvement offers these DOs and DON'Ts to parents. Do provide a quiet place for your child to study. Do provide books and magazines at home to help increase your childrens' interests and vocabulary. Do make sure your children are well rested, and have a well-balanced diet. Do make sure your child attends school regularly. Do help your children to have positive self-images and positive outlooks toward learning. Do meet you're childrens' teachers as often as possible and discuss your children's progress, attitude, and activities. Do ask the teacher what you can do to help. Do encourage and praise your children so they will feel good about theirselves and not be afraid to make an educational "stretch". Don't be too anxious about your children's test scores. Don't judge your children on the basis of a single test score.

Finally, its important to review the test results. Most material is sequential in its learning pattern, therefore it is vital to understand each building block. Discuss the wrong answers with your children and find out why they answered as they did. Discuss any comments made by the teacher and discuss how they prepared for the test. Help them to see all the connections in the test-taking process.

Well, thats it for this newsletter. We hope you find this information helpful. See you at Ravelles family Halloween party.

Sincerely,

Lorena Caldwell, Ph.D.
Principal

cf

CHAPTER 12

Review

Every once in a while, it's a good idea to take a breather from presentations on new material. It gives your mind a chance to regroup—to go back over the material already learned. Because this review chapter contains errors from all chapters already covered in the text, it won't allow your mind to take a rest. It will, however, allow you to reinforce and verify your knowledge of the major topics already covered:

Apostrophes	Reading for meaning
Capitalization	Run-on sentences
Commas	Semicolons
Comma splices	Sentence fragments
Divisions	Spelling
Parallelism	Subject-verb agreement
Pronouns	Troublesome words

The following exercises are presented as simulated documents you would proofread and correct for Marketing Management, Inc. Make all necessary corrections using standard proofreaders' marks.

PROOFREADING POINTER

When in doubt, check it out!

EXERCISE 12-A *Directions:* Correct this letter using standard proofreaders' marks.

February 2, 1999

Sue Fieldstone
District 5 Sales Manager

SALES CONFERENCE

Your trip to the Maricopa District Sales Meeting has been approved by the Board of Directors. The meeting should provide an excellent opportunity for you to promote our organization as wll as promote our professional development seminars, furthermore, you should be able to make several contacts with perspective trainers in the field.

The board feels that Kerry Redington is an excellant choice to present the keynote address at the conference; Kerrys address will be "Developing a Personality that sells."

One of the directors suggested that you might want to consider setting up an hospitality table. Why don't you talk with the coordinator to see if this idea is feasable. If you think we should persue this idea, we'll need a list of the the promotional items, the food, and the other expenses involved in this project.

Jason Wickline
Sales Manager

yr

EXERCISE 12-B *Directions:* Correct this letter using standard proofreaders' marks.

February 4, 1999

Ms. Almeda Mertz
National Graphics
458 Edison Road
Riomedina, TX 78066

Dear Ms. Mertz:

Marketing Management, Inc., is currently considering sponsoring a hospitality table at the Maricopa District Sales Meeting in June. If we carry through on this project we will need several items for use as promotional pieces. Could you give us prices on the following:

1. *Pencils.* We would like No. 2 pencils with the name of our company and our slogan, "Sales can be managed." We'll need about 5000 of these pencils.

2. *Coasters.* About three years ago, we used leather coasters with our logo and name imprinted. We would like to use these again this year for the conference. We will need 1000 of these coasters.

3. Napkins. We estimate we'll need about 5000 napkins with our name and logo inprinted. We are planning to use only the name of our organization so the napkins can be used for other functions.

If you have any other ideas for promotional items, for a conference of salesmen who specialize in small appliances, send samples and prices. We should be making a decision by April 31 and will discuss contract terms at that time if we decide to continue with the project.

Sincerely,

Ms. Sue Fieldstone
District 5 Sales Manager

fh

EXERCISE 12–C *Directions:* Correct this letter using standard proofreaders' marks.

February 3, 1999

Mrs. Joanne Homala
One Masterville Circle
Maricopa, AZ 85239

Dear Mrs. Homola

We are pleased to confirm that Kerry Redinton will be able to speek to the Marcopa District Sales Meeting on June 9, 1999. Our company is always pleased to be able to participate in your activities.

I have included the information you requested regarding our vender display at the conference. If you have any problems with the specifications, let me know, I will see if I can modify our arrangments.

Our company is also considering setting up a hospitality table at the conference. We would have coffee and beverages available for your members during the early morning hours, and the scheduled break times. The refreshments would be available at know cost to your members.

Could you let me know as soon as possible weather your group would like us to cover the hospitality duties. We have included a press release on Kelly for your use.

Sincerely,

Ms. Sue Fieldstone
District 5 Sales Manager

mw

Enclosure

EXERCISE 12-D *Directions:* Correct this news release using standard proofreaders' marks.

May 15, 1999 **NEWS RELEASE**

FOR IMEDIATE RELEASE

KERRY REDINGTON TO SPEAK
AT Maricopa DISTRICT SALES MEETING

Kelly Redington, author of a series of internationally acclaimed books on the art of selling. will speak at the Maricopa District Sales Meeting. Redington, noted crusader for drug- and alcohol-free living, combines his sales techniques with humor to emphasize the joy of life.

The meeting, held on June 9, is open to the Public. As is his custom, Redington charges no fee for the lecture if the local high school marketing and business classes are invited to attend.

BIOGRAPHY

Kerry Goldwyn Redington, popular authority on the art of selling, is known for his ability to turn any chance meeting into a golden opportunity—for sales. His gift for sales is certainly noteworthy, he's a billionaire. What is even more remarkable, is his need to use that gift to sell the younger generation on living a drug- and alcohol-free life.

Born in 1949 Redington grew up in a rural community in the Appalachian hills of West Virginia. His family was always helping a neighbor, even when there was little money for anything but the necessities. The Redingtons were never wealthy but the love of the strong family circle always reached out to include others. In edition to raising their five biological children, Redington's parents raised four orphans.

A college scholarship and a dozen part-time jobs helped put Redington through

NEWS RELEASE
Kerry Redington
Page 2
May 15, 1999

college in five years. After graduating with honours from Eagleton College, Redington was hired to sell land for a real estate firm specializing in farm sales. Although never successful at selling farms, he found he had a talent for selling residential property.

Redigntonn eventually found his niche as a sales agent for Kensington Medical Supplies. He was so successful that he was able to help put the other nine children thru school. Even that wasn't enough; he still felt he needed to do more. When a neice was killed in a accident caused by a drunk driver; he found what was missing in his life—a cause to fight for. He says he's always selling—either medical supplies or clean living.

In 1982, Redington moved his family to a small town in southeastern Ohio near Ohio University. A profesor friend convinced him to try his hand a writing. His book was an instant success, his sales techniques have been adapted by major corporations throughout the world. Recently the successful author joined the staff of Marketing Management, Inc. as a sales trainer.

Today Redington lives in The Plains, OH with his wife Martha; his two children, Kyle and Nathan; and his English Setter, Ikabod. When asked what he fells is the most satisfying part of his life, he always answers, "My family."

EXERCISE 12–E *Directions:* Correct this letter using standard proofreaders' marks.

June 1. 1999

Mr. Kerry Redington
23400 Westminster Hill Road
The Plains, OH 45780

Dear Mr. Reddington:

We are pleased you have agreed to speak at the Maricopa Sales District Meeting as your first assignment with Marketing Management, Inc. This conference is the weekend before you actually begin employment with our firm, but this is probably the most important sales conference in the northwest. We know you are going to enjoy you're new career. Your still selling, but now your selling your sales procedures to other salesmen.

You should plan to arrive at the Columbus, OH, airport an hour before your 10:45 a.m. departure on June 8. Wally Andres will meet your plane in Phoenix and serve as your escort for the conference. Wally is the District 10 sales manager for our company.

I will be joining you and Wally for dinner that evening. I am looking forward to meeting you, and to hearing about your presentation. I'll also be able to brief you on the back ground of the Maracopa District.

If you have any special requirements concerning equipment or setup, please be sure to give me a call. My business card is enclosed.

Sincerely,

Jason Wickline
Sales Manager

kl

Enclosure

EXERCISE 12-F *Directions:* Correct this itinerary using standard proofreaders' marks.

ITINERARY FOR

Kerry Redington

June 8, 1999

9:45 a.m.	Arrive at Columbus international airport at CarPARK. You will leave your car and be taken to the Airport.
10:45 a.m.	Departure from Columbus International Airport. The flight is a non-stop flight to Phoenix, Arizona abored Air Traveler Flight 245. The flight, which departs from Gate 28 in Concourse B, includes dinner.
2:04 p.m.	Arrive Phoenix, Arizona, where you will be met by Wally Andres, district 10 sales manager.
4:00 p.m.	Arrive at Maricopa Inn.
6:30 p.m.	Dine with Wally Andres and Jason Wickline in the inn's Dining Room. This should be an early evening since you indicated you like time to rest the evening before a speach.

<u>November 9</u>

9:15 a.m.	Meet with Sue Fieldstone in the Lobby of the inn. She will escort you to the Marketing Management, Inc., Hospitality table for the Maricopa District Sales Meeting. Leave your luggage packed in your room. We will have it transfered to the company van.
10:30 a.m.	Give keynote presentation. Following the keynote address, you will have lunch with the conference delegates. You will also need to be available at the hospitality table for questions, book signing, and general goodwill building.
5:00 p.m.	Diner with Almeda Merts, promotional consultant for the conference; Sue Fieldstone; and Wally Andres. Following dinner Wally will escort you to the airport for the 8 p.m. USA Flight 3487 to Columbus.
10:30	Arrive at Columbus international airport. You will be met at the East Entrance by a representative of Car PARK, the representative will give you the keys to you car.

EXERCISE 12-G *Directions:* Correct this report using standard proofreaders' marks.

HOSPITALITY REPORT

Maricopa Sales District Meeting

Approximately 2000 delegates representing 78 businesses attended the Maricopa District Sales Meeting in Phoenix, AR, on June 9 and 10.

The topic of this conference was "Selling Tough." Marketing Management, Inc., director of Sales Training, Kerry Redington, author of *Selling with Conviction* was the featured speaker. Various appliance vendors were present to demonstrate the technology of the future.

Kerry Redingtons keynote was a resounding success with the conference. He is certainly a dynamic speaker and was extremely popular with the conference delegates. Already a proven success on the college lecture circuit, he will undoubtedly be even more successful with salesmen trying to move merchandise in a tight-money market.

Our Role in the Conference

Marketing Management, Inc. participated in this worthwhile conference in two ways. As has been our custom for the past several years, we hosted a display in the vendor area on merchandise and sales-training books appropriate for the conference. The sales from books at the conference amounted to $1982, compared with $858 last year—an increase of $1116.

This year we also sponsored a hospitality table during the early morning and after-noon brakes. In the morning our table featured fresh fruit in addition to the usual fair of doughnuts, coffee, and juice. During the midafternoon break, we served fresh fruit and vegetables, coffee, and an assortment of decaffienated beverages. Our logo was imprinted on the blue napkins used at both sessions. Furthermore, we supplied pencils and a Company coaster at each place on the first day of the conference.

This was the first time we had offered to run a hospitality table, and we were initially concerned about the cost-benfit ratio of the service. We found we really had nothing to be concerned about. The hospitality table was well received by the sales personnel at the conference. Even more valuable though was the opportunity to meat with the salesmen in a setting not directly associated with sales. We also received several enquiries concerning upcoming sales-training conferences.

Sponsoring the hospitality service was definitely worth the effort involved. At a total cost of $650 the goodwill we generated was worth far more then the expense we incurred. I would certainly recommend that Marketing Managers, Inc., consider sponsoring the hospitality service at the conference next year.

CHAPTER

13

Other Punctuation

RULES

Semicolons

13.1 Spacing After a Semicolon

13.2 Semicolon Between Two Independent Clauses

13.3 Semicolon Between Two Independent Clauses With Internal Punctuation

13.4 Semicolons in a Series Containing Internal Punctuation

Colons

13.5 Spacing After a Colon

13.6 Colon Preceding a List Following an Anticipatory Expression

13.7 Colon With Items Listed on Separate Lines

13.8 Word, Phrase, or Clause Defining a Preceding Independent Clause

13.9 Colon With Proportions

13.10 Colon With Quotations

Dashes

13.11 Spacing Before and After a Dash

13.12 Dashes Separating Nonrestrictive Elements Containing Internal Commas

13.13 Dashes to Indicate an Abrupt Break in Thought

13.14 Dashes Before a Source

13.15 Dashes After a Summarizing List

13.16 Dashes for Emphasis

Parentheses

13.17 Spacing Before and After a Parenthesis

13.18 Parentheses With Explanatory Nonessential Material

13.19 Parentheses With References and Directions

13.20 Parentheses With Enumerated Lists in a Sentence

RULES (CONTINUED)

In Chapters 6, 8, and 9, you worked almost exclusively with the proper use of commas. You may recall that Chapter 9 referred to punctuation marks as the street and road signs for the written word. With this analogy in mind, we might say you have worked on the part of the driver's test that asks you to recognize signs for stopping and yielding. Now comes the part where you identify all those other signs—everything from railroad crossings to one-way streets and from no U-turns to school crossings. In other words, this chapter reviews the use of all those other not-quite-so-basic but equally important pieces of punctuation: semicolons, colons, dashes, parentheses, ellipses, quotation marks, and underlining or italics.

As you read through this chapter, remember to study the examples that accompany each rule and to analyze the patterns of use for each punctuation mark. When you apply these rules during your own proofreading, you will be looking for patterns or road signs to aid the reader's understanding.

SEMICOLONS

Spacing After a Semicolon

13.1 Space once after a semicolon.

➤ Martha was promoted to assistant manager; her twin sister became the personnel officer.

Semicolon Between Two Independent Clauses

13.2 Use a semicolon to join two closely related independent clauses. Generally, the semicolon is used in place of a coordinate conjunction.

➤ Leslie Juarez received a swimming scholarship to Cal State; his sister Susan had received a track scholarship the year before, also from Cal State.

➤ Mr. Ruggles retired this year; he had spent 35 years with Vanguard Tires.

Semicolon Between Two Independent Clauses With Internal Punctuation

13.3 For clarity, use a semicolon (instead of a comma) before a coordinate conjunction joining two independent clauses when either clause contains internal punctuation.

➤ According to the latest statistics, Williams Widgets annually manufactures 6 tons of widgets, 1500 pounds of weskets, and 800 pounds of wiskets; and it is ranked fourth in the state for production output.

➤ Roy Deals had been assigned the new territory; but Marty Edwards, top sales representative, demanded and was given the area, even though the company had made it a policy not to reassign territories.

Semicolons in a Series Containing Internal Punctuation

13.4 Use a semicolon instead of a comma to separate items in a series when any item in the series contains an internal comma.

➤ To promote the new tax package, the President plans to travel to Wilton, North Carolina; Madison, Wisconsin; and Boise, Idaho.

➤ The officers appointed to the Unified Committee are Alan Answan, director of training of Answan Industries; Ethel Phoebe, coordinator of adult learning at Community Tech; and Ayako Sunahara, public service administrator of Fordham Steel Corporation.

PROOFREADING POINTER

The semicolon as a conjunction: The semicolon is used to join closely related independent clauses. Frequently, although it is not necessary, an adverbial conjunction is used to show that connection. Be sure not to confuse adverbial conjunctions with coordinate conjunctions. Remember the clue: FAN BOYS.

➤ Nancy Hultz was awarded the promotion; she also received an extra week of vacation. (no conjunction)

➤ Nancy Hultz was awarded the promotion; moreover, she received an extra week of vacation. (adverbial conjunction)

➤ Nancy Hultz was awarded the promotion, and she also received an extra week of vacation. (A semicolon would be incorrect if it were used in addition to this coordinate conjunction when neither independent clause contains internal punctuation.)

EXERCISE 13-A

Directions: Make all necessary corrections by using standard proofreaders' marks. If no corrections are needed, mark the sentence with a C. This exercise covers Rules 13.1 through 13.4.

1. You invite Ms. Chanteuse; I'll invite Mr. Write.
2. Although Rita Margoal emphasized the importance of a powerful cover letter, correct grammar, and a professional-looking résumé; I thought a dynamic interview was the key to getting a job, perhaps it's a combination of written and verbal skills.
3. The candidates for the job were Joyce Cramblett, an M.A. from Purdue, Ralph Drybinski, an M.B.A. from Wharton, and Liselle Paulee, a Ph.D. from Rutgers.
4. Frankly, I think Joyce Cramblett is the best candidate, but it's not my decision.
5. I can't read this application, however, I bet Rose Wong can do it.
6. Howard lost the report but found it later;   unfortunately, it was too late for the meeting.
7. I can't believe that ordering four egg salad sandwiches, two salads, and a hero sandwich is the proper procedure for entertaining an important business client, but you must know what you're doing.
8. Her one-week lecture takes her through Lexington, Kentucky, Cincinnati, Ohio, Indianapolis, Indiana, and Chicago, Illinois.
9. Winston Pinnley, the CEO of National Widgets, restructured his organization after he considered the new equipment, the work force, and the training requirements, however, he forgot to estimate the failing economy's effect on the need for the company's manufactured products.
10. Secondhand smoke is finally being banned in the workplace; because insurance companies have become increasingly demanding in their cost coverage.

PROOFREADING POINTER

Spacing after a semicolon and a colon: An easy way to remember the proper spacing after these two punctuation marks is to remember how many *periods* there are in each mark.

Put one space after a semicolon because it contains only one period.

➤ Sarah bought a stapler; Ralph bought the staples.

Put two spaces after a colon because it has two periods.

➤ Sarah bought the following: staples, pens, folders, and scissors.

COLONS

Spacing After a Colon

13.5 Use two spaces after a colon. With expressions of times, proportions, and Biblical and technical citations, no spaces are required after a colon.

➤ The club purchased these items: 20 roles of bunting, 2 staple guns, 4 boxes of staples, 2 rolls of white paper, and 4 cans of spray paint.

➤ I never saw such a terrible disaster: demolished homes, flooded basements, mangled street signs, uprooted trees, and strewn rubbish.

7:55 P.M.	51:1 (Biblical citation—Chapter 51, verse 1)
3:2 ratio	10:23 (technical citation—Volume 10, page 23)

Colon Preceding a List Following an Anticipatory Expression

13.6 Use a colon between an independent clause and a list when the clause is short or an anticipatory expression (*as follows, follows, thus, these, the following*) appears near the end of the clause.

➤ These are the antiques to be sold: one butter churn, two butter stamps, and one wooden coffee grinder.

➤ The grocery list includes the following items: green beans, lettuce, ground beef, chicken, cereal, sugar, and cheese.

➤ Santa delivered the following gifts: electric trains, tricycles, video games, and talking teddy bears.

PROOFREADING POINTER

A colon that introduces a list must be preceded by a complete sentence. Don't be fooled into thinking that a subject and a verb always form a complete sentence. Study the following examples and think about the sentence pattern that must occur before a colon may be used to introduce a list.

Incorrect: The antiques to be sold are: one butter churn, two butter stamps, and one wooden coffee grinder.
Correct: The antiques to be sold are one butter churn, two butter stamps, and one wooden coffee grinder.
Correct: The antiques to be sold are as follows: one butter churn, two butter stamps, and one wooden coffee grinder.

Incorrect: The grocery list includes: green beans, lettuce, ground beef, chicken, cereal, sugar, and cheese.
Correct: The grocery list includes green beans, lettuce, ground beef, chicken, cereal, sugar, and cheese.
Correct: The grocery list includes these items: green beans, lettuce, ground beef, chicken, cereal, sugar, and cheese.

Incorrect: Santa delivered: electric trains, tricycles, video games, and talking teddy bears.
Correct: Santa delivered electric trains, tricycles, video games, and talking teddy bears.
Correct: Santa delivered these presents: electric trains, tricycles, video games, and talking teddy bears.

PROOFREADING POINTER

***Such as* is like a punctuation mark.** The phrase *such as* frequently introduces a list. Even if you do hear yourself take a deep breath before you start that list, do not use a colon or a comma immediately after *such as*. Take a look at these examples:

Incorrect: Sharon has many varied interests such as, computers, cooking, tennis, origami, and taxidermy.

Incorrect: Sharon has many varied interests such as: computers, cooking, tennis, origami, and taxidermy.

Incorrect: Sharon has many varied interests: such as computers, cooking, tennis, origami, and taxidermy.

Correct: Sharon has many varied interests, such as computers, cooking, tennis, origami, and taxidermy.

Colon With Items Listed on Separate Lines

13.7 Use a colon after an incomplete sentence when the items needed to complete the sentence are listed on separate lines. Double space before and after the list.

➤ The meetings will be:

March 5
April 12
May 2

➤ The committee consists of:

John Fayette
Susana García
Terry Lee

Word, Phrase, or Clause Defining a Preceding Independent Clause

13.8 Use a colon before a word, phrase, or clause that defines or illustrates the preceding independent clause.

➤ We had the worst vacation imaginable: rain, heat, lost luggage, and food poisoning.

➤ The Tremble Company hired a person with "from-the-ground-up" experience: Winona Wininsky has worked in five of the seven departments and has been an employee for over 14 years.

Colon With Proportions

13.9 Use a colon in place of the word *to* in a proportion. The colon is typed without spaces on either side.

➤ Sampson's Delight is favored at 5:1 for Saturday's race.

➤ The ratio of widgets to wiggets is 3:2.

Colon With Quotations

13.10 Use a colon before a long quotation following an independent clause. Use a colon if the quotation contains more than one sentence.

➤ In 1884 Susan B. Anthony had this to say: "We women have been standing before the American republic for thirty years, asking the men to take yet one step further and extend the practical application of the theory of equality of rights to all the people—to the other half of the people—the women."

➤ In his fiery oration entitled "Sun-Beams May Be Extracted from Cucumbers, But the Process Is Tedious" on July 4, 1799, David Daggett compels his audience to appreciate the sacrifices the American settlers have made for this country:

> They fought—they bled—they died.—At this expense of ease, happiness and life, they made establishments for posterity—they cemented them with their blood—they delivered them to us as a sacred deposit, and if we suffer them to be destroyed by the tinselled refinements of this age, we shall deserve the reproaches, with which impartial justice will cover such a pusillanimous race.

(Notice how punctuation rules have changed in two centuries.)

EXERCISE 13-B

Directions: Use standard proofreaders' marks to make all necessary corrections. If no corrections are needed, mark the sentence with a *C*. This exercise covers Rules 13.5 through 13.10.

1. That would be a difficult bet to win: 100:1 against.
2. Rena purchased: three computers, two printers, and one shredder for the office.
3. Mr. Scrooge is the meanest man I know, he would take a lollipop away from a small child.
4. Think how many people have uttered these words, "To be or not to be. That is the question."
5. Standing before the congregation, the child recited John 3: 16 from the heart.
6. Loretta Ping wanted these characteristics: integrity, competency, and punctuality.
7. I heard Ms. Lomez say these exact words: "I won't tolerate that behavior. Do you hear me? Everyone will have to stay after class."
8. Janice read four stories to the child: the little girl enjoyed the one with the talking animals the most.

9. For his own dinner, Harry Kulwalski ordered: two double cheeseburgers, three fries, one garden salad, and two diet soft drinks.

10. Ralph never arrived at a dinner party before 8: 30 p.m.

11. For graduation Lynn asked for:

    A car.

    A computer.

    A new boyfriend.

EXERCISE 13-C *Directions:* Make all necessary corrections by using standard proofreaders' marks. This exercise covers Rules 13.1 through 13.10.

MEMORANDUM

TO: Leslie Barrons, Senior Clerk
Marsha Kinnley, Secretarial Pool Officer
Martin Williams, Office Manager

FROM: Juanita Park, Senior Accountant

DATE: May 27, 1999

SUBJECT: Ordering Supplies

The next half year is upon us, therefore, it's time for reviewing the budget. Consequently, we all need to take stock of our current office supplies, fill out those requisition forms, and turn them in, and we have only two weeks in which to do these things. After checking with Ian Thatcher in the General Supply Department, we know we have more than enough of the following items. staples, pencils, notebook dividers, legal-size tablets, proofreading pens, and blue, green, and yellow memo and telephone pads.

We will be using a different form this year: the PO 2382, which is color-coded and has triplicate forms. Routing will be the same, but there is one difference, send *all three* copies to your immediate supervisor. After signing the copies, your supervisor will log the order onto the computer system, send the blue and green copies to the Purchasing Department, and keep the yellow copy as a departmental record, and then the Purchasing Department will be able to file the blue form and send back the green one with your order. Please keep the green form as your individual record in case there is a question with the half-year tallies.

As you look at your supplies and think of the equipment purchases you would like to make, remember these clichés; "A penny saved is a penny earned." "Waste not, want not." "The ole' gray mare [meaning the economy] ain't what she used to be." I am sure we can accommodate the necessities if we can keep down the extras.

Remember to have your requisitions in by June 10, to use the new PO 2382 form, and to consider sharing supplies, forms, and equipment whenever it is feasible.

ds

DASHES

Spacing Before and After a Dash

13.11 Do not use a space on either side of a dash (two hyphens) when the dash occurs within a sentence. If the dash is used to break off a sentence (an abrupt break in thought), space twice after the dash.

➤ This magic potion—snake oil—will cure all ailments.

➤ I wonder if— Oh, I don't really need to know that!

Dashes Separating Nonrestrictive Elements Containing Internal Commas

13.12 Use dashes instead of commas to set off nonrestrictive clauses and phrases that contain internal commas.

➤ Three individuals—Alice Toms, Ralph Kikko, and Dolores Benard—won top honors.

➤ I finally have completed—I know that's hard to believe, isn't it?—my manuscript.

Dashes to Indicate an Abrupt Break in Thought

13.13 Use a dash to indicate an abrupt break in thought.

➤ Alex Stone—that horrid, beady-eyed little man—committed the murder.

➤ If only Sam could have saved the dog before he— Well, it's over now.

Dashes Before a Source

13.14 Use a dash before a source that immediately follows a quotation.

➤ "I only regret that I have but one life to lose for my country."—Nathan Hale

Dashes After a Summarizing List

13.15 Use a dash after a summarizing list of items preceding *these, they*, or *all* used as the subject.

➤ Fried chicken, potato salad, and watermelon—these are true picnic foods!

➤ Mason Willis, Ralph Spinner, and Mary Worstall—all have been asked to speak at the banquet.

Dashes for Emphasis

13.16 Use a dash—sparingly—for emphasis in place of a colon, semicolon, comma, or parentheses.

➤ He said the magic word—*abracadabra.*

➤ I felt Siobhan Kalley was the most qualified—and I do mean qualified!

➤ Talk to Wells—he's at Ajax Inc.—if you want to know the real reason.

PARENTHESES

Spacing Before and After a Parenthesis

13.17 Use one space before an opening parenthesis and one space after a closing parenthesis.

➤ Kelby International (founded in 1889) is facing bankruptcy.

Parentheses With Explanatory Nonessential Material

13.18 Use parentheses to set off explanatory nonessential material within a sentence.

➤ I saw President Knox with Suzanne Juarez (she's the new person in accounts) last night.

➤ Mary does not agree (nor is she ever likely to) with the health plan as it stands now.

➤ James Madison (1751–1836) was the fourth U.S. President.

➤ The invention of the Gatling gun (1862) was made possible only after the invention of the percussion cap.

Parentheses With References and Directions

13.19 Use parentheses to set off references and directions.

➤ The second graph (see Figure 3) will chart the Wayco Industry stocks.

➤ The committee discussed (see the April 12 minutes) the Wilson complaint but did not reach a decision.

Parentheses With Enumerated Lists in a Sentence

13.20 Use parentheses to enclose letters or numbers used in enumerations within a sentence.

➤ Mr. Onocky has requested three forms: (1) the accident report, (2) the insurance coverage information, and (3) the doctor's statement.

➤ Bring the following items to the test: (a) two pencils, (b) typing paper, (c) eraser, and (d) two pieces of identification.

Parentheses With Other Punctuation

13.21 Place punctuation directly related to a parenthetical clause or phrase within the parentheses. Sometimes a parenthetical independent clause that is enclosed in parentheses requires the same final punctuation used at the end of the main clause. In such cases, omit the final punctuation in the clause.

➤ I interviewed all three candidates (Lillian D'Antonio, Arthur Marple, and Joseph Warner) yesterday.

➤ Ms. Smith dictated (have you ever listened to her?) for three hours.

➤ That computer program was impossible (and I do mean totally)!

➤ That is the hardest task I have ever completed (don't you think?).

13.22 Punctuation directly related to the main clause is placed outside of the parentheses. Colons, semicolons, and commas follow the closing parenthesis.

➤ On Thursday Lena Jones talked to Sam Wilder (the tall, skinny man at the party), and she said he was really quite nice.

➤ I purchased these items (they certainly weren't cheap, either): a gold-plated letter opener, a Spanish silver money clip, and a designer umbrella.

EXERCISE 13–D

Directions: Use standard proofreaders' marks to make all necessary corrections. If no corrections are needed, mark the sentence with a *C*. This exercise covers Rules 13.11 through 13.22.

1. The cost of the stocks and last month's selling trend may be seen in this report—see Figure 3a.
2. He used the only weapon he had— his brains.
3. The following items should be brought to class every day: 1) No. 2 pencils, 2) your journal, 3) a dictionary and English handbook, and 4) your completed homework.
4. The following items: No. 2 pencils, your journal, a dictionary, an English handbook, and your completed homework should be brought to class every day.
5. No. 2 pencils, a dictionary, an English handbook, and a thesaurus: these are the tools of a good student.
6. Matthew Hurzler (have you seen him lately) received the scholarship award.
7. Ms. Leslie said that growing old—I wonder what her age is—does not guarantee the accumulation of—Quiet! She just walked into the room.
8. Have you contacted the officers, Les Albert, Georgia Leith, and Ralph Nichols, about the new meeting time?
9. I nearly exploded with laughter when I saw the results of Winston's latest battle, two shiners!
10. Sir Frederick William Herschel (1738–1822) is responsible for the reflecting telescope.
11. Catherine Mitchell made the motion—see the September 20 minutes—after the committee argued for half an hour.
12. There Lynn was when—Did you see what just happened out there?
13. Dana was shopping (that's a new one, isn't it) when the phone call came in.

EXERCISE 13–E *Directions:* Make all necessary corrections by using standard proofreaders' marks. This exercise is a text review.

PANIC DISORDER

Have you ever had the feeling of being overwhelmingly terrified of an unknown impending doom over which you felt you had no control? Have you ever had an intense fear of losing control and do something embarrassing? Have you ever had dreamlike sensations or perceptual distortions? If these symptoms appeared suddenly without any apparent cause, and lasted for several minutes you probably had a panic attack.

When someone has repeated attacks, or feels severe anxiety about having another attack, they are said to have panic disorder. Approximately 3 million people in the United States will have panic disorder at some time in their lives.

The panic attack is often just the beginning of the problem. For example, a panic attack can occur in a mall where there is a large amount of people. After the attack, the individual becomes irrational about the fear, and where and why it happens. To avoid another attack, the individual soon refuses to enter crowded places. This avoidance pattern may become so severe that the person will not go out in public, some people literally have not set foot out of their homes in years. These people are said to have panic disorder with agoraphobia. Obviously, these are nonfunctioning indivduals whom are suffering a great deal. Fortunately there is treatments for panic disorder.

There are two treatments for panic disorder; medication and psychotherapy. Improvement is usually noticed in a fairly short period of time--about six to eight weeks.

Significant relief occurs for 70 to 90 percent of the sufferers.

The illnesses that often accompany panic disorder are these (depression and drug and alcohol abuse). In addition suicide attempts are more frequent in people with this health problem. All of these conditions may be successfully treated.

Theories about the causes of panic disorder or varied. Some scientists believe it is hereditary, others point to the many people who have this ailment but whose family members have never been effected. Some scientists feel the bodys normal response to threat (certain mental and physical symptoms that occur when we are afraid) are set off unnecessarily, but they don't know what causes this. In panic disorder, the first attacks are often triggered by: physical illnesses, a major life stress, or medications that increase activity in the part of the brain involved in fear reactions.

Tragically many people with panic disorder do not seek or receive treatment. To encourage recognition and treatment of panic disorder, the National Institute of Mental Health (NIMH) is sponsoring a major information campaign to acquaint health care professionals and the public with this disorder.

For further information write to either of these addresses: Anxiety Disorders Association of America, 6000 Executive Boulevard., Suite 20, Rockville, MD 2852, or National Institute of Mental Health, Panic Campaign, Room 15C-05, 56 Fishers Lane, Rockville, MD 20857.

ELLIPSES

Ellipses Used to Indicate Omitted Material

13.23 Use an ellipsis (three periods with a space before and after each period) to indicate omitted material within a quote. Place the end punctuation after the ellipsis.

➤ Dean Kinnley said, and I quote, ". . . the meeting dissolved into a screaming match. I was not amused."

➤ Dean Kinnley said, and I quote, "I had never been so embarrassed. . . . I was not amused."

➤ Dean Kinnley said, and I quote, "I had never been so embarrassed for someone else. Moreover, the meeting dissolved into a screaming match. . . ."

QUOTATION MARKS

Spacing Before and After Quotation Marks

13.24 Do not space after an opening quotation mark or before a closing quotation mark. All other spacing connected to quotation marks follows traditional spacing patterns.

➤ Martha shouted, "If you don't stop that, I'm going to tell." I stopped.

Quotation Marks With Direct Quotes

13.25 Use quotation marks to enclose the exact words of a speaker or an exact quotation from a text. If the quotation is longer than three typewritten lines, the quoted material is indented a half inch on each side, and the quotation marks are omitted.

➤ Ms. Davees said, "Don't you think you should redo this agenda?"

➤ "I don't know why," replied Mr. Torelly.

Quotation Marks for Emphasis

13.26 Use quotation marks to emphasize technical terms, business jargon, coined words, and colloquial expressions.

➤ "Booting" a computer system is not as violent as it sounds.

➤ "As the crow flies" is probably not a common expression among young people.

Quotation Marks With Titles of Portions of Published Works

13.27 Use quotation marks around the titles of portions of a complete published work (articles, chapter titles, columns, conference themes, episodes of television programs, essays, short poems, sermons, and songs).

➤ Read the chapter entitled "Pronoun Usage" again.

➤ Jes Gilley wrote "Around and About Town" in today's paper.

➤ Have you seen his article, "Lead Poisoning: A Silent Threat," in the latest edition of that magazine?

PROOFREADING POINTER

Entitled: Use a comma when a work is followed by its title in apposition.

➤ Estelle Smith's book, *Perfect Manners,* is a best seller.

Do not use a comma when the word *entitled* falls between a work and its title.

➤ Estelle Smith's book entitled *Perfect Manners* is a best seller.

Quotation Marks With Other Punctuation Marks

13.28 Periods and commas are placed inside quotation marks.

➤ Officer Hennesey spoke quietly, "Do you like ice cream? It is my favorite food."

➤ "No," sniffled the small child with the tear-streaked face.

13.29 Colons and semicolons are placed outside of quotation marks.

➤ I have seen what Madge calls "collectors' items": 20-year-old eggbeaters, her mother's clothespins, and her children's diaper pins.

➤ In the 1960s many things were "cool"; 20 years later things were "cool" again.

13.30 Place question marks, exclamation points, dashes, and parentheses inside the quotation marks if they are directly related to the quote; place them outside the quotation marks if they are directly related to the main part of the sentence. Do not use double punctuation at the end of a sentence; use only the stronger punctuation mark.

➤ "Going somewhere?" asked Mrs. Kaughman.

➤ Why is that man saying, "Down with Dumont"?

➤ Was Willis trying to scream, "Leave me alone!"

UNDERLINING OR ITALICIZING

Underline or Italicize Titles of Published Works

13.31 Underline (or use italic type if available) titles of complete published works (books, long poems, magazines, movies, musicals, paintings, plays, operas, and television programs). Some sources use all capital letters for titles, but underlining or italicizing is preferable.

➤ I just finished reading the latest edition of *Harper's Bazaar.*

➤ *The Sound of Music* is one of the top-grossing movies of all time.

Underline or Italicize Words Used as Words

13.32 Underline (or use italic type if available) words used as words.

➤ The word *alot* drives English teachers wild: it is not only misspelled but also imprecise.

➤ I will scream if I hear the term *meaningful dialogue* one more time.

HYPHENS

Hyphens in Compound Words (Nouns and Verbs)

13.33 Compound nouns and verbs may be hyphenated or written as one word or two words. For current usage, consult a dictionary preferred in your field. Some examples follow:

Verb	Noun
kick back	kickback
print out	printout
trade in	trade-in
trade off	tradeoff

Hyphens After Prefixes With Proper Nouns

13.34 Use a hyphen between a prefix and the capital letter in a proper noun.

anti-American	post-Civil War
mid-December	pro-Castro

Hyphens in Compound Adjectives

13.35 Hyphenate most compound adjectives when they appear immediately before a noun. Consult a dictionary for current usage.

stop-and-go driving	up-to-date report
three-year-old child	well-known banker

PROOFREADING POINTER

Adverbs ending in *-ly*: When a compound adjective before a noun contains an *-ly* adverb, the compound adjective is not hyphenated.

➤ Toby Wallace is a *highly respected* individual. (Adverb ends in *-ly*.)

➤ Toby Wallace is a *well-read* individual. (Adverb does not end in *-ly*.)

Suspended Hyphens

13.36 When two or more hyphenated adjectives modify the same noun, place a hyphen after each adjective. (This is called a *suspended hyphen*).

two- and four-year colleges 12- or 13-page report

EXERCISE 13-F

Directions: Use standard proofreaders' marks to make all necessary corrections. If no corrections are needed, mark the sentence with a C. This exercise covers Rules 13.23 through 13.36.

1. Molière (1622–1673), France's greatest comic dramatist, is known for plays such as "Tartuffe" (1664) and "Le Misanthrope" (1666).
2. The American Journal of Psychology, founded by Granville Stanley Hall, was the first psychology journal published in the United States.
3. " Don't you think that tearing up his résumé was a cold hearted thing to do "? asked Jason.
4. The anti-American demonstration was a decidedly-emotional event for both participants and onlookers.
5. On and off-line job descriptions were written for every position in the Beckley manufacturing plant.
6. Have you read *The Post-Civil War Days* (Chapter 12) in your American history book?
7. According to The American Heritage Dictionary, the word stake means "a pointed piece . . . driven into the ground". . . .
8. Sandra Stoecker requested a 10 or 12-page report that is to be done as an in-house publication.
9. It is bizarre to hear people say, "I have to boot the computer;" what does that word boot mean?
10. In the 1960s "going to my pad" meant going to one's home.
11. What did Franklin mean when he said, ". . . early to rise makes a man . . . wise?"
12. Was it Robert Frost or Carl Sandburg who wrote the poem *The Road Not Taken*?
13. Carl Sandburg won a Pulitzer Prize for *Complete Poems* in 1951.
14. More and more businesses are changing their approach to "total quality management".
15. Sarah reported that Frank shouted, "I have had it with this give and take!".

EXERCISE 13-G *Directions:* Make all necessary corrections by using standard proofreaders' marks. This exercise is a chapter review.

THE ATTIC

The steps are steep, the stairway dark. I wonder how many times she made this trip, carrying "treasures" to be stashed away for another time and another pair of eyes.

The word *treasures* accurately describes the contents of this mystical wonderland. I never tire of making this trip into Never-Never Land for these reasons. Voices drift up from cracked photographs holding little more than a hint of the experiences and emotions of the faces that pass in front of me. Musty smells escape from the yellowed, flaking pages that make time travel possible. Minuscule dust storms emerge from soot covered packages when their contents are exposed.

Some of the photographs and pictures have meaning to me: others will remain anonymous. In one time-worn photograph, a chunky child proudly straddles a dappled pony. I find myself remembering the voice of the ninety-year-old "child" saying, "I wasn't much to look at, but I sure had a good time with Cricket." She must have had a good time for the carefully-preserved saddle dangles by one stirrup in the farthest corner of the attic. Leaning against the wall is a stack of picture frames, cracked glass, scratched paint, and chipped corners, housing their unblinking, unsmiling denizens with their high-browed, firm-jawed, and time-honored faces.

There are more treasures, I can hardly wait to discover them!, that are tucked between the disintegrating pages of autograph books, old schoolbooks, and century-old magazines and newspapers—all fantastic! In an 1890 autograph book, this was written: When the name that I write here is dim on the page and the leaves of your album are yellowed with age, still think of me kindly and do not forget that wherever I am, I remember you yet. From an 1890 small-town newspaper—The Cyclone and Fayette Republican, a column entitled Missionary Society yielded this information;

> "Not withstanding the inclemency of the weather and the muddy condition of our streets, the entertainment given by the Young Ladies Missionary Society of the

2

> Presbyterian Church . . .was a decided success. A delightful literary and musical program was rendered, and refreshments were served. . . . The entertainment was a decided success throughout, and all seemed to enjoy themselves.

In the same society section, this report was given: ". . . There were present about twenty young people, who enjoyed themselves to the fullest extent in a pleasant social way. An elegant supper was served, and all went home recognizing the fact that Mr. and Mrs. Patton and family are splendid entertainers." Prices were interesting too. The paper advertised this list of wholesale grain prices, 1) wheat, new, 93 cts. per bushel, 2) corn, 50 cts. per bushel, 3) butter, 15 cts. per pound, and 4) poultry, young, 8 cts. per pound. I wondered what an average salary was.

A camel back trunk was filled with boxes— each box a separate mystery in itself. Some boxes were tied: some were lined with yellowed tissue paper. Sometimes there were original cases that, like clams, still had their prize *pearls* enclosed. What pearls they were, too—a family Bible with a Civil War veteran's honorable discharge paper signed by Abraham Lincoln, a violin and bow with broken strings, a tarnished brooch nested in tissue, a china teapot with no handle, wire-rimmed glasses, should I say spectacles, that had perched on a nose and were equipped with a retractable fob, and twine-bound stacks of 1903–1906 Cosmopolitan. The list is truly endless.

I speculate about my elderly cousin's ancestors; I think of questions I would like to ask her if she were here today. I know she rode a pony as a child and drove a Model T as a youth. She learned to read from The McGuffey Readers but quit college when her father forbade her to be a doctor. ("It is not a woman's profession"). For over 30 years she took care of aging parents and the county automobile club. It was a full life, but was it enough? Who were you really, Fern Chaffin? For that matter, who are we? What will we leave in our attics?

EXERCISE 13-H *Directions:* Make all necessary corrections by using standard proofreaders' marks. This exercise is a text review.

THE ALLERGY CLINIC

ONE BENTWOOD AVENUE
KANSAS CITY, KS 66110

May 18, 1999

Mr. Samuel Driscoll
348 Bennington Way
Overland Park, KS 66204

Dear Mr. Driscoll:

Our results are back from your allergy test. Since your last tests with us at The Allergy Clinic in 1997 you have become allergic to two more food additives; sulfites and tartrazine, FD&C—Food, Drug, and Cosmetic—Yellow No. 5. Fortunately, both of these substances are listed with the ingredients in all food products, therefore, read you're labels carefully before you purchase your food.

Sulfites have been banned from use on fresh fruits and vegetables since 1986 because a small segment of the population, you are one of these people, have been found to develop hives, nausea, diarrhea, shortness of breath or even fatal shock after sulfite consumption. Sulfites added as a preservative in packaged and processed foods must be listed on the product label.

FD&C Yellow No. 5--tartrazine--is used to color beverages, dessert powders, candy, ice creams, and other foods. Tests reveal that fewer then 1 in 10,000 people may get hives from tartrazine. Therefore the Color Additive Amendments to the Food, Drug, and Cosmetic Act of 1960 require dyes used in foods, drugs, cosmetics, and certain medical devices to be approved by the Food and Drug Administration prior to marketing. The Nutrition Labeling and Education Act of 1990 require than any certified color added to food be listed in the ingredient statement by its common or usual name.

If you have any questions, please do not hesitate to call the main office anytime between 9 a.m. and 4:30 p.m. We appreciate your confidence in letting us be a part of your health-care team.

Sincerely,

THE ALLERGY CLINIC

Austin Barsalow, M.D.

rb

EXERCISE 13-1

Directions: Make all necessary corrections by using standard proofreaders' marks. This exercise is a text review.

March 10, 1999

Dear Home Owner:

According to a recent survey done by the county engineering office, most of the homes in your subdivision were built before 1870. This means that there is more than a reasonable possibility that your home contains asbestos. Asbestos may be found in the following places in older homes, around pipes and furnaces as insulating jackets and sheathing, in some vinyl flooring materials, in ceiling tiles, in exterior roofing, shingles, and siding, in some wallboards, in patching compounds or textured paints, and in door gaskets on stoves, furnaces, and ovens.

As you are probably aware, asbestos is a carcinogen. The biggest danger is to people who have extensive exposure to it, however, research does not report conclusively what even small amounts of asbestos will do. Home health risks arise when age, accidental damage, normal cleaning, construction or remodeling activities cause the asbestos containing materials to crumble, flake or deteriorate. When this happens, minute asbestos fibers are released into the air and can be inhaled through the nose and mouth. The fibers can cling to almost anything, clothing, tools, and exposed flesh. Cleanup operations can than dislodge the fibers, and cause them to circulate in the air, thus the cycle starts all over again.

Be very careful when handling, cleaning, or you work with any material suspected to contain asbestos. Sometimes the removal of asbestos takes special equipment and training. That's were we at Aston's Asbestos Removal Inc. comes to your service. Aston's is offfering free inspection and testing for the presence of asbestos in your home. We will also provide you you with a free estimate for the removal of this unwanted hazard. Please see the enclosed brochure for more information and prices. Give us a call today. Astin's Asbestos Removal Inc. want to make your home a healthy and worry free "castle."

Sincerely,

Miss Joan Aston, President

cp

Enclosure

CHAPTER

14

Letters, Memorandums, and Reports

Formatting is, stated simply, arranging material on a page. Many people say, "It's what you have to say that is important, not the way you say it," and to some extent that is true—creativity should be applied to the content of the letter.

But in business it is just as important for the format to be correct as it is for the message to be accurate. When a reader opens an envelope and finds the entire letter on the top half of the page, the credibility of the writer is immediately in question. Accuracy and format contribute equally to that important first impression—the impression that is so difficult to change.

Documents generally fall into one of three categories: letters, memorandums, and manuscripts. We first examine letters—their formats, punctuation styles, and parts, and the rules that govern them.

Formatting Letters

There are many styles of letters used in the business world. Three styles, however, are most popular.

Full Block This is the letter style used most frequently today. In full-block style, all lines of the letter start at the left margin. Because paragraphs are not indented, letters in this style can be typed more quickly and are less prone to retyping. An example of a full-block letter appears in Figure 14.1.

Modified Block In a modified-block letter, the date, complimentary close, and signature block all begin at the center of the page (see Figure 14.2). The first line of each paragraph may begin at the margin or may be indented. Unless you are given specific instructions to indent, paragraphs should be blocked.

Simplified The simplified letter is the newest letter style. In place of a salutation, a subject line, typed in capital letters, appears below the address of the person who will receive the letter. Three line spaces are placed above and below the subject line (see Figure 14.3). The complimentary close is also eliminated in a simplified-style letter. The writer's identification lines are typed in capital letters in the usual location at the bottom of the letter.

Although formatting varies among different sources, the styles illustrated in Figures 14.1 through 14.3 are commonly used.

Punctuation Style

The two punctuation styles commonly used in letters are open punctuation and standard punctuation.

Open Punctuation This punctuation style derives its name from the absence of punctuation after the salutation and the complimentary close. Open punctuation may be used with full-block or modified-block letters (see Figure 14.1, for example).

Standard Punctuation In a letter using standard punctuation, a colon is placed after the salutation, and a comma is placed after the complimentary close. This punctuation style also may be used with full-block or modified-block letters (see Figure 14.2).

Margin Settings

Once the letter style and punctuation style have been selected, the next step is deciding on margin settings. To give a document a centered look, the right and left margins should be approximately equal. The top and bottom margins should also be approximately even. Chart 14.1 presents some guidelines for setting margins.

CHART 14.1 FORMATTING LETTERS

Length of Letter	Number of Words	Top Margin* in Lines	L/R Margins in Spaces** Pica	Elite	L/R Margins in Inches
Short	100 or fewer	18	23–63	28–78	2
Average	101–200	15	18–68	22–82	$1\frac{1}{2}$
Long	201–300	13	13–73	16–88	1
Two pages	Over 300	13	13–73	16–88	1
6" Line	As above	As above	13–73	16–88	1
1" Side	As above	As above	11–75	13–90	1

*The top-margin, or date-line setting, is only an approximation. The letter should be adjusted so the top and bottom margins are approximately even, something done easily on a computer or word processor.

**If you are using a typewriter instead of a computer, add 5 spaces to the right-margin setting.

PROOFREADING POINTER

Centering the page: Business letters are either placed a specified distance from the top of the page or centered vertically in the middle of the page. Word-processing packages have features that make either method of letter placement easy. For example, WordPerfect has both an *advance feature* that allows the text to start at a specified point on the page and a *center-page feature* that centers a page vertically (when letterhead stationery is not used). Check your word-processing package for these time-saving features.

SALYARD • ALASKAN • CRUISE • LINES

One Hundred Thirty Five Washington Drive ♦ Fairbanks, Alaska 99701

September 15, 1999

4 or 5 returns

Mr. Jesse Roberts
65 East Fourth Street
McAllen, TX 78501

2 returns

Dear Mr. Roberts

2 returns

Letter styles are confusing at first glance; but once you study the layout of the three main letter styles, you'll find there are several similarities that make learning the styles easier. All you need to do is memorize the differences.

1. The easiest style to learn is the **full-block** (sometimes called block) style. All the letter parts start at the left margin, creating blocked paragraphs (no indent). The spacing is as indicated on this letter.

2. **Modified-block**-style letters are very similar to full-block-style letters with similar spacing between letter parts. There are only two mandatory changes and one optional change (blocked and indented paragraphs) in the layout of the modified-block-style letter.

   a. The date begins at the center of the paper.

   b. The closing lines (the complimentary close and the name block) start at the center point of the letter.

   c. The letter can have blocked or indented paragraphs; unless you have specific instructions to use indented paragraphs, do not use them. Forgetting a required indent can force retyping, a costly process.

3. The third commonly used style is the **simplified style**. This style differs from block and modified block in four ways.

   a. The salutation is omitted.

   b. In place of the salutation, there is a subject line typed in capital letters; two blank lines precede and follow the subject. The word *subject* is not used in the subject line in letters in simplified style.

   c. The complimentary close is omitted.

   d. The writer's identification lines are typed in capital letters.

These three letter styles are by far the most commonly used in business today. They should be simple to remember.

2 returns

Sincerely

4 returns

James P. Bailey
Office Manager

2 returns

cl

FIGURE 14.2 MODIFIED-BLOCK LETTER STYLE WITH STANDARD PUNCTUATION

SALYARD ♦ ALASKAN ♦ CRUISE ♦ LINES

One Hundred Thirty Five Washington Drive ♦ Fairbanks, Alaska 99701

start at center

September 15, 1999

4 or 5 returns

Mr. Jesse Roberts
65 East Fourth Street
McAllen, TX 78501

2 returns

Dear Mr. Roberts:

2 returns

Letter styles are confusing at first glance; but once you study the layout of the three main letter styles, you'll find there are several similarities that make learning the styles easier. All you need to do is memorize the differences.

1. The easiest style to learn is the **full-block** (sometimes called block) style. All the letter parts start at the left margin, creating blocked paragraphs (no indent). The spacing is as indicated on this letter.

2. **Modified-block**-style letters are very similar to full-block-style letters with similar spacing between letter parts. There are only two mandatory changes and one optional change (blocked or indented paragraphs) in the layout of the modified-block-style letter.

   a. The date begins at the center of the paper.

   b. The closing lines (the complimentary close and the name block) start at the center point of the letter.

   c. The letter can have blocked or indented paragraphs; unless you have specific instructions to use indented paragraphs, do not use them. Forgetting a required indent can force retyping, a costly process.

3. The third commonly used style is the **simplified style**. This style differs from block and modified block in four ways.

   a. The salutation is omitted.

   b. In place of the salutation, there is a subject line typed in capital letters; two blank lines precede and follow the subject. The word *subject* is not used in the subject line in letters in simplified style.

   c. The complimentary close is omitted.

   d. The writer's identification lines are typed in capital letters.

These three letter styles are by far the most commonly used in business today. They should be simple to remember.

2 returns

Sincerely,

4 returns

James P. Bailey
Office Manager

2 returns

start at center

cl

FIGURE 14.3 SIMPLIFIED LETTER STYLE

SALYARD ♦ ALASKAN ♦ CRUISE ♦ LINES

One Hundred Thirty Five Washington Drive ♦ Fairbanks, Alaska 99701

September 15, 1999

4 or 5 returns

Mr. Jesse Roberts
65 East Fourth Street
McAllen, TX 78501

3 returns

THREE POPULAR LETTER STYLES

3 returns

Letter styles are confusing at first glance; but once you study the layout of the three main letter styles, you'll find there are several similarities that make learning the styles easier. All you need to do is memorize the differences.

1. The easiest style to learn is the **full block** (sometimes called block) style. All the letter parts start at the left margin, crreating blocked paragraphs (no indents). The spacing is as indicated on this letter.

2. **Modified-block**-style letters are very similar to full-block-style letters with similar spacing between letter parts. There are only two mandatory changes and one optional change (blocked or indented paragraphs) in the layout of the modified-block-style letter.

    a. The date begins at the center of the paper.

    b. The closing lines (the complimentary close and the name block) start at the center point of the letter.

    c. The letter can have blocked or indented paragraphs; unless you have specific instructions to use indented paragraphs, do not use them. Forgetting a required indent can force retyping, a costly process.

3. The third commonly used style is the **simplified style**. This style differs from block and modified block in four ways.

    a. The salutation is omitted.

    b. In place of the salutation, there is a subject line typed in capital letters; two blank lines precede and follow the subject. The word *subject* is is not used in the subject line in simplified style.

    c. The complimentary close is omitted.

    d. The writer's identification lines are typed in capital letters.

These three letter styles are by far the most commonly used in business today. They should be simple to remember.

4 returns

JAMES P. BAILEY
OFFICE MANAGER
2 returns
cl

EXERCISE 14–A

Directions: In the space provided on page 235, indicate whether each of the following letters looks correct in placement and spacing. If a letter is correct, write *C*. If a letter is incorrect, identify the problem.

EXERCISE 14-A

1

December 4, 1999

Mr. Jonathan Durbin
234 Mayberry Drive
Jackson, MI 49201

Dear Mr. Durbin:

I am pleased to be able to send you the information you requested on letter styles. I am sure you will find the information helpful as you use it in the office situation.

There are three basic letter styles in use in the office environment today. The first style is Modified Block. The date, the complimentary close, and the writer's identification block all begin at the center of the page. In all other respects the modifiec block letter is similar to the Full Block letter style.

The second letter style is the Full Block. In a Full Block letter all the lines begin at the left margin. This is the simplest and quickest letter style in use today.

The final letter style is Simplified. In a simplified letter the salutation (Dear Mr. . . .) is omitted. In its place an all-cap subject line is inserted with a triple space (2 blank lines) above and below the subject line. the word<u>subject</u> is never used. Additionally, the complimentary close is omitted, and the writer's identification block is typed in all capital letters.

I have enclosed copies of all three letter style with the proper spacing marked on the letters. Let me know if you have additional questions.

Sincerely,

Edith Wharbler
Office Manager

xx

Enclosure

2

December 4, 1999

Mr. Jonathan Durbin
234 Mayberry Drive
Jackson, MI 49201

Dear Mr. Durbin:

I am pleased to be able to send you the information you requested on letter styles. I am sure you will find the information helpful as you use it in the office situation.

There are three basic letter styles in use in the office environment today. The first style is Modified Block. The date, the complimentary close, and the writer's identification block all begin at the center of the page. In all other respects the modifiec block letter is similar to the Full Block letter style.

The second letter style is the Full Block. In a Full Block letter all the lines begin at the left margin. This is the simplest and quickest letter style in use today.

The final letter style is Simplified. In a simplified letter the salutation (Dear Mr. . . .) is omitted. In its place an all-cap subject line is inserted with a triple space (2 blank lines) above and below the subject line. the word<u>subject</u> is never used. Additionally, the complimentary close is omitted, and the writer's identification block is typed in all capital letters.

I have enclosed copies of all three letter style with the proper spacing marked on the letters. Let me know if you have additional questions.

Sincerely,

Edith Wharbler
Office Manager

xx

Enclosure

3

December 4, 1999

Mr. Jonathan Durbin
234 Mayberry Drive
Jackson, MI 49201

Dear Mr. Durbin:

I am pleased to be able to send you the information you requested on letter styles. I am sure you will find the information helpful as you use it in the office situation.

There are three basic letter styles in use in the office environment today. The first style is Modified Block. The date, the complimentary close, and the writer's identification block all begin at the center of the page. In all other respects the modifiec block letter is similar to the Full Block letter style.

The second letter style is the Full Block. In a Full Block letter all the lines begin at the left margin. This is the simplest and quickest letter style in use today.

The final letter style is Simplified. In a simplified letter the salutation (Dear Mr. . . .) is omitted. In its place an all-cap subject line is inserted with a triple space (2 blank lines) above and below the subject line. the word<u>subject</u> is never used. Additionally, the complimentary close is omitted, and the writer's identification block is typed in all capital letters.

I have enclosed copies of all three letter style with the proper spacing marked on the letters. Let me know if you have additional questions.

Sincerely,

Edith Wharbler
Office Manager

xx

Enclosure

4

December 4, 1999

Mr. Jonathan Durbin
234 Mayberry Drive
Jackson, MI 49201

Dear Mr. Durbin:

I am pleased to be able to send you the information you requested on letter styles. I am sure you will find the information helpful as you use it in the office situation.

There are three basic letter styles in use in the office environment today. The first style is Modified Block. The date, the complimentary close, and the writer's identification block all begin at the center of the page. In all other respects the modifiec block letter is similar to the Full Block letter style.

The second letter style is the Full Block. In a Full Block letter all the lines begin at the left margin. This is the simplest and quickest letter style in use today.

The final letter style is Simplified. In a simplified letter the salutation (Dear Mr. . . .) is omitted. In its place an all-cap subject line is inserted with a triple space (2 blank lines) above and below the subject line. the word<u>subject</u> is never used. Additionally, the complimentary close is omitted, and the writer's identification block is typed in all capital letters.

I have enclosed copies of all three letter style with the proper spacing marked on the letters. Let me know if you have additional questions.

Sincerely,

Edith Wharbler
Office Manager

xx

Enclosure

5

December 4, 1990

Mr. Jonathan Durbin
234 Mayberry Drive
Jackson, MI 49201

Dear Mr. Durbin

I am pleased to be able to send you the information you requested on letter styles. I am sure you will find the information helpful as you use it in the office situation.

There are three basic letter styles in use in the office environment today. The first style is Modified Block. The date, the complimentary close, and the writers identification block all begin at the center of the page. In all other respects the modifiec block letter is similar to the Full Block letter style.

The second letter style is the Full Block. In a Full Block letter all the lines begin at the left margin. This is the simplest and quickest letter style in use today.

The final letter style is Simplified. In a simplified letter the salutation (Dear Mr. . . .) is omitted. In its place an all cap subject line is inserted with a triple space (2 blank lines) above and below the subject line. the word<u>subject</u> is never used. Additionally, the complimentary close is omitted, and the writers identification block is typed in all capital letters.

I have enclosed copies of all three letter style with the proper spacing marked on the letters. Let me know if you have additional questions.

Sincerely,

Edith Wharbler
Office Manager

xx
Enclosure

6

December 4, 1990

Mr. Jonathan Durbin
234 Mayberry Drive
Jackson, MI 49201

LETTER STYLES

I am pleased to be able to send you the information you requested on letter styles. I am sure you will find the information helpful as you use it in the office situation.

There are three basic letter styles in use in the office environment today. The first style is Modified Block. The date, the complimentary close, and the writer's identification block all begin at the center of the page. In all other respects the modifiec block letter is similar to the Full Block letter style.

The second letter style is the Full Block. In a Full Block letter all the lines begin at the left margin. This is the simplest and quickest letter style in use today.

The final letter style is Simplified. In a simplified letter the salutation (Dear Mr. . . .) is omitted. In its place an all-cap subject line is inserted with a triple space (2 blank lines) above and below the subject line. the word<u>subject</u> is never used. Additionally, the complimentary close is omitted, and the writer's identification block is typed in all capital letters.

I have enclosed copies of all three letter style with the proper spacing marked on the letters. Let me know if you have additional questions.

EDITH WHARBLER
OFFICE MANAGER

xx

Enclosure

1. ______________________

2. ______________________

3. ______________________

4. ______________________

5. ______________________

6. ______________________

Letter Parts

Letters always contain some required sections—the date, the inside address, the body, and the writer's identification block. Many letters contain additional sections, depending on how the letter is written and what letter style is used. Chart 14.2 lists all letter parts, in correct order; the required sections are set in bold type.

The U.S. Postal Service sometimes makes recommendations concerning attention lines and addressing styles. Consult the U.S. Postal Service for current recommendations.

CHART 14.2 LETTER PARTS

Letterhead or return address

Date

Personal or confidential notation

Inside address

Attention line

Salutation

Subject line

Body of the letter

Complimentary close

Company signature

Writer's identification block

Reference initials

Enclosure notation

Delivery notation

Copy notation

Postscript notation

LETTER RULES

Letterhead or Return Address

14.1 Business letters should be typed on letterhead stationery or should include a return address immediately preceding the date.

> 45690 Westward Ho Drive
> Jackson, MI 49201
> October 10, 1999

Date

14.2 Every letter begins with a date. The date should include the month, the day, and the year. No abbreviations should be used in the date line.

Personal or Confidential Notation

14.3 A personal or confidential mailing notation is typed two lines below the date, at the left margin. The notation could be typed in any of the following formats:

Personal	**Personal**	PERSONAL
Confidential	**Confidential**	CONFIDENTIAL

Inside Address

14.4 The inside address should include the name of the person or organization you are writing; a street address, post office box number, or route number; and the city, state, and ZIP Code. The inside address, preceded by three or four blank lines, is typed single-spaced, beginning at the left margin.

14.5 When you write to an individual, always include a courtesy title (such as *Dr.*, *Mr.*, or *Ms.*). The only time the courtesy title is omitted is when the gender of the name is unknown. For example, Lynn could be a woman's name or a man's name.

14.6 When you write to an organization, try to identify an individual in the inside address. If you cannot identify any individual, use an appropriate position title. These practices are a courtesy to those distributing mail, and they also help ensure that your letter will reach its proper destination.

Mr. Jason Lippitt
Ogilvie Corporation
23 Kelvey Drive
Naili, HI 96791

Personnel Director
Ogilvie Corporation
23 Kelvey Drive
Naili, HI 96791

14.7 In the street address, do not abbreviate words such as *Street*, *Drive*, and *Boulevard*.

14.8 The street address is placed on a line by itself.

14.9 Use figures for house and street numbers. The only street number that is spelled out is *One*.

Ms. Mildred Jones
One Arrowwood Drive
Peoria, IL 61601

Mr. Ed Smith
18 Miller Drive
Peoria, IL 61601

14.10 Do not abbreviate a compass point that appears before a street name.

Ms. Frazier Brooks
23 East Morton Circle
Lenoir, NC 28645

Ms. Edith Warder
One Northwest Line Street
Lenoir, NC 28645

14.11 When a compound compass point (*NW, SE,* and so on) appears after a street address, the street address is followed by a comma and the compound compass point is abbreviated. If the compass point is not compound (*N, S, E,* or *W*), the direction is spelled out.

2350 Wolverton Place, NW 345 Jural Street, East

14.12 When a number is used as a street name, use an ordinal number, spelled out, for the numbers 1 through 10: *First, second, third, . . . tenth.* Use numerals for ordinals above ten: 11th, 22d, 44th, and so on.

947 Second Street 203 72d Boulevard

14.13 The city, state, and ZIP Code appear on one line. Do not abbreviate the names of cities. Only one space is required between the state abbreviation and ZIP Code.

➤ Washington Court House, OH 43701

14.14 Use the two-letter abbreviations preferred by the post office in the inside address. Both letters are capitalized with no periods used. Leave only one space between the state abbreviation and the ZIP Code. A listing of the two-letter state abbreviations is found on the inside front cover of this book.
Note: The two-letter state abbreviation is used only in the inside address and on the envelope. State names used in sentences within the body of the letter are never abbreviated.

Attention Line

14.15 The attention line is typed two line spaces below the inside address at the left margin. The following forms are acceptable.

➤ Attention Director of Personnel

➤ Attention: Director of Personnel

➤ ATTENTION: DIRECTOR OF PERSONNEL

Note: If you are using a window envelope, type the attention line as the first line of the inside address.

➤ Attention Director of Personnel
Marvey Products, Inc.
885 Brighton Boulevard
Essex, CT 06426

Salutation

14.16 The salutation is typed on the second line below the attention line if one is present. Otherwise, type the salutation on the second line below the inside address.

14.17 Capitalize the first word of the salutation.

14.18 Use a courtesy title in the salutation if one is known.

14.19 If the gender of the person receiving the letter is unknown, then *Dear* is followed by the full name of the individual.

Dear Lynn Wells Dear Dale Glacier

14.20 If the letter is addressed to an organization, use one of the company salutations, such as *Gentlemen* (if the organization is 100 percent male), *Ladies* (if the organization is 100 percent female), or *Ladies and Gentlemen*. This is done to avoid gender bias. A second option open to writers wishing to avoid gender bias is to adopt the simplified letter style, which eliminates the salutation.

14.21 If a letter contains an attention line, the letter is technically being sent to an organization. One of the organizational salutations discussed in Rule 14.20 should be used.

Gentlemen Ladies Ladies and Gentlemen

Forms of Address

14.22 Chart 14.3 lists the most commonly used forms of address for correspondence with officials. A comprehensive reference manual will contain a more complete listing.

CHART 14.3 COMMONLY USED FORMS OF ADDRESS FOR OFFICIALS

Addressee	Inside Address	Salutation	Complimentary Close
Lawyer	(Mr., Mrs., Ms.) _____ Attorney-at-Law Address	Dear (Mr., Mrs., Ms.) _____	Sincerely
Physician Doctoral Degree	Dr. _____ Address	Dear Dr. _____	Sincerely
College President	Dr. (Mr., Mrs., Ms.) _____ President, [college name]	Dear President _____ (or) Dear Dr. _____	Sincerely
Dean of College	Dr. (Mr., Mrs., Ms.) _____ Dean, [college name] Address	Dear Dean _____ (or) Dear Dr. _____	Sincerely
Professor	Professor _____ Department of _____ Address	Dear Professor _____	Sincerely
Military Personnel	[military rank] _____ Address	Dear [military rank] _____	Sincerely
President of United States	The President The White House Washington, DC 20500	Dear Mr. President	Respectfully
U.S. Senator	The Honorable _____ United States Senate Washington, DC 20510	Dear Senator _____	Sincerely
U.S. Representative	The Honorable _____ House of Representatives Washington, DC 20515	Dear (Mr., Mrs., Ms.) _____	Sincerely

CHART 14.3 (CONTINUED)

Addressee	Inside Address	Salutation	Complimentary Close
State Senator	The Honorable _____ [state] State Senate Address	Dear Senator _____	Sincerely
State Representative	The Honorable _____ [state] House of Representatives Address	Dear (Mr., Mrs., Ms.) _____	Sincerely
Governor	The Honorable _____ Governor of [state] Address	Dear Governor _____	Sincerely
Judge	The Honorable _____ [name of court] Address	Dear Judge _____	Sincerely
Mayor	The Honorable _____ Mayor of [city] Address	Dear Mayor _____	Sincerely
Catholic Clergy	The Reverend _____ Address	Dear Father _____	Sincerely
Protestant Clergy	The Reverend _____ Address	Dear Reverend _____	Sincerely
Jewish Clergy	Rabbi _____ Address	Dear Rabbi _____	Sincerely

Subject Line

14.23 In the *simplified letter* style, the subject line is typed on the third line below the inside address and three lines above the body of the letter. The subject line is typed in capital letters; the word *subject* is not used.

➤ WELCOME TO HARVEY HOUSE

➤ PROMOTIONAL SALES IDEAS

14.24 In a *modified-block letter* or *full-block letter,* the subject line is typed on the second line below the salutation. It can be centered or typed at the left margin in modified-block style. In the full-block style, however, it should be typed at the left margin. All of the following styles are commonly used. The word *subject* may be included in a modified-block letter or a full-block letter.

➤ Subject: Welcome to Harvey House

➤ SUBJECT: PROMOTIONAL SALES IDEAS

➤ PROMOTIONAL SALES IDEAS

Body of the Letter

14.25 The body of the letter is typed single-spaced with a blank line between paragraphs.

Complimentary Closing

14.26 The complimentary closing is omitted in a simplified letter.

14.27 Use one of the acceptable forms of complimentary closings in Chart 14.4. Notice that only the first word of the complimentary close is capitalized.

CHART 14.4 COMPLIMENTARY CLOSINGS

Standard Closings	Formal Closings*
Cordially	Respectfully yours
Cordially yours	Very cordially yours
Sincerely	Very sincerely yours
Sincerely yours	Very truly yours

*For the appropriate complimentary close for official situations, see Chart 14.3.

Company Signature

14.28 A company signature is not ordinarily used with letterhead stationery. On occasions when it is used, the letter usually represents the official view of the company. The company signature is then typed in capital letters, on the second line below the complimentary close.

Writer's Identification Block

14.29 The name of the writer is located on the fourth line below the complimentary close in a modified-block or full-block letter. In simplified style, it is located on the fourth line below the body of the letter, and it is typed in capital letters.

14.30 A man's name never requires a courtesy title in the writer's identification block. A woman's name, however, does require one so that the person responding to the letter will know the title she prefers. A woman writer can choose instead to sign her title (in parentheses) before her written signature. The courtesy title should be indicated in either the written or the typed name but not in both.

Sincerely yours,	Sincerely,
Marion Browne	(Ms.) Marion Browne
Ms. Marion Browne	Marion Browne

14.31 If an academic title is preferred by the person sending the letter, the person's degree is indicated by an abbreviation, which is placed after the name and is preceded by a comma.

➤ Mark Jenkins, M.D.

➤ Ellie Albertson, D.D.S.

➤ Doug Shatto, Ph.D.

Reference Initials

14.32 The reference initials of the typist, if the person sending the letter did not also type it, are placed on the second line below the writer's identification line. Neither initial is capitalized.

14.33 If the person writing or dictating the letter is different from the person signing the letter, the initials of the dictator, in capitals, are placed before the typist's initials. Some acceptable styles are the following:

➤ MC:js

➤ MCjs

➤ MC/js

Enclosure Notation

14.34 If other materials are to be enclosed with the letter, an enclosure notation is added. The enclosure notation is placed on the second line below the reference initials (if they are required) or the second line below the body of a letter that has no reference initials. The following styles are acceptable.

Enclosure

Enclosures

Enclosures (2)

2 Enclosures

Enclosures:
Contract
Verification Form

Delivery Notation

14.35 If a letter specifies the delivery instructions, a notation is made on the second line below the enclosure notation or below the reference initials if no enclosure notation exists.

By certified mail

By [delivery service name]

By messenger

By two-day Priority Mail

Copy Notation

14.36 If a copy of the letter is being sent to any other individuals, a copy notation is placed at the left margin, on the second line below the delivery notation, the enclosure notation, or the reference initials, whichever occurs last. Although few businesses now use carbon paper, *cc* is still used to represent copies. Various choices are available; some examples follow.

cc Ms. White	Copy to: Ms. White
c Ms. White	Copies to: Ms. Alma White
pc Jason White	Mr. Morgan Dennis

14.37 Sometimes the writer may want to send copies of the letter to other individuals but may not want the person receiving the letter to know about the copies. In such cases, a blind copy notation—*bc* or *bcc* is added to the copies of the letter, including the file copy; it does not appear on the original.

bcc Ms. Blanchet   bc Ms. Blanchet

Postscript Notation

14.38 A postscript notation may be deliberately used to emphasize some material; it might occasionally be added to include accidentally omitted material. The postscript notation is the last notation on the page, and it begins at the left margin. All of the following formats are acceptable.

- PS: Why don't we consider including a dinner after the formal initiation ceremony? Maybe the culinary arts students would agree to prepare a dinner.
- PS. Why don't we consider including a dinner after the formal initiation ceremony? Maybe the culinary arts students would agree to prepare a dinner.
- Why don't we consider including a dinner after the formal initiation ceremony? Maybe the culinary arts students would agree to prepare a dinner.

Continuation Pages in Letters

14.39 If a letter requires a second (or third) page, a heading is used in case the continuation page becomes separated from the first page. Only the first page appears on letterhead stationery; all continuation pages are on plain paper. The heading begins on line 7 and can use either of the following formats. In both cases, two blank lines follow the heading.

- **Block style—used with full-block or modified-block letters:**

Mrs. David Martin

Page 2

December 5, 1999

- **Horizontal style—used only with modified-block letters:**

Mrs. David Martin   2   December 5, 1999

EXERCISE 14-B *Directions:* Proofread the following letter and make corrections using standard proofreaders' marks. This is a text-review exercise.

January 30, 1999

Ms. Susan Haney
2905 Culbertson Avenue
Freeport, TX 77541

Dear Ms. Haney:

It is a pleasure to write this letter to you. I always enjoy extending a position for summer internship to the candidate we select.

Prairie Research Intensive Naturals (ORIN) is a research organization located in the Galveston, TX. We do research on the Texas prarie dog, an animal recently placed on the endangered speces list. Each Summer we hire three interns to work along with our professional staff members. This arrangment helps us and provides valuable field experience for the students.

We know you don't have much field experience but we also know you have the qualities that make a good intern--determination, a desire to learn, and a interest in preserving the prairie dog communities. You were recommended by George Houghton, your botany field-experience instructor. George's students have been selected from the list of over 100 names for the past four years.

The postion pays $500 per month, plus room and bored. You will need to be in Galveton by Saturday, June 4 at 10 a.m. The internship will end on September 4. We do need to know by March 1, if you want to accept this position. We hope you'll be as anxous to join us as we are to have you join us.

Sincerely

T. Clayton Selander

ko

EXERCISE 14-C

Directions: Proofread the following letter and make corrections using standard proofreaders' marks. This is a text-review exercise.

Exotic PAPERS UNLIMITED
324 Webb Street • Coldwater, MI 49036 • 517/555-3498

January 22, 1999

Ms. Becca Baughman
907 Kodak Drive
Coram, New York 11727

WELCOME TO THE WORLD OF EXOTIC PAPERS

Welcome to the exciting world of Exotic Papers Unlimited. We are sending, under seperate cover, the **Rainbow Cloud** paper you ordered. Now that you have found a supply of exotic papers, we know you will find many uses for our products.

We are inclosing a catalog that explains the variety of styles we have available. We are also sending you the free sample case that all first-time buyers recieve. The sample case contains over 200 samples of the paper styles we have available. We couldn't think of a better way for you to experience the wonderful world of exotic textures. Be sure to check out the **Leopard Spot** paper under the Wildlife Shadows section. What better paper to make you're party invitations stand out then to print them on paper that represents an animal skin.

All are paper stock is made from recycled paper; EPU is doing its part to save the trees. We're proud of our advanced processing that allows us to produce quality paper from recycled products. Our toll free number is listed on the outside front cover of the catalog; you won't have trouble finding the number. We're open 24 hours a day, except Christmas. Orders over $50 are shipped next-day delivery; all other orders are shipped standard five-day delivery.

Sincerely

Janice Brinkman

dd

enclosure

Memorandums

Memorandums are commonly used for correspondence within an organization. Since they are in-house documents, it is not necessary to use courtesy titles. Many organizations use printed memorandum forms, which sometimes are only half sheets.

Formatting Memorandums

14.40 When memorandums are typed on printed forms, a double space is left following the headings TO, FROM, DATE, and SUBJECT. The memorandum begins on the third line following the heading. The headings may be aligned at the left or aligned at the colons (see Figures 14.4 and 14.4A).

14.41 Material following the TO, FROM, DATE, and SUBJECT in printed-form memorandums is typed in capital and lowercase letters (see Figures 14.4 and 14.4A). Capitalize all significant words: the first word, the first word after a colon, the last word, both parts of a hyphenated compound, and all other words except articles, short prepositions, and short conjunctions. A preposition is short if it is made up of three or fewer letters.

Memorandums are frequently typed on the printed forms supplied by the organization. When such forms are not provided, either letterhead stationery or plain paper may be used. All three of the formats in Figures 14.4, 14.4A, and 14.5 are commonly used. Spacing is indicated in the two samples. Notice that in all three of these formats the memo occupies the top portion of the paper. Memorandums should not be centered vertically on the page.

FIGURE 14.4 STANDARD MEMORANDUM WITH COLONS ALIGNED

1½-inch top margin

TO: Mark Williams

FROM: Lynn Wells

DATE: January 12, 1999

SUBJECT: We Need Your Help to Save a Tree

TS

I know we are in the habit of always using full sheets of paper for our memorandums. If the memo is long and fills more than half a page, we need the full sheet. If the memo is short—and probably half of them are—we could just as easily put two copies of the memo on the same piece of paper. We'll be doing our part to save a tree. Besides, it is more cost-effective to use one sheet of paper rather than two.

The software we are all using for word processing will easily copy the memorandum and place the second copy below the first on the same page. You'll find the directions for the internal copy feature on page 14 of the instruction manual for our software package.

Thanks for your help in this paper-saving matter.

DS

op

FIGURE 14.4A STANDARD MEMORANDUM WITH BLOCK ALIGNMENT

1½ inch top margin

TO: Mark Williams

FROM: Lynn Wells

DATE: January 12, 1999

SUBJECT: We Need Your Help to Save a Tree

TS

I know we are in the habit of always using full sheets of paper for our memorandums. If the memo is long and fills more than half a page, we need the full sheet. If the memo is short—and probably half of them are—we could just as easily put two copies of the memo on the same piece of paper. We'll be doing our part to save a tree. Besides, it is more cost-effective to use one sheet of paper rather than two.

The software we are all using for word processing will easily copy the memorandum and place the second copy below the first on the same page. You'll find the directions for the internal copy feature on page 14 of the instruction manual for our software package.

Thanks for your help in this paper-saving matter.

DS

op

FIGURE 14.5 SIMPLIFIED MEMORANDUM

1½-inch top margin

January 12, 1999

DS

Mark Williams

DS

WE NEED YOUR HELP TO SAVE A TREE

DS

I know we are in the habit of always using full sheets of paper for our memorandums. If the memo is long and fills more than half a page, we need the full sheet. If the memo is short—and probably half of them are—we could just as easily put two copies of the memo on the same piece of paper. We'll be doing our part to save a tree. Besides, it is more cost-effective to use one sheet of paper rather than two.

The software we are all using for word processing will easily copy the memorandum and place the second copy below the first on the same page. You'll find the directions for the internal copy feature on page 14 of the instruction manual for our software package.

Thanks for your help in this paper-saving matter.

QS

Lynn Wells

DS

kl

Continuation Pages in Memorandums

14.42 If a memorandum requires a second (or third) page, a heading is used in case the continuation page becomes separated from the first page. Continuation pages are done on plain paper, not on letterhead stationery. The format of the heading can be either of the following. In both cases, the heading begins on line 7 and is followed by two blank lines.

➤ **Block style:**

Mark Williams

Page 2

January 12, 1999

➤ **Horizontal style**

Mark Williams 2 January 12, 1999

EXERCISE 14-D *Directions:* Proofread the following memorandum and make corrections using standard proofreaders' marks. This exercise is based on all material covered earlier in this text.

March 15, 1999

All Employees

Handle-Your-Stress Seminar

Early last year all of you hear in the Central office of Rational Solutions, Inc., filled out a survey on office morale. Much to hour admitted surprize, you overwhelmingly listed one topic as an idea for professional development—stress Reduction.

You didn't mention anything in the work environment as the primary problem. After conducting an additional investigation, we have determined that the problem is in the type of work we do. We are, of course, in the middle of client problems on a continuous bases. Although we try to avoid becoming personally involved, we are unable to avoid the stress that goes along with the complicated problems we are trying to solve.

Since we can't avoid the stress the next best thing is to learn to reduce it to the lowest possible level. LL (which stands for Lower the Level) is a private company that studies stress in the work environment and then trains employees to handle the stress in the best possible manner.

LL will be joining us next Monday, March 15, at 8 p.m. for there survey. Then on Monday, May 10, they will be joining us at our annual spring retreat for a one-week training program on stress reduction.

We know we can't eliminate the stress, but were hopeful that we can reduce it to the lowest level possible.

Michael Denton

tr

EXERCISE 14–E

Directions: Proofread the following memorandum and make corrections using standard proofreaders' marks. This exercise is based on all material covered earlier in this text.

To: All Staff Members

FROM: Wylie Jones

DATE: January 30, 1999

SUBJECT: Parking Lot lightning Improvements

Starting this Friday, the workmen will be here from Anders Electric to replace our current parking lot lights with new automatic-sensor lights. These lights will be photosensitive, therefore, they will turn on automatically when available light is low.

At the same time, we will replace the pavement in the existing lot and expand the lot on the east side. We have done only repair work on the lot since it was first poured 10 years ago and the lot is in in desperate of need of renovation.

All of this work will make the lot safer and more convenient for you, but for the two weeks the work is being done, we will experience some inconvenience. We won't be able to park in our lot; we have, therefore, made arrangements for you to park in the Telly Towers lot on Third Street.

Sorry for the inconvenience, but its going to be a definite improvement for you and for our customers.

jg

Manuscripts

Manuscripts can take many forms. They vary from simple business reports to specialized manuscript formats, including agendas, minutes, and itineraries. All manuscripts follow a bound or an unbound format, depending on whether the final pages are to be bound or left unbound. Chart 14.5 presents guidelines, including those for setting margins, for these two formats. It also includes guidelines for top-bound manuscripts, although they are seldom used today.

CHART 14.5 FORMATTING MANUSCRIPTS

	MARGINS (IN INCHES)					
Format	**Left**	**Right**	**Top**	**Bottom**	**Page No. Location**	**Page No. on Line**
Unbound						
First pages	1	1	$1\frac{1}{2}$	1	N/A	N/A
Continuation pages	1	1	1	1	upper right	7
Bound						
First pages	$1\frac{1}{2}$	1	$1\frac{1}{2}$	1	N/A	N/A
Continuation pages	$1\frac{1}{2}$	1	1	1	upper right	7
Top-Bound						
First pages	1	1	2	1	N/A	N/A
Continuation pages	1	1	$1\frac{1}{2}$	1	bottom centered	62

Headings and Subheadings in Manuscripts

Various headings may be used in reports and other manuscripts, including titles, side headings, and paragraph headings. Examples of these headings and the proper spacing for each can be found in the sample unbound manuscript in Figure 14.6.

Title Reports always contain a title, a main heading that is typed in capital letters on the first line of the first page. The title is horizontally centered and is followed by two blank lines if no subheading immediately follows.

If the title is followed by a subheading, the subheading is typed on the second line below the main heading, in capital and lowercase letters. The subheading is then followed by two blank lines.

Side Heading Side headings are typed at the left margin, either in capital letters or in capital and lowercase letters. These headings may be underlined or set in bold. They are preceded by two blank lines and followed by one blank line.

Paragraph Heading Paragraph headings are typed (initial capitals only) following the paragraph indent, and they are underlined or set in bold. They are followed by a period, two spaces, and the regular text.

Specialized Manuscripts

Agendas, itineraries, and minutes are specialized forms of manuscripts. One-inch side margins are standard. Samples of these formats, with appropriate spacing marked, are found in Figures 14.7 to 14.9. Formatting may vary from company to company, so be sure to check your company's style.

FIGURE 14.6 AN UNBOUND MANUSCRIPT WITH SIDE HEADINGS AND PARAGRAPH HEADINGS

1½ inch top margin

ARCHERY

TS

The phrase "bow and arrow" brings to mind either the Old West and the Native American or Robin Hood and his Merry Men. However, the origin of the bow and arrow goes farther back in history than Medieval England (476–1453); references to the bow and arrow are found in the Bible as well as in the literature and art remaining from ancient civilizations. The Greeks and Romans used the bow as a standard military weapon. The Egyptians were best known for their mounted archers, but other groups of that time were also versed in "horse archery." Native American groups were known for their skills in the use of the bow and arrow for hunting, and their hunting skill was enhanced by their ability to track game.

TS

THE HAND BOW

DS

Although there are several types of bows, the plain hand bow is by far the best known. The bow is a single piece of wood shaped so a string can be tied between the ends. The arrow has a notch on the end that fits onto the string. The string is pulled back with the arrow notched on the string and then released. The amount of force it takes to draw the arrow back so just the tip of the arrow extends beyond the bow is called the "pounds pull."

Early Bows. Before the Norman Conquest in Europe, bows and arrows were considered unimportant as military weapons. Most of the bows were short—3 to 5 feet—and were used primarily for hunting. It wasn't until late in the twelfth century that the longbow evolved. Up to 6 feet long with a pull between 80 and 140 pounds, the longbow was used extensively by the legendary Robin Hood. The longbow was considered an important military weapon and continued to maintain its popularity until the mid-1500s.

Today's Bows. While the bow and arrow have been replaced by other weapons in today's military arsenal, archery as a sport has grown in popularity. The strength of the bow can be modified to match the strength of the archer, making archery a sport for people of all ages and strengths. Competitions in both target archery and field (hunting) archery are popular with enthusiasts and keep the "romance" of the bow and arrow alive today.

FIGURE 14.7 AN ITINERARY

1½ inch margin

ITINERARY

DS

For William C. Cover

DS

April 5, 1999

TS

Tuesday, April 13, 1999

DS

7:00 a.m. Arrive at Columbus International Airport for 8 a.m. departure via Flyaway Flight 2365 to Des Moines, Iowa

1:14 p.m. Arrive at Des Moines, Iowa. Catch Executive Shuttle Service at Henning Desk (just to the right of the baggage claim area) to the Des Moines Domain.

Des Moines Domain
129 Wheaton Avenue
Des Moines, Iowa
Phone: 569-4999

3:00 p.m Meet with Charlene Coomer and Dwight Farmer. They will pick you up at your hotel and take you to the meeting site. They have also made dinner arrangements.

9:00 p.m. Megan Christine Desmond will pick you up at your hotel for the 9:30 performance of *The Fantastiks*.

TS

Wednesday, April 14, 1999

8:00 a.m. 9 a.m. board meeting of *Publishing Today*. Dwight Farmer will pick you up in the hotel lobby.

1:00 p.m. Meet Dwight Farmer in the lobby of *Publishing Today* to return to Des Moines airport for 2 p.m. departure via Flyaway Flight 543 to Columbus.

6:00 p.m. Arrive in Columbus.

FIGURE 14.8 AN AGENDA

1½-inch top margin

BUSINESS DIVISION

DS

Agenda

DS

Division Meeting

DS

January 12, 1999

DS

Conference Room, TC408

TS

1. Call to order
2. Approval of minutes of previous meeting
3. Report on new building project
4. Report from North Central steering committee
5. Discussion of "Education for the Future" report
6. Discussion of grade-distribution report
7. Overview of faculty preparation week
8. Old business
9. New business
10. Adjournment

FIGURE 14.9 MINUTES OF A MEETING

1½-inch top margin

PROFESSIONAL BUSINESS ALLIANCE OF AMERICA, MATC CHAPTER

DS

Minutes

DS

Regular Meeting of Executive Committee

DS

September 12, 1999

TS

A regular meeting of the Executive Committee of the MATC chapter of Professional Business Alliance of America was called to order at 4 p.m. in the Magi Conference Room of College Hall.

The following officers were present: Dawn Lucas, president; Annette Kendal, vice president; Mark Nykile, secretary; Juanetti Yester, treasurer; Steve Johnson, historian; and Ted Bailey, parliamentarian. Dawn Hargus and Angel Wickham, student senate representatives, were excused to attend the student senate meeting.

Dr. Rebecca Smith was present by special invitation.

Dawn Lucas introduced Dr. Rebecca Smith, state adviser for Professional Business Alliance of America, Ohio Division. Dr. Smith explained changes in the state competitive events this year and extended a formal invitation to our chapter to attend the events. Our chapter has been selected to present the emblem-building ceremony during the competition.

It was moved by Steve Johnson and seconded by Annette Kendall that the executive committee of the MATC chapter of Professional Business Alliance of America endorse presenting the emblem-building ceremony at the state competition. The motion passed unanimously. The recommendation will be presented at the November meeting.

The next meeting of the executive committee will be held on October 12 at 4 p.m. in the Magi Conference Room of College Hall.

The meeting adjourned at 5:05 p.m.

QS

____

Mark Nykile, Secretary

EXERCISE 14–F *Directions:* Proofread the following minutes for Parts, Inc., and make corrections using standard proofreaders' marks. This exercise is based on all material presented earlier in the text.

BUSINESS SERVICES

Minutes

Regular Departmental Meeting

September 20, 1999

A regular meeting of the Business Services department was called to order at 10 a.m. on Monday, September 20, in the Craynell Conference Room of Wilber Hall.

The following employee were present; David Darringer, Kevin Erickson, Ms. Andrea Jones, Julie McClain, Reece Roberts, Allison Smitye, and Cindy Willard. Steve Kline was excused.

Doug Georges, present by special invitation, distributed information to the department on budget requests for the coming year. All departments in Parts, Inc., have exceeded budget ceilings for the upcoming year, which should present unusual challenges as the need for computer parts increase. The corporation is projecting a doubling in income, but, unfortunately the increased spending power our organization will have form the increase in sales will not occur until the year after the growth. Our bu-dget for 1999 will have to remain the same as it is for this year. All section managers are to reduce budget requests for the coming year to match the current years' spending level. Final budget requests are due by November 1.

The corporate membership in Exercise, Plus has been authorized. We will be participateing in a modified Jogger Plan, which allows each employee to visit the facility five times per week, and enroll in two classes. Evaluation visits, monitoring, and nutrition counseling are also availiable as part of the plan. For a fee of $10 per month, each employee has the option of adding family members to the plan. Familiy members would have the same benefits as employees. Interested employees should contact Leslie Morsek who is in charge of this personnel package. Benefit information on the corporate membership will be distributed early next week.

The no-smoking policy was discussed. It was moved by Allison Smitye and seconded by Kevin Erickson that we adopt a smoke-free policy for our department. Following a discussion, the motion passed by a unanimous vote.

The next meeting will be held on Monday, October 4, at 10 a.m. in the Craynell Conference Room.

The meeting adjourned at 11:43 a.m.

____

Cindy Willard, Secretary

EXERCISE 14-G *Directions:* Proofread the following report and make corrections using standard proofreaders' marks. This exercise is based on all material covered earlier in the text.

PAYING THE PRICE OF TECHNOLOGY

Technology is changing the picture of American life in ways we only dreamed about years ago. We just need to look around to see the evidence of those changes. Computers, more then any other symbol of progress, can be found everywhere—in businesses, homes, banks, libraries, schools, and even church offices.

Many people are finding that while they are able to perform routine tasks more rapidly and efficiently, they are having to pay a price that wasn't listed on the sticker. Carpal Tunnel Syndrome, (CTS) sometimes called the disease of the '90s, is an injury to the wrist caused by performing repetitive motions. Anyone who repeats vigorous hand motions in the same way for prolonged periods of time is at risk for CTS. The computer keyboard and the mouse is responsible for most CTS cases, but other occupations also require motions that can lead to the disease. Mail sorters, meat cutters, check-out clerks, hairdressers, musicians, and auto workers are also at risk.

What Is CTS?

Carpal Tunnel Syndrome often develops in the tendons of the wrist and arm from strain caused by repetitive motions. The tendons can swell, pinching the nerves running between the wrist and the arm. This can cause numbness of the the thumb, index finger, middle finger, and half of the ring finger. Sometimes this numbness extends up the arm into the shoulder.

While the numbness itself is irritating, it can also be dangerous. The accompanying loss of sensitivity in the hand can be hazardous around hot surfaces. CTS victims may exhibit weakness in the hand and a loss of dexterity.

Can CTS Be Prevented?

Anyone performing repetitive motions should try to avoid using the wrist in a bent or twisted position. When you sit at a computer, don't rest your palms on the keyboard. When you use a mouse, don't depress the mouse keys with just the tips of your fingers; use the whole finger.

Setting up strait or rearanging a desktop can help eliminate the twisted or bent postions of the wrist. Sometimes the height of the chair or the desk simply needs to be adjusted.

What Can Be Done?

If you think you have CTS you should see a doctor who may prescribe a wrist brace. A second suggestion for treatment may be to eliminate the repetitve motion. While this will diminish the CTS symptoms, it is often impossible to do. Computer operators can't eliminate the keyboard, mail sorters can't stop sorting mail.

If the symtoms are cronic, surgery is an alternative. The relatively uncomplicated surgery severes the ligament that creates the tunnel. The good news is that the surgery is usually successful. Approximately 90 percent of CTS victims improve immediately after the surgery. The bad news is that the symptoms may reappear if the conditions which caused the disease is not changed.

More Changes Ahead

As technology continues to evolve, many suggest that jobs will become even more repetitve; consequently, more workers will develop Carpel Tunnel Syndrome. Permanant solutions to the problem are yet to be found. Several major companies, including Priceman Inc., is studying ways to reduce assembly-line injury. Research is continuing on on keyboards and mice designed to reduce the strain that leads to CTS. It's a start, but we've got a long way to go.

EXERCISE 14-H *Directions:* Proofread the following letter and make corrections using standard proofreaders' marks. This exercise is based on all material covered earlier in the text.

September 12, 1999

Ms. Anastasia Farquelin
12398 Milestone Pk.
Eufaula, Alabama 36027

DEAR MS. FARQUELIN:

Air Travelers, Inc., have built its reputation on prompt efficient travel anywhere in the United States. We've always prided ourselves on our written guarante that "You and Your lugguage will arrive together every time you travel through **Air**." Your letter about delayed luggage was therefore very upsetting to all of us. We are, of course, sorry for the inconvenience you experienced because of the misplaced luggage.

Being sorry is not enough. We hope the two enclosed round-trip-ticket coupons for travel to any city that AT serves will be enough.

We did some checking to discover the cause of the problem and have found that the mix-up occurred at the Columbus, OH, airport. It seems that a ground squirrel entered the airport through the sliding glass doors, somehow the squirrel made it back to the the luggage area, where he was spotted by the luggage handlers. While they were trying to catch him your bag was accidently knocked off the cart where it was waiting to be placed aboard your flight to Bangor, Me. It was discovered by the handlers shortly after you flight departed. We were able to get the luggage aboard a flight arriving in Bangor about six hours after your flight arrived. The luggage was immediately delivered to your hotel.

Ms. Anastasia Farquelin
Page 3
September 23, 1999

We know the tickets won't make up for the inconvenience, but may be it will convince you to fly through **Air** again in the fuutre.

Sincerely,

RONALD RESTON,
PRESIDENT

dj

Enclosures

PS I know this sounds like a "squirrelly story, but strange things do happen, even in modern airports. The squirrel, however, is delighted; one of the baggage handlers took him to the Dawes Arboretum, where he is, by all accounts, happily adjusting to his new surroundings.

EXERCISE 14-1 *Directions:* Proofread the following memo and make corrections using standard proofreaders' marks. This exercise is based on all material presented earlier in the text.

March 15, 1999

Sally Johansen, COE

REPORT ON CORPORATE MEMBERSHIP IN EXERCISE PLUS

Last month you asked me to survey our employees to determine if there might be sufficient interest in Exercise Plus to warrant purchasing a corporate membership. The answer to the survey is an unqualified "YES!"

Exercise Plus has three types of corporate memberships. The plans and the benefits are listed in the table below:

Stroller Plan	**Jogger Plan**	**Sprinter**
Three visits weekly per employee	Five visits weekly per employee	Unlimited visits weekly per employee (unlimited)
Use of all facilities	Use of all facilities	Use of all facilities
One class per year per employee	Two classes per year per employee	Four classes per year per employee
Evaluation visit	Evaluation visit and mon-itoring	Evaluation visit, mon-itoring, and coaching
Nutrition Counseling	Nutrition counseling and classes	Nutrition counseling, classes, and follow-up
$2000 per year	$3,000 per year	$4000 per year

My contact at Exercise, Plus, Melvin Miskanen, has a formal proposal ready for our corporation on a recomendation for our group. He will be out of town next week, but could make the presentation any time during the week of April 5. Is there a time during that weak that would be best for you?

Sally Johansen, CEO
Page 2
March 15, 1999

The employees have been asking about the types of plans available. Some wonder if there is a way we could negotiate a family fee with Exercise Plus. The employees would be willing to pay for the additional cost of the family plan.

One final thought—do you think it would be a good idea to bring in two or three employees to hear the presentation? I think it would be good for the moral of the group. I recommend Walter Davis and Kitty Jergens.

June Kingston

ff

CHAPTER

15

Type Styles, Typefaces, and Justification

CHAPTER OUTLINE

- Type Styles for Emphasis
- Typefaces
- A Word of Caution—Use Restraint
- Fixed Spacing and Proportional Spacing
- Justification

When we dress up, we do so because we want to look our best. Our culture seems to feel it is necessary to have a coordinated appearance in order to make a good impression. Unfortunately, we do not apply the same principle to our written communications—but we should! We take time to comb our hair and make sure our shoes match our outfit, but we don't take time to make sure all parts of our letters match. We make sure our accessories are just right, but we don't make sure our punctuation marks are just right.

As we noted in Chapter 14, formatting is simply the way a document is arranged on the paper. The format includes margins, tab settings, spacing, spacing between parts of a document, and questions of document style. Additionally, with the availability of word-processing packages that offer a variety of typefaces, choice of typeface has become a part of document formatting. Typefaces are different designs of type, such as Futura, Helvetica, and Times Roman.

The overriding principle of formatting is that documents should be arranged in one style. Don't change typefaces more than once or twice in a document. Don't combine letter styles in the same letter. Don't use inconsistent margins, unless a document requires special treatment, as does a bound report. Treat similar column headings in the same way—if one is underlined, then all column headings should be underlined.

Type Styles for Emphasis

The only way to emphasize type on older typewriters or in handwritten material was to underline it or to put quotation marks around it. Today most electronic typewriters and almost all word-processing packages give us three type styles: boldface, italic, and underline. Here are some guidelines for choosing which of these three type enhancements to use in documents.

Underline	Underlining used to be the favorite type enhancement. However, underlining has the disadvantage of being hard to read. Underlining, although still used for column titles and in other special cases, should be used sparingly.
Bold	**Boldface type appears darker than other type in the document. Boldface is a practical way to emphasize type in documents, and it has the advantage of being much easier to read than is underlined text. Boldface type is often used for headings, subheadings, and titles.**
Italic	*Until recently, italic type, which has a slanted appearance, was found primarily in printed materials, mainly because typewriters could not produce italic type. Many word processors now offer italic as an option. When italic type is available, it should be used as a substitute for underlined text.*

EXERCISE 15–A *Directions:* Using standard proofreaders' marks, correct any errors in the following letter. Check for consistent use of type styles for emphasis. This letter was produced on a printer with italic type.

SALYARD ♦ ALASKAN ♦ CRUISE ♦ LINES

One Hundred Thirty Five Washington Drive ♦ Fairbanks, Alaska 99701

September 9, 1999

Ms. Lynn Ann Johnson
One Chevington Circle
Kahului, HI 96732

Dear Ms. Johnson:

We were pleased to receive your application for employment with *Salyard* Alaskan Cruise Lines. I noticed, however, that you did not list a specific job classification in the job preference category. Although we do employ students in several positions on our cruise ships, we need to have **specific** classifications listed before we can process the application. To help you with the decision, we have listed several of the positions, their qualifications, and a description of the duties.

Position	**Qualification**	Duties
Life guard	Red Cross Life Saving Certificate	Life guarding for a six-hour shift
Child-Care worker	Completed *freshman* and *sophomore* years in an elementary education curriculum	On-call babysitting for passengers. When no on-call assignments are available, cover at drop-in care center.
Food server	Completed *one* year of college	Serve food at outdoor food concessions
Table server	Completed *two* years of college	Serve food for inside meals
Entertainment host	Completed three years of college	Assist show coordinator with audience participation activities
Librarian	Completed *three* years of college	Staff library of the ship during open hours

Ms. Lynn Ann Johnson
Page 2
September 9, 1992

Your résumé does indeed look interesting; if you'll make your selection from the listed positions, we'll process your application. Thank you for your interest in a position with Salyard Alaskan Cruise Lines.

Sincerely,

Robert Worstall
President

EXERCISE 15–B

Directions: Using standard proofreaders' marks, correct any errors in the following article, which was produced on a printer with italic type. This exercise reviews all material previously covered in this text.

ETIQUETTE

In rearing children, parents are expected to teach them the rules governing their society. Where did those rules originate? And why do we have them.

The rules that govern acceptable behavior in a society are called the rules of etiquette. Etiquette is defined in The American Heritage Dictionary as the practices and forms presecribed by social convention or by authority. They are a combination of good sense and tradition that have become custom.

The rise of civilization provided a climate where eitiquette could flourish. The oldest book on etiquette is The Instructions of Ptahhotep, a book on the conduct of life by an Eqyptian in 2650 B.C. Ancient Roman and Greek civilizations alsol had rules for the conduct of life. Cicero wrote a book--at great length--about matters of civility and polite conduct. Aristotle wrote on the conduct of life within a family.

The bible provided many of the rules of conduct. The golden rule. "Do unto others as you would have others do unto you," forms the basis of our current rules of etiquette.

In the early Middle Ages. the rules were often developed by clergy. Chivalry and the pomp and ceremony surrounding knighthood inspired many of the traditions prized by the citizens. The Book of the Order of Chivalry was one of the most popular books of instruction on courtly behavior.

The changes in civilization from the renaissance to modern day have continued to influence changes in the rules governing behavior. Etiquette in the seventeenth century stressed table manners to an extreme. (This may have been due to the emergence of knives and forks as common tableware.) Etiquette in the United States following the Civil War placed increasing emphasis on the elaborate formalities practiced by high society.

Since the Second World War, etiquette in the United States has emphasized the concepts of human dignity, worth, and equality.

EXERCISE 15-C *Directions:* Using standard proofreaders' marks, enter any needed changes in the following letter. This exercise covers material presented in Chapters 1 through 15.

October 13, 1999

Ms. Alameda Jaminez
1 Atherton Plaza
Zanesville, OH 43701

Dear Ms. Jaminez

It's too late to start saving for your holiday shopping this year, but its not too late to start your savings plan for next year—Christmas 2000. The Zanes Trace Bank has put together a special program to help you save for the first holiday season in the new century.

We're calling our plan, appropriately enough, **Christmas 2000**. The plan requires that you make payments to the bank on a monthly basis. Then, on November 20, you'll receive an additional check with your paycheck . So far it sounds like all other holiday savings plans, but just wait!

* When you first enroll for the plan, you'll be asked to fill out your application, indicating your place of employment. All payments to the **Christmas 2000** plan will be made on a payroll-deduction basis.

* Payments for the **Christmas 2000** plan are made for 10 months at the rate of $180 per month. The check you'll receive for your holiday shopping will be for $2000, a return of 15.1 percent on your investment.

* If you successfully complete the **Christmas 2000** plan, you'll receive an extra bonus from your employer of $100; the extra money will be nice, but it will be even nicer since your boss will be delivering the money to you personally! The best part is that he'll be dressed as Santa Claus—or Mrs. Claus— when he hands you your bonus. Yes, your boss has agreed to this!

* Finally, you will receive a special hand-crafted **Christmas 2000** ornament for your tree. Santa will also deliver this in person.

The interest rate on this program is higher than on other savings plans. After all, you'll be receiving $200 from the plan and $100 from your employer. We are able to do this only through a special cooperative effort of the Zanes Trace

Ms. Alameda Jaminez
Page 2
October 31, 1999

Bank and all local employers. The area businesses have agreed to the program as a boon for the local economy. And would you believe it--*every* employer in the Zanesville area has agreed to participate in this program! It's a sure sign that cooperation will be an important aspect of life in the year 2000.

Don't miss out on this unusual program. Call Lorraine Julian at 555-2000 to sign up for Christmas 2000. Make the first holiday season in the new century a season to remember.

Sincerely,

Ronald McDougal
ZANES TRACE BANK

cs

Typefaces

One of the challenges facing today's proofreaders is a direct result of advanced technology. Typefaces come in many different forms and patterns, a radical change from the days of the typewriter, when only two or three choices were available. Typefaces are divided into three families—serif, sans serif, and decorative. Each serves a different purpose, and proofreaders should be aware of their traditional uses.

Serif Typefaces Letters in the serif typefaces contain small cross-strokes (serifs) at the bottom and top of letters. These cross-strokes help the eye travel across the page, thus making the text easier to read. Consequently, the serif faces are used within the body of the text rather than for headlines and titles. Some common serif typefaces are Times Roman, Prestige Elite, and Courier.

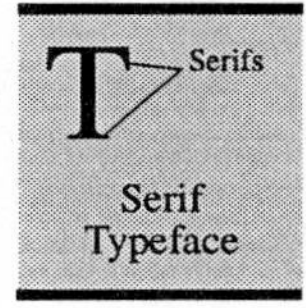

Sans Serif Typefaces The word *sans* in French means "without." Sans serif letters, then, are "without" the cross-strokes found in serif typefaces. Sans serif faces are used for titles and headlines. Some common sans serif typefaces are Helvetica and Letter Gothic.

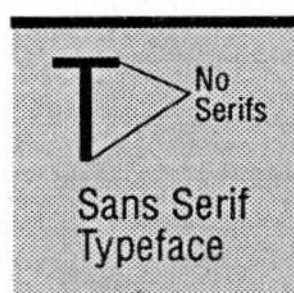

Decorative Typefaces Decorative typefaces, whether serif or sans serif, are definitely novel. They can be very effective when used in small amounts, but they are extremely difficult to read. As a result, they should be used sparingly. Some examples of decorative types are shown in the column at the right.

Black Chancery

WILL

Frankenstein

A Word of Caution—Use Restraint

Perhaps the greatest temptation for many of us—and one we must all resist—is the tendency to use many different typefaces in a letter or report. The general rule of thumb is to use only two or three typefaces to a page. Using too many faces causes the document to resemble a ransom note in which words have been cut from different publications to ensure the writer's anonymity.

Word-processing packages make typeface and type-style changes so easy that sometimes these changes are made unintentionally. A proofreader needs to be alert for unwanted changes in typefaces, which can be hard to spot. The lines below are in different typefaces, although they are similar in appearance. The middle, boldfaced line is obviously a different face, but the differences in the top and bottom lines are not so evident. If you examine them carefully, however, you will see subtle variations in the shape of the letters *g* and *o* and in the width of the letters, even though the general shape of the typefaces is similar.

Now is the time for all good men

Now is the time for all good men

Now is the time for all good men

Now is the time for all good men

Now is the time for all good men

PROOFREADING POINTER

Wrong font: In addition to unwanted typeface and type-style changes, sometimes type will appear in a different size where no change in size was intended. Some of these changes are easy to spot, but some of the changes are not so easy to recognize.

There is a change in size in this line

There is a change in size in this line

If an unwanted change in typeface, type style, or type size occurs, circle the text and write the proofreaders' symbol for **wrong font:** *wf*

EXERCISE 15–D

Directions: In the spaces below, indicate whether the typeface is serif or sans serif. Also identify those that are decorative.

1. This is Architect Typeface. ______________________
2. THIS IS POSTCRYPT TYPEFACE. ______________________
3. This is Lucida Sans typeface. ______________________
4. This is Bookman typeface. ______________________
5. This is Mystical typeface. ______________________
6. This is Chaucer typeface. ______________________
7. This is Bahamas typeface. ______________________
8. This is Arial typeface. ______________________
9. This is Paradise typeface. ______________________
10. This is Memorandum typeface. ______________________

Fixed Spacing and Proportional Spacing

Type is classified not only by typestyles and families but also by the spacing of the characters, which is either fixed or proportional. In fixed spacing each character occupies the same amount of space on the line. For example, the letter *i* takes up the same amount of space as the letter *M*. Fixed spacing is standard on typewriters, and it presents no special problem to proofreaders.

Proportional spacing does present a special problem to proofreaders. In proportional spacing, an *i* occupies less space on the line than is taken up by an *M*. For text to align properly, the typist must put in tabs, not spaces. If an error occurs, the proofreader must request an alignment rather than a deletion of a space, as in the following example:

> Mollie, I would like you and Susan Snyder to check the following items for the party:
>
> ||
> Favors
>
> Place cards
>   Napkins
> Door prizes

In general, a passage set with proportional spacing will produce a shorter line than the same passage set with fixed spacing. Proportional-spaced type resembles typeset text rather than typewritten copy. Examples are shown below.

Proportional Spacing

> The man found the car located in a run-down used-car garage at Stonewall Corners. The garage, owned by Alley Hill, was not the type of place where one would expect to find a 1957 Chevy in "mint" condition.

Fixed Spacing

```
The man found the car located in a run-down used-
car garage at Stonewall Corners.  The garage,
owned by Alley Hill, was not the type of place
where one would expect to find a 1957 Chevy in
"mint" condition.
```

Another proofreading problem that arises from proportional spacing is that the two spaces following a period do not show up easily on a computer screen. They do not always show up well on the printed line, either, especially if the line is tight (very little space between words). This tight fit is a direct result of the proportional spacing and should not be marked as an error. (See the second line in the proportional spacing example above.)

Justification

Text can be set in several different alignment styles—left, full, center, or right justification. The style chosen will depend on the message being sent.

Left Justification Left justification is the most commonly used style. Lines begin evenly on the left side of the page and end in what is commonly called a "ragged right"—the lines are of uneven length and do not extend to the right margin. This is considered the easiest style of justification for the reader.

Full Justification Fully justified text is also considered easy to read; it is commonly used in textbooks and magazines. This style of justification produces a block of text because both the right and left ends of the lines abut the margins.

Center Justification Center justification means that every line is centered horizontally. Center justification is used for tables and titles. Centered text is considered formal and stiff, but it may be used for emphasis.

Right Justification Right-justified text has an even right side and a "ragged left." It is not often used since it is considered difficult to read. It is useful, however, for creating an index or a table of contents.

CHART 15.1 JUSTIFICATION STYLES

LEFT JUSTIFICATION	CENTER JUSTIFICATION
This text is left-justified. It aligns on the left side of the page and has a ragged-right edge. This style of justification is the most commonly used.	This text is center-justified. Notice that every line of the text is centered. Center justification is used for announcements and formal documents.
FULL JUSTIFICATION	**RIGHT JUSTIFICATION**
This text is fully justified. Notice that both the left and right margins end evenly. This style of justification is commonly used in magazines and newspapers.	This style is rarely used since it is very difficult to read. It is sometimes used in a table of contents or an index.

EXERCISE 15-E *Directions:* Using standard proofreaders' marks, enter any needed changes in the following letter. This exercise covers material presented in Chapters 1 through 15.

Courteous Canine Conservatory
6519 Shawick Lane • Kennesaw, GA 30144

March 3, 1999

Mr. Daniel Schwartz
Eleven Madison Place
Kennesaw, GA 30144

Dear Mr. Schwartz:

We have received your application for Ambrose's enrollment in the Courteous Canine Conservatory. We are pleased to let you know that you and Ambrose have been approved for admission to the 3C Novice Class.

Your class meets on Thursday nights from 7 p.m. to 8:15 p.m.. We ask that you try to arrive at the conservatory on Mussleman Road by 7 p.m., so Ambrose will have time to socialize for 15 minutes prior to class, he should then be ready to work when class begins.

Our classes hear at the 3C are small--only eight to a class. Your instructor will be Cassandra Jeffers. Cassandra has been with us for four years and has received excellant evaluations from here classes.

The first class will meet on March 19. For this class only, we ask that you leave Ambrose at home. You the handler, must be absolutely certain that you know what you are doing before you begin working with your dog. We can't send her mixed signals or she will be confused about what the correct behavior should be.

We're looking forward to seeing you on the 19th.

Sincerely

Courteous Canine Conservatory

Ruth Rogavin,
Owner

nk

EXERCISE 15-F

Directions: Using standard proofreaders' marks, enter any needed changes in the following report. This exercise covers material presented in Chapters 1 through 15. (Information for this report has been taken from the third edition of *The American Heritage Dictionary.*)

HOW MANY WORDS DID SHAKESPEARE USE?

You might think it would be easy to count the number of words in someone's book by a simple count of the words in the text. Indeed, Shakepeare's complete works contain 884, 647 words of text. Of those 884, 647 words, there are 29,066 different words—at least by one way of counting.

There are, however, several ways of counting words. Typing teachers define words in timings as five strokes on the keyboard. Dictation speeds are also counted in five-stroke words. Reading speeds are often computed the same way.

Students writing papers are likely to count every word, even those of one letter; it does, after all, help students to complete a 500-word paper a few words earlier. A few computer programs that do word counts include every word bounded by a space on either side. This method of counting was used to count the words in the complete works of Shakespeare mentioned in the first paragraph.

But is this method of counting words really accurate. Consider, for example, the words play, playing, plays, played. These words are all forms of the base word play, and together with the base word, they form a lemma, which is defined as a "set of grammatical forms, differing only in inflection". Counting lemmas may be a more accurate indication of word content than counting actual words. Shakespeare's complete works contain approximately 18,000 lemmas.

An even more startling fact is the finding that the 100 most often used lemmas account for 49.6 percent of all the words in the text. Indeed, 80 percent of the Shakespeare's complete works (just short of one million words) is made up of 2854 different word forms belonging to 2124 lemmas.

Does all this mean that Shakespeare didn't have a good vocabulary? The answer to this is, of course, no, but it does go to prove that it's not only what you say that is important, but how you say it.

Note: The word count on the above article, as computed by the Word Perfect for Windows software program, is 311 words.

EXERCISE 15–G *Directions:* Using standard proofreaders' marks, enter any needed changes in the following announcement. This exercise covers material presented in Chapters 1 through 15.

Its a Neighboorhood Block Party

Saturday, October 31

Lets Celebrate!

Its

HALLOWEEN

The fun begins at 6 a.m. and runs until midnight.
We'll be haunting the grounds at Marvin Frankensteens house
(28 Kensingham Lane).
Come dressed as your favorite hysterical figure.

Prizes for the best costume will be awarded
at the bewitching hour—Midnight.

IF YOUR NOT RIP THEN RSVP!

CHAPTER

16 Review

Proofreaders can never know exactly what types of mistakes they will encounter; they must always be alert for errors of any kind. The minisimulation in this review chapter is designed to allow you to practice your proofreading skills in locating errors based on any material covered in the first 15 chapters of this text. The following major topics are reviewed.

Apostrophes	Parallelism
Capitalization	Parentheses
Colons	Pronouns
Commas	Reading for meaning
Comma splices	Run-on sentences
Dashes	Semicolons
Divisions	Sentence fragments
Document format	Spelling
Document layout	Subject-Verb agreement
Other punctuation	Troublesome words

All exercises should be marked with standard proofreaders' marks. All documents in this minisimulation were prepared for Glascow Computers Inc. These documents pertain to a job search conducted through the office of Terri Martin, Personnel Manager.

PROOFREADING POINTER

When in doubt, check it out!

EXERCISE 16–A *Directions:* Correct this memo using standard proofreaders' marks.

MEMORANDUM

TO: Anton Schneider

FROM: Joe Christie, President

DATE: January 12, 1999

SUBJECT: Employee Search Committee

We have excepted, with regrets, the resignation of Rob Wright from his position of computer software specialist. Rob plans to move to California with his wife, we will certainly miss him. Even though we understand the need for the move, we are now faced with the difficult task of finding someone to replace Rob.

I know it is extra work to serve on employee search committees, but I feel that employees hired thru this process are the best assets are company can have. Anton would you be willing to serve on this search? If you will serve on the committee, please notify my secretary, Anita Friel at Ext. 234 by noon this Friday, January 14. I hope to schedule the first meeting next Wednesday morning.

af

EXERCISE 16-B *Directions:* Correct this memo using standard proofreaders' marks.

January 14, 1999

Anton Schneider

SEARCH COMMITTEE Meeting

The committee is now set and I think we have a great group of people ready to tackle the difficult task of filing the computer software specialist position. The first meeting will be held on January 20 at 9 a.m. in the Balistar Conference Room.

We'll be writting the position announcement and designing a candidate screening form. (The first advertisment will appear in the Sunday, January 23 paper). Terri Martin, Personnel Director, will be present to brief the committee on employment law.

The other members of the committee are: Sara Gibson, Ron Redferns, Gayle Jenkins. Barb Davis will be chairing the committee. If you have any questions, call Barb at Ext. 179.

af

EXERCISE 16-C *Directions:* Correct this job announcement using standard proofreaders' marks.

Announcing

Computer Software Specialist Position

POSITION: Computer Software Specialist

THE FIRM: Glascow Computers Inc. is a national company involved in the development and sales of computer software, hardware, and services. The corporate headquarters, which employs more than 3000 employees, is located in McLean, TX., at 1714 Mobeetie Road.

JOB DESCRIPTION: The computer software specialist operates and maintains computers in offices and training centers in the corporate headquarters. Responsibilities include establishing a priority system for control of network access; provide training for corporate office personnel; developing in-house training materials; developing software plans, suggestions, and solutions for office personnel, and ordering, maintaining, and installing all computer software.

QUALIFICATIONS: An associate degree or equivalent and three years' of related work experience are required. The successful canidate must be able to relate to and work with many diverse groups of company personal. Strong organizational skills are needed to handle the fast changing software environment; the technican must be able to quickly learn and evaluate new software packages.

EMPLOYMENT PERIOD This is a 12-month position. The salary is $28,000 -$34,000, based on qualifications. An excellent fringe-benefit package includes medical insurance, dental insurance, vision insurance, life insurance and a retirement plan.

APPLICATION: Interested applicants must submit a completed Glascow Computers Inc. application form, résumé, college transcripts, and the names and telephone numbers of four references. The search will continue until the position is filed.

CONTACT: Ms. Terri Martin, Personnel Manager
(806) 555-7269

GLASCOW COMPUTERS INC. IS AN EQUAL OPORTUNITY EMPLOYER

EXERCISE 16–D

Directions: Correct this letter using standard proofreaders' marks.

February 2, 1994

Ms. Ellen Casterline
567 Roberts Drive
Amarillo, Texas 79105

Dear Mrs. Casterline:

Our office received your resume, transcripts, and references, along with your request for more information about the computer software specialist position open here at the corporate headquarters.

Enclosed with this letter is the standard application form, which must be returned by February 24. This is the one piece of documentation needed to complete your application for the position of computer software specialist. The committee will be meeting that week to select the top three candidates for interviews, and you should here something within the next weak to ten days.

I can't answer all your questions about computer software and equipment used here in the corporate headquarters, but I can answer two of them.

1. The Pentium DOS system handles the majority of the computer load. Several of the Pentium DOS systems also have access to the mainframe computer which handle all company sales transactions. The computer software specialist is responsible for software installation and operation on the DOS systems only.

2. The primary software programs used in the building is WordPerfect for Windows, DATAB (Windows version), Excel for Windows, Calendar Creator Plus, Office Organizer, Instant Artist, and CorelDraw.

The search committee will be able to answer more of your questions if you are selected for and interview. I'll look forward to recieving your completed application form so you can be considered for the position.

Sincerely

Terri Martin
Personnel Manager

mw

EXERCISE 16-E *Directions:* Correct this letter using standard proofreaders' marks.

GLASCOW COMPUTERS INC.

1714 Mobeetie Road
McLean, TX 79057

February 23, 1999

Ms. Tammie Seevers
7612 El Dorado Way
Sayre, OK 73662

APPLICATION FOR EMPLOYMENT

We received your application for employment as a Computer Software Specialist. We are very impressed with your experience and background, especially in the computer networking system LANTIE.

While your background does not fit our needs in the computer software area, it matched perfectly with another position that has just opened up within are company. Our network specialist has had to move to Arizona to help take care of an ailing parent, we must replace him without delay since much of our sales system is on the LANTIE network.

Would you be willing to meet with our network administrator and discuss the position. If the network background is a match-—and we think it should be—we would be able to offer you a three month temporary position as a computer software specialist at a salary of $33,000 per month.

Glascow Computers, Inc., staff all positions through a search committee process. First consideration being given to in-house candidates. If you take on the temporary position, you would be considered an in-house candidate, and would be considered for the position before all outside candidates.

If you are interested in discussing this position, call my secretary, Mark Watton, at EXT. 224 before March 1. After that date, we will try to fill the position through one of the temporary services.

Ms. Terri Martin
Personnnel Director

mw

EXERCISE 16–F *Directions:* Correct this memo using standard proofreaders' marks.

M E M O R A N D U M

TO: Gayle Jenkins

FROM: Barb Davis, Chairman
Search Committee

DATE March 1, 1999

SUBJECT: Schedule for Search Committee Meetings

Following our meeting on January 21, the position announcement we designed appeared in Sunday paper for two consecutive weeks. We received 14 replies to the advertisement. Between the three papers we used, the advertisement in The Texas Star produced the most responses.

You will need to spend some time this week reviewing the applications and rating them on the evaluation tool we developed. Mark will be keeping the copies of the applications in his office, where you can also schedule time to use the small conference room adjoining my office for privacy. The evaluations need to be completed this week.

While I don't know how long it will take to finish the forms. I would like to suggest that you go through and scan the applications for the basic requirements—the required work experience and associate degree. Any applicant not meeting these requirements can be eliminated you won't have to spend time on those applications.

Our next schedule meeting will be on March 8 in the Balistair Conference Room at 9 a.m. We'll be ranking the candidates and setting up an interview schedule. If you have reviewed and ranked the applications prior to the meeting, the ranking and candidate selection should not be too time consuming.

mw

EXERCISE 16-G *Directions:* Correct this letter using standard proofreaders' marks.

GLASCOW COMPUTERS INC.
1714 Mobeetie Road
McLean, TX 79057

March 10, 1999

Ms. Billie Lou Harris
9909 East Oleta Way
McLean, Texas 79057

This letter confirms your interview for the Computer Software Specialist position at Glascow Computers Inc. on March 17 at 10 a.m. You will need to arrive promptly at the gate 3 entrance on Mobeetie Drive. Since our plant and offices are under tight security, my secretary, Mark Watton, will meet you and escort you to the personnel office.

The days' activities will consist of an interview with our company president, Edna Lemay Glascow, a tour of the facilities, a meeting with a represenative group of software users, lunch (on us, of course), and a group interview with our search committee. You can expect the entire interview to run from 10 a.m. until 3 p.m. Yes it is a long time for an interview but we want to make sure you would be as happy with us as we would be with you.

We have scheduled interviews for this position through March 25; The committee should make a recommendation on March 26. We will do reference check's early the following week, and should be able to make an offer of employment near the end of that week.

Would you please call Mark Watton at Ext. 242 to confirm your acceptance of the interview and your arrival time?

Sincerely,

Ms. Terri Martin
Personnel Manager

mw

CHAPTER

17 Number Usage

CHAPTER OUTLINE	RULES
Proofreading Tables and Columns	Number-Usage Rules
Proofreading Numbers in Text	**17.1** Basic Number Style
	17.2 Numbers Beginning a Sentence
	17.3 Fractions
	17.4 Commas
	17.5 Millions and Billions
	17.6 Related Numbers
	17.7–17.8 Side-by-Side Numbers
	17.9 Dates
	17.10–17.11 Clock Time
	17.12 Telephone Numbers
	17.13 Ages
	17.14 Anniversaries and Birthdays
	17.15 Ordinal Numbers
	17.16 Money, Measurements, Percentages, Decimals, and Numbers Used as Numbers
	17.17 Even-Dollar Amounts

RULES (CONTINUED)

Numbers present a special challenge to the proofreader. Imagine these situations:

- You've waited two weeks for your paycheck, which should amount to $724. The check you receive is for $72.40.
- Congress approves a one-time national deficit-reduction tax of $10 to be paid by each U.S. worker. With more than 100 million workers in the United States, that tax would reduce the deficit by $1 billion.
- When you type in your employer's income tax return, you accidentally add an extra 0 to the net income line. The Internal Revenue Service won't miss the error, and your boss certainly won't be amused when the audit notification arrives.

Errors in numbers, whether transpositions or inaccuracies, can create dramatic results.

Proofreading Tables and Columns

When proofreading tables and columns, use the back of a plain, solid-color ruler to mark your place as you check the columns. The front of the ruler contains lettering and numbers that could confuse or distract you as you read. The back is generally free of marks, and the solid color gives a visual guide for the eye. The following hints can help you catch errors that might otherwise be difficult to spot.

- When you check a column, move down, not across, the column, reading the entries one at a time.
- Add the columns, even if they're not totaled in the text. If your totals for the original and the copy are the same, the two versions probably have the same numbers.
- Check numbers to be sure they have the correct number of digits. For example, a social security number with eight digits should be checked because all social security numbers have nine digits.
- Make sure the decimal points, commas, parentheses, and dollar signs align in the column.
- Dollar signs should be placed on the first and last items in the column. They should be followed by enough space to allow them to clear the longest item.
- Check the headings and make sure they are consistently placed over columns. All should be either centered or flush with the left column; don't mix the two styles.
- Divide longer items into sections for easier reading. For example, 546,290,345 could be checked by threes (546 290 345).

➤ Have a co-worker read the numbers aloud while you check them. This is especially effective if the figures are complicated or extremely technical.

Proofreading Numbers in Text

PROOFREADING POINTER

When proofing numbers, it helps to:

➤ Use the back of a solid-color ruler to mark your place.

➤ Use a calendar to check whether dates and days of the week are correct.

➤ Use a calculator to check percentages, totals, and balances.

➤ Total columns on the original and the copy to be sure they agree.

Proofreading numbers in written text creates special problems. The numbers, especially when spelled out, are easily lost in the text; so they are hard to spot. Even as figures, numbers may appear jumbled because they are not in columns. Practice the following helpful hints when proofreading numbers in text.

➤ Check the text first. This will allow you to separate the numbers and words visually so that you can then concentrate on the numbers as if they were an isolated math problem without being distracted by reading the words between the numbers.

➤ Check all the numbers after you finish checking the text. This will allow you to concentrate on the numbers.

➤ Make sure all the numbers are logical. A letter containing a reference to an order placed in 1899 should raise an obvious question in a proofreader's mind.

➤ If possible, use a calculator to check totals, percentages, and balances.

➤ Make sure dollar amounts have a dollar sign. An omitted dollar sign can confuse the reader.

EXERCISE 17–A

Directions: You have been asked to verify the outstanding checks for the bank reconciliation statement for your employer. Compare the written information in the left column with the numbers in the right column. Assume the handwritten column is correct. Using standard proofreaders' marks, correct any errors in the column on the right. If both items in the right column are correct, circle the line number.

1.	23710	23710
	$225.90	$235.90
2.	23772	23712
	$23,711	$23,711
3.	23717	23717
	$123.83	$123,83
4.	23720	23720
	$29.95	$29.95
5.	27311	23711
	$234.96	$234.69
6.	23715	23715
	$45.09	$45.09
7.	23173	23713
	$98.59	98.59
8.	23719	23719
	$390.01	$390.01
9.	23714	23714
	$15.50	15.50
10.	23718	23718
	$5,667	$56.67
11.	23716	23716
	$515.93	155.93

EXERCISE 17–B

Directions: The two columns on the left are correct. Compare the columns on the right with the columns on the left and circle any errors.

	A		B	
1.	73296	13.24	73276	13.24
2.	70030	7.17	70030	7.19
3.	62235	32.44	62325	32.44
4.	81723	24.37	81723	24.37
5.	83179	13.26	83197	13.26
6.	56261	7.23	56261	7.33
7.	30349	11.49	30349	11.49
8.	30356	21.38	30356	21.38
9.	71179	32.75	71719	32.75
10.	63917	11.84	63719	11.89
11.	59640	11.27	59640	11.27
12.	52316	12.64	52396	12.67
13.	77815	14.33	74815	14.33
14.	94637	10.21	94637	10.21
15.	85073	15.72	85073	15.72

EXERCISE 17–C

Directions: For each of the following items, compare the numbers in columns *A*, *B*, and *C*. Then, in the blank space beside each entry, write the letter of the column that differs from the other two. If all three columns are identical, write an *S*.

		A	B	C
1.	_____	23988145	23988154	23988154
2.	_____	78954412	78954412	78954412
3.	_____	12569883	12659883	12659883
4.	_____	45678911	45678911	45679811
5.	_____	23544001	23544001	23544OO1
6.	_____	89712653	89712553	89712653
7.	_____	32987544	32987544	32987544
8.	_____	46509381	46509381	46509381
9.	_____	71146904	71196404	71146904
10.	_____	09786523	09786523	09768523

NUMBER-USAGE RULES

Basic Number Style

17.1 Spell out numbers one through ten. Use figures for numbers above ten.

➤ The manager hired *three* new employees.

➤ The coach benched *two* players for unruly conduct.

➤ According to state code, the banquet hall can hold *250* people.

➤ The classroom was so full that *11* students were forced to stand.

Numbers Beginning a Sentence

17.2 Spell out numbers when they begin a sentence.

➤ *Twenty-five* people were invited to the party.

➤ *Five* UFOs were spotted in the sky last Friday night.

Fractions

17.3 Spell out fractions that stand alone. Use figures for fractions that occur in mixed numbers (whole number and a fraction).

➤ When the plane took a nose dive, *one-half* of my pistachios rolled off the table tray.

➤ The club needed a *two-thirds* majority to elect new officers.

➤ Add $1\frac{1}{3}$ cups of flour to the pancake batter.

Commas

17.4 Use commas in numbers with five or more digits. Use a space instead of a comma in metric measurements.

➤ The candidate received *32,318* votes in the November election.

➤ The park manager needs *4231* tulip bulbs for the spring planting.

➤ The underground tank at the filling station in Ontario, Canada, holds *45 216* liters of gasoline.

Millions and Billions

17.5 Use figures and words when expressing large numbers with millions and billions.

➤ David won *$5.4 million* in the lottery.

➤ The earth's population will grow to *6.3 billion* by the end of the decade.

Related Numbers

17.6 Related numbers in a document should be written in the same style. If any of the numbers are above ten, use figures for all of the numbers.

➤ Mary Jo packed *7* pairs of jeans, *10* sweaters, and *12* pairs of socks.

➤ The office manager ordered 2 reams of laser paper, *12* boxes of paper clips, and *24* ink pens.

➤ Of the *75* glasses shipped, only *3* were broken.

Side-by-Side Numbers

17.7 When two numbers written in the same style appear side by side, separate the numbers with a comma. When the two numbers are written in different styles, no comma is needed.

➤ On page *654, 12* names were omitted from the guest list.

➤ In *1492 three* ships sailed from Spain to the New World.

➤ He received *six $20* bills as a Christmas bonus.

17.8 When two numbers appear side by side and one is a compound adjective, use figures for the larger number and spell out the smaller number.

➤ Did you pick up *7 six-pack* cartons of root beer?

➤ Will you be able to bring *five 20-pound* boxes in your car?

EXERCISE 17-D

Directions: Using standard proofreaders' marks, correct any errors in the following sentences. Indicate the rule number for each error you mark. If a sentence contains no errors, circle the number of the sentence. This exercise is based on Rules 17.1 through 17.8.

1. 25 employees attended the proofreading seminar held on March 25 in Columbus, Ohio.
2. According to the census taken in 1990 $2635 is spent annually per student in our public schools and universities.
3. Our company purchased three printers, 12 computers, and two and a half boxes of diskettes.
4. The former employee embezzled $7,000,000 from the profit-sharing fund.
5. On June 6 9 students attended the band camp held in Normal, Illinois.
6. Former Soviet President Mikhail Gorbachev spent 3 days in captivity following the August 18 coup.

7. The sun has a diameter of 864000 miles.
8. In Bangladesh approximately $\frac{1}{4}$ of primary-age children attend primary school.
9. The real estate agent showed us four 3-bedroom houses.
10. The real estate agent showed us three 4-bedroom houses.

EXERCISE 17–E

Directions: Using standard proofreaders' marks, correct any errors in the following letter, which is based on Rules 17.1 through 17.8.

June 15, 1999

Mr. John Calvinson
One Wilmington Circle
Elco, NV 89801

Dear Mr. Calvinson:

We received your letter of June 26 requesting 2 copies of our newest book, Writing in the Age of Computers. We are sending the copies you requested, along with some other information you may find useful as you prepare for your class at Wilton Career Center.

We publish 3 books dealing with writing. Of the three, one should be useful to you in your class. Approximately 1/2 of the book deals with composition skills; the remainder of the book deals with developing proofreading skills. 3 chapters in the beginning of the book train students to locate spelling and typographical errors. The remaining chapters cover basic writing and organization skills. In addition, all 1,234 pages contain logic errors for the student to correct. Starting on page 1201, you will find a listing of all rules presented in the text.

The book is designed to be used for 2 ten-week quarters. Appropriate overhead transparency masters and a test bank have been included.

As you mentioned, teaching an adult education class for the first time is indeed a challenge. If we can be of any further help, please let us know. Best of luck with your first teaching experience.

Sincerely,

Robin West
Western Region Sales Representative

kl

Enclosures

EXERCISE 17-F *Directions:* Using standard proofreaders' marks, correct any errors in the following manuscript. This exercise covers all material previously covered in this text.

COMPUTER VIRUSES

Virus is a word that has always brought to mind a cold with all the accompanying aches and pains. More recently, however, the word virus brings to mind another illness—this time a computer illness. For example, in 1988 a goverment computer in the Department of Defense was infected by a *virus* that ultimately shut down thousands of computers.

Some viruses destroy by using all the available memory in a computer; this will cause the computer to stop operating. Other viruses destroy data that cannot be recovered. Both types of viruses cost U.S. businesses millions of dollars.

Individuals creating viruses do for a variety of reasons. One group thinks setting a virus loose is "fun". The thrill comes from proving the system can be beaten. While no data are destroyed, time is lost in trying to repair the program.

Revenge seekers sometimes create viruses in an attempt to correct a perceived wrong. These viruses usually destroy data, the sabotage generally effects others as well as the intended target.

Criminally motivated saboteurs use computer terror in the some way bombs were used forty years ago. Extortion and violence are all too common in today's society, and coporations with large computer systems are at high risk. Bringing down a computer system with over three-hundred-thousand computers can cost millions. Unfortunately, protecting against this type of sabotage can also cost millions.

The fanatic or foreign agent is potentially the costliest of all computer saboteurs. Using the computer to launch missiles or destroy a countrys security will cost lives, not just money.

Much effort is currently being invested in creating vacines to prevent computer viruses. Unfortunately, while some minds are working to create vacines for existing viruses, other minds are working to create new types of viruses.

Dates

17.9 Use figures (without a *th*, *st*, or *d*) to express specific dates when the month appears before the figure. When the month appears after the figure, use the ordinal form (*th*, *st*, or *d*).

➤ The adorable baby was born on *December 18, 1992.*

➤ She was inducted into the army on the *3d of March.*

➤ The company picnic was held at Dillon State Park on *September 12.*

Clock Time

17.10 Use figures with *a.m.*, *p.m.*, or *o'clock.* Do not use a colon and two zeros to indicate that the time is on the hour.

➤ The breakfast meeting of the Board of Trustees was held at *7 a.m.* in the conference room.

➤ The plane was scheduled to land at *6:23 p.m.*

➤ It was *7 o'clock* in the morning when the phone rang.

17.11 If the clock time is expressed without the *a.m.*, *p.m.*, or *o'clock*, spell out the number.

➤ We planned to meet the candidate at *ten.*

➤ The student was scheduled to take the proficiency test at a *quarter past two* in the afternoon.

Telephone Numbers

17.12 Use figures to express telephone numbers. If an area code is given, it is preferable to enclose the area code in parentheses. Check your company's style, however; an alternate style hyphenates the area code.

➤ You may reach me at *(614) 555-7839* after 6 p.m.

➤ The receptionist left a message for the exterminators to call *555-1234.*

Ages

17.13 Spell out ages in general business writing. Use figures when the age appears immediately after a name; when the age is expressed in years, months, and days; or when the age appears in highly technical or legal material.

➤ Nancy Smith will turn forty this spring.

➤ David McKay, 52, was nominated for the Pulitzer prize.

➤ The reorganization of the company took 2 years, 5 months, and 17 days.

Anniversaries and Birthdays

17.14 Spell out anniversaries and birthdays if the number can be expressed in one word or two words. If the number is more than two words, use figures.

- ➤ My boss and her husband will celebrate their *twenty-fifth* anniversary this Friday.
- ➤ The company held an open house to celebrate its *131st* anniversary of service to the community.

Ordinal Numbers

17.15 Except for specific dates (see Rule 17.9), spell out ordinal numbers (first, second, twenty-second) that can be expressed in one word or two words.

- ➤ Kris Wortman won *first* place in shorthand transcription at the Business Professionals of America State Competitive Events.
- ➤ I wonder what computer technology will be like in the *twenty-first* century.

EXERCISE 17–G

Directions: Using standard proofreaders' marks, correct any errors in the following sentences. Indicate the rule number for each error you mark. If a sentence contains no errors, circle the number of the sentence. This exercise is based on Rules 17.9 through 17.15.

1. Please call me at 614-555-8889 before 7 o'clock this evening.
2. Susan B. Anthony Day, the birthday of a pioneer crusader for equal rights for women, is celebrated on February 15th every year.
3. Sadie Hawkins Day is celebrated the 1st Saturday in November.
4. The social hour will begin at 8.
5. John Adams and Thomas Jefferson, the second and third presidents of the United States, both died on July 4th, 1826, the 50th anniversary of the Declaration of Independence.
6. Molly Boggs's class begins at 8:15 a.m. on Fridays.
7. Rachel Smith, renowned expert in computer applications, will begin lecturing at 7:00 p.m. on Monday, September 15.
8. Bob Johansen, 55, was named president of the local small business management association.
9. Arnold Dietz was 45 in 1992.
10. On July 16th, 1994, Vanity Software agreed to sell its remaining assets, including its European rights to 45 patents, to International Widgetware for $60 million.

EXERCISE 17-H

Directions: Using proofreaders' marks, correct any errors in the following memorandum. This exercise covers Rules 17.9 through 17.15.

TO: Dale Armbruster

FROM: Ramone Inez

DATE: January 23, 1999

SUBJECT: Search Committee Orientation

Thank you for agreeing to serve on the search committee to hire a replacement for the business department chair who is retiring this June. As you are aware, this is an extremely important position, so we need to take special care in choosing this individual.

Our 1st meeting to discuss the requirements for this position will be held in the board room at seven o'clock on February 5th. If you are unable to attend, please call Sarah at 721-555-3923 by four. Dessert will be served.

We have already placed advertisements for this position in 7 magazines and newspapers. The Key to Education will not be able to include the advertisement until the 28 of January. The Local Press has run the advertisement 3 times and The Daily Dispatch twice. All the others will have run the advertisement weekly during January.

We have received several responses from potential candidates. Frances LaCourt, 42, has a doctorate in curriculum with 20 years of teaching experience. Steve Billings, 38, has finished his 6th year as the coordinator for the Adult Learning Center at Smith Community College. Mannie Jawoski, 52, is well published in the area of business management. Ruth Arpeggio, 47, has finished her 12th year as a coordinator for a training and consulting firm.

We have decided to keep all the applicant materials at Human Services with Imogene. Please set aside some time to review these materials before 5:00 next Friday.

We would like to have this position filled in time for our 50th anniversary celebration in order to maximize publicity.

Again, thank you for joining the committee. I look forward to working with you.

py

EXERCISE 17–1 *Directions:* Using standard proofreaders' marks, correct any errors in the following letter. This exercise covers all material previously discussed in the text.

June 31, 1999

Mr. Don Lambrusco
Dependible Dons Delivery Service
1579 Park Avenue
Springfield, IL 62703

Dear Mr. Lambrusco:

Musical Notes has appreciated you prompt accurate delivery service. We felt we could trust Dependable Don's Delivery Service to reach our special-order customer's with the merchandise in tax. We have also depended upon receiving supplies that were delivered by you in order to complete those special requests. Indeed, it seemed to be good business for both of us.

Unfortunately, there have been several mistakes these past 3 weeks that Musical Notes feel they can no longer overlook. 1st, we had sent Brown and Associates 3 8-pack containers of metronomes. Brown called us and said only 2 had a-rrived. On May 20, 2 cases of music stands, four guitars, and 13 record albums were delivered to 1 Parkway Avenue instead of 1 Park Avenue. Our Mesa Avenue store sent the main store an antique piano light, which arrived in twelve pieces. The shipment of specially designed paper, Invoice 372-411, was 8 days behind its usual delivery time, which made it impossible for us to use it in our 25th anniversary special. The 4th problem occurred on May 27th, only half of the xylophone parts arrived at the downtown location.

Whatever is causing these problems at your delivery service, we at Musical Notes hope you can remedy the situation immediately or we will be forced to take our business elsewhere. We

Mr. Don Lambrusco
Page 2
June 5, 1999

also request compensation for the problems listed above. Please call Ernest Wong at 713-555-3027 to discuss an equitable compensation settlement. We would expect to hear from you by the fourteenth of June.

Sincerely,

MUSICAL NOTES

Mr. Eric Masterson

js

Money, Measurements, Percentages, Decimals, and Numbers Used as Numbers

17.16 Use figures for amounts of money, measurements, percentages, decimals, and numbers used as numbers. Spell out the word *percent.*

➤ The employee was reimbursed *$27.15* from the petty cash fund for supplies.

➤ The executive's desk was *7* feet wide.

➤ We plan to offer the employees a *5 percent* increase in salary and benefits.

➤ The numbers *9* and *6* are easily transposed.

➤ The error we're trying to locate in this account is *79 cents.*

(Use of the dollar sign and decimal point for amounts under one dollar serves only to maintain consistency with other figures or to save space in tables.)

Even-Dollar Amounts

17.17 In even-dollar amounts, do not use a decimal point or zeros.

➤ The salary for the position is *$27,500* and is stated in the job description.

➤ I just spent *$110* on two new tires for the company van.

Indefinite Numbers

17.18 Spell out indefinite numbers and indefinite amounts of money.

➤ The average employee hopes to earn *millions of dollars* during a lifetime.

➤ The agency claimed there were *thousands of people* at the concert.

Numbers Paired With Nouns

17.19 Use figures when a number is paired with a noun and is part of a sequence. If the paired noun is the word *number, number* is abbreviated and capitalized. *Number* is not abbreviated if it is the first word of the sentence.

➤ I will be working on *Lesson 20.*

➤ Your new account is *No. 2365.*

➤ Number 2365 is your new account.

Omission of the Word *Number*

17.20 Omit the abbreviation for *number* when an identifying noun such as *room, page, invoice, check,* or *order* precedes the figure.

➤ In the process of moving, we have misplaced your Check 4599.

➤ The seminar will be held in Room 23 of College Hall.

Abbreviations and Symbols

17.21 Use figures with abbreviations and symbols in tables and forms. Avoid using abbreviations and symbols in standard business writing.

20%	I-70
SR 146	2 in.

EXERCISE 17–J

Directions: Using standard proofreaders' marks, correct any errors in the following sentences. Indicate the rule number for each error you mark. If a sentence contains no errors, circle the number of the sentence. This exercise is based on Rules 17.16 through 17.21.

1. According to the 1990 census, the average American without a high school diploma earned $452.00 monthly; with a high school diploma, $921.00; with a bachelor's degree, $1829.00; with a doctorate, $3637.00; and with a professional degree, $4003.00.
2. In 1990, 46% of school-age children used computers.
3. The Statue of Liberty was originally shipped from Rouen, France, in June 1885 in 100s of packing cases.
4. The head of the Statue of Liberty measures ten feet from ear to ear.
5. Kevin hoped to hear number three read as the winning number in the lottery.
6. The business card we found told us the owner of the wallet worked at Branch No. 23 of the Seldon National Bank.
7. We received your Check No. 235 for forty dollars in payment of your account.
8. We hope to collect 50 cents from every resident in the city to buy new uniforms for the band.
9. The government has indicated that higher education can expect budget cuts of 20% next year.
10. The winning ticket was announced as Number 4519.

EXERCISE 17–K *Directions:* Using standard proofreaders' marks, correct any errors in the following exercise. This exercise is based on the rules for number usage only.

SUPER LOTTO

On June 21st Suzanna was feeling unusually lucky. The Super Lotto jackpot was $22,000,000, so she stopped by a lottery ticket outlet. Suzanna knew that she would not be able to find much money since she had been unable to cash her paycheck that day and had changed purses that morning. Scrounging around in the bottom of her purse, Suzanna found less than $1.00. In fact, she could find only $0.88. She bowed her head in disappointment but suddenly was distracted by a shiny object on the ground. It was a dime, and now Suzanna had $.98, but only $.98! Where would she find two pennies? Suzanna was desperate! She just knew she would have the lucky number, so she sat down on the bench to think. Her back ached, and her feet throbbed. She thought disgustedly about having purchased shoes that were really too tight. Why had she insisted on penny loafers? Penny loafers! Yes, pennies! Suzanna kicked off her loafers, dug out the two pennies, and dashed back into the store with the final 2% that she needed to earn millions. Within minutes she was holding her lottery ticket—number 235200. In her mind she had begun to spend her 1,000,000s.

EXERCISE 17-L

Directions: Using standard proofreaders' marks, correct any errors in the following letter. This exercise covers all material previously discussed in this text.

June 3, 1999

Esther Dawson
The McMillan Hotel
28 East 23 St.
Dix Hills, NY 11746

Dear Ms. Dawson

We appreciate the time you spent with our committee last Wednesday. Our committee feels the Jefferson Lounge will be a delightful place to hold the social hour preceding the meeting; we anticipate that about 45 employees will attend the social hour on June 30. We do need to point out, however, that we have reservations for 60 for dinner in the Davis Room.

No special equipment will be necessary for the social hour, but we will need a projection screen for the after-dinner presentation. We plan to bring our own projecter. The table arrangements should be made so all seats have a restricted view of the screen. Additionally we will need a podium for the head table; there should also be 6 seats at the head table.

As we agreed at our meeting, we are enclosing a check for $250.50 to cover the initial deposit. Our singed copy of the contract is also enclosed.

Our company is certainly looking forward to our employee-appreciation night at the McMillan Hotel, Mrs. Dawsen.

Sincerely,

Mr. Kevin Masterson

ss

Enclosures (2

EXERCISE 17–M *Directions:* Using standard proofreaders' marks, correct any errors in the following manuscript. This exercise covers all material previously discussed in the text.

WHOSE THE MONKEY?

Mention the word *evolution* and most people think of either Charles Darwin or the Scopes Monkey trail. While Darwin's theory of evolution is the better known of the 2 topics, the Scopes Monkey Trial is popular in its own write. It didn't prove that the human race evolved from monkeys, but it did prove that man is quite capable of making a monkey out of themselves.

The trial, which ran for eleven days in 1925, was the 1st national radio broadcast of a trial in America. 200 or more media representatives covered the trial with over 65 telegraph operators on hand to send reports to newspapers and magazines. Prominent newspapers gave it front page coverage.

Clarence Darrow defended John Scopes, who was accused of teaching a theory that denied the story of the Divine Creation as taught in the Bible. William Jennings Bryan spearheaded the prosecution. Although charged with teaching evolution, Scopes's only experience with teaching biology had ocurred as a substitute, and that wasn't when the class was covering evolution. In addition to the issue of creationism versus evolutionism, the trial also raised concerns over the 1st Amendments right to the freedom of speech and the 14th Amendments provision for personnel liberty.

In actuality, religion was never the issue—money was. George W. Rappleyea and

F. E. Robinson, co-chairman of the county school board in Dayton, Tennessee conspired with other town officials in an effort to provide a boost for the local Dayton economy by bringing potential investors to the area. In order to preserve the publicity stunt they had to have the grand jury trial moved ahead 3 months on the schedule, organize an evolution protest, bring Scopes back from a vacation, and set up a private tutoring session in the back seat of a taxi so witnesses could truthfully say Scopes had taught evolution.

If the reasons for the trial was a hoax, the reported information about the trial was just as much a hoax. The storys about the trial concentrated on two issues—the freedom of speech for teachers in the classroom and a bias against Bryan who was rarely given credit for his logic and skilful argumentation. The coverage tended to ignore the unimportant issues of academic freedom of students and parental involvement in curricular decisions.

The jury deliberated for a mere nine minutes; the verdict was "quilty." Scopes was fined $100.00.

Evolutionism has never again been the issue it appeared to be in 1935. However, the effectiveness of the publicity stunt has lasted much longer than the effectiveness of the ver-dict. Bryant College was established by some trial participants as a memorial to Bryant, a 3rd edition of the trial transcript has been published, a Scopes Trial Museum exists as a National Historic Landmark, and a play and festival help the local community's economy every year. Today however, the festival and the play doesn't monkey with the truth; may be we have evolved after all.

CHAPTER

18

Numbered Lists

RULES

How many of the following lists have you ever used—perhaps even on a regular basis?

"To-do" list	Learning objectives	Job-duty descriptions
Grocery list	Assignments	Procedures
Sale items	Experiment directions	Inventories
Items to pack	Grade reports	Stock market figures
Recipes	Class lists	Agendas
Travel directions	Minutes of meetings	Sports scores

After looking over this "list of lists," you probably realize you, too, are a producer, reader, and user of lists or enumerations. Lists are handy items; since all the "extras" have been cut out, what is left is an easily discernible and highly visible piece of information. Items in a list can be used within a sentence or placed on separate lines, but should be consistent within a document. As with all writing, there are rules to make your numbered lists clear and effective pieces of communication.

NUMBERED-LIST RULES

Lists Within a Sentence

18.1 Use figures (or letters) enclosed in parentheses to number lists included within a sentence.

➤ We need to purchase the following items for the office: (1) plastic paper clips, (2) desk chairs, and (3) staplers.

18.2 Do not allow a line of text to break between the item's list number and the first word of that item.

➤ We need to purchase the following items for the office: (1) paper clips, *(2)*
desk chairs, and (3) staplers. (*Incorrect*)

➤ We need to purchase the following items for the office: (1) paper clips,
(2) desk chairs, and (3) staplers. (*Correct*)

➤ We need to purchase the following items for the office: (1) paper clips, *(2) desk*
chairs, and (3) staplers. (*Correct*)

Lists on Separate Lines

18.3 Use a figure (or letter), a period, and two spaces before items listed on separate lines.

➤ We need to purchase the following items for the office:

1. Paper clips
2. Desk chairs
3. Staplers

Format of Numbered Lists on Separate Lines

(See sample letters on pages 315 and 316 of this chapter.)

18.4 Allow an extra line space before and after a numbered list.

18.5 Capitalize the first word of items listed on separate lines.

18.6 Single-space the lines within the items in a numbered list.

18.7 In general, allow an extra line space between the items in a list. If space is limited, it is permissible to single-space the items if no item has more than one line, but double-spacing is preferred.

18.8 Listed items in a document can be typed the full width of the line or can be indented five spaces (or half an inch) on both sides. Be consistent within a document.

18.9 Two spaces follow the period and the number in listed items. Remember to align the periods. In documents with indented paragraphs, a list indention can be more than two spaces to enable either the numbers of the list or the first word of the entries to align with the first word in the indented paragraph.

18.10 A period follows listed items that are sentences, dependent clauses, long phrases on separate lines, or short phrases (if the phrases are needed to complete the sentence). No period is needed following short listed items if the statement preceding the listed items is a complete sentence.

18.11 If any item occupies two lines, the first word on the second line aligns with the first word on the line above.

Parallel Structure

18.12 Items in a numbered list should be presented in parallel structure.

FIGURE 18.1 NUMBERED LISTS (BLOCK)

July 27, 1999

Pandora's Box
456 Easter Walk
Cornwall Bridge, CT 06754

Ladies and Gentlemen:

I recently received a copy of your catalog in the mail. Along with the catalog came a gift certificate good for 50 percent off the items listed on pages 112 through 117 if I placed an order between July 20 and July 28. Since I am always interested in a bargain, I turned quickly to page 112 and started looking through the catalog. You can imagine my surprise when I found that I had no pages 115 or 116. What happened? Was my catalog a misprint? I feel sure that this was not intentional since you run a mail-order service and the order form was also missing.

This is not really a complaint letter, but since I found several items of interest on the pages in my catalog, I wondered what delights might appear on the missing pages. Could you possibly supply me with another copy of your catalog and then extend the deadline on the sale to give me the opportunity to order the "invisible" items on pages 115 and 116.

I would like to order the following items:

1. Felt-tip markers with holder (120) with the name of my business printed on the stand.

2. Dictionaries (120) with the name of my business printed on the outside leather cover.

3. Digital alarm clocks (50) with the name of my business printed on the face of the case of the clock.

The information form for the company name is enclosed with this letter along with a copy of our PO 6890.

I am looking forward to receiving a copy of the complete catalog. Your executive gift items are delightful.

Sincerely,

Ms. Andrea Karmody

kd

Enclosure

FIGURE 18.2 NUMBERED LISTS (INDENTED)

July 27, 1999

Pandora's Box
456 Easter Walk
Cornwall Bridge, CT 06754

Ladies and Gentlemen:

I recently received a copy of your catalog in the mail. Along with the catalog came a gift certificate good for 50 percent off the items listed on pages 112 through 117 if I placed an order between July 20 and July 28. Since I am always interested in a bargain, I turned quickly to page 112 and started looking through the catalog. You can imagine my surprise when I found that I had no pages 115 or 116. What happened? Was my catalog a misprint? I feel sure that this was not intentional since you run a mail-order service and the order form was also missing.

This is not really a complaint letter, but since I found several items of interest on the pages in my catalog, I wondered what delights might appear on the missing pages. Could you possibly supply me with another copy of your catalog and then extend the deadline on the sale to give me the opportunity to order the "invisible" items on pages 115 and 116.

I would like to order the following items:

1. Felt-tip markers with holder (120) with the name of my business printed on the stand.

2. Dictionaries (120) with the name of my business printed on the outside leather cover.

3. Digital alarm clocks (50) with the name of my business printed on the face of the case of the clock.

The information form for the company name is enclosed with this letter along with a copy of our PO 6890.

I am looking forward to receiving a copy of the complete catalog. Your executive gift items are delightful.

Sincerely,

Ms. Andrea Karmody

kd

Enclosure

EXERCISE 18–A

Directions: Using standard proofreaders' marks, correct any errors in the following letter. This exercise covers the rules in this chapter.

THE SUPERSAVER CLUB

Sponsored by Ferdinand's Food Emporium

783 McCallister Road • Cornwall Bridge, CT 06754

September 7, 1999

Mr. Edward Eskels
4590 Jessup Drive
Cornwall Bridge, CT 06754

Dear Mr. Eskels:

With your last visit to Ferdinand's, you completed the eligibility visits to our store. It is a great pleasure for Ferdinand's Food Emporium to welcome you as a member of the SuperSaver Club; you'll find your membership card enclosed. This small card is your passport to the large savings that only members of the SSC circle enjoy. The details of your membership benefits are listed below:

(1.) You are entitled to a 10 percent bonus savings on all 20 items listed in the front of the store. The list changes every Wednesday and is posted only in our store.

(2) You are entitled to a 5 percent discount if you shop on Tuesday morning between the hours of 9 a.m. and noon.

(3) You will receive automatic check approval without the lengthy waits you sometimes encounter in other stores. Just show your card when you check out.

(4) You will have a chance at our $25 shopping spree every time your SSC number is entered in the cash register. One number is selected at random by the computer on Monday, and that number will remain in the computer for the entire week. If your SSC number is keyed in, you'll hear the cash register bell sound (loudly, we might add), and the store manager will credit you with $25.

We hope that all of these activities will add to your enjoyment of shopping in Ferdinand's Food Emporium. We're looking forward to your continued patronage in our store.

Happy shopping,

Miss Felicia Ferdinand, Owner

lg

Enclosure

EXERCISE 18-B *Directions:* Using standard proofreaders' marks, correct any errors in the following memorandum. This exercise covers the rules in this chapter.

TO: Andrea Lutz

FROM: Susan Kee
Chair, Seasonal Encounter Committee

DATE: November 1, 1999

SUBJECT: Plans for 1999 Seasonal Encounter

Last year Jeff Grimes, CEO, discovered that only 50 percent of the employees attended our Christmas party; he was disturbed, to say the least. During January of this year, he made an informal survey of the 23 employees who did not attend our holiday social event. What he found was surprising.

1. Four employees did not attend for religious reasons.
2. Seven employees did not attend because of other obligations that occurred on the same evening.
3. Twelve employees did not attend because of illness, including illness of children when no baby-sitter was available.

The charge of the Seasonal Encounter Committee was to find a party format that would bring as close to 100 percent attendance as possible. Since the goal of the party was to reward all employees for productivity during the year, we felt a change in format was needed.

This year we will be holding a seasonal encounter day here at work with entertainment, refreshments, activities, a scavenger hunt, and a catered lunch. The offices will be officially closed during the encounter day; no appointments will be scheduled. All employees will be dismissed at 1:30 p.m. and will receive full pay for the day.

We felt this would solve the problem of poor attendance for the following reasons: (a) All employees would be at work since this is a normal work day, (b) Employees would have access to day care since their regular baby sitters would be watching their children, (c) employees will not have conflicts with this seasonal observance since no religious themes will be followed. We hope you approve of our solution; if this does not work out as expected this year, we can change the format again next year.

sj

EXERCISE 18-C

Directions: Using standard proofreaders' marks, correct any errors in the following letter. This exercise is a text review.

September 9, 1999

Ms. Mai Li, Editor
The Publishing Company
501 Washington Avenue
Rowley, MA 02127

Dear Ms. Li

Here is the manuscript— at least part of it. Only a day or two late and probably ten reams of paper later, the first 12 of the 20 chapters are in this box. Its been quiet a project but we are pleased with the outcome.

You will find in this pandora's box the following:

1) Camera ready copies of our work.

2) A double spaced copy of the manuscript. We were not concerned with spacing or page breaks on this copy since this is for editing purposes. This copy also includes your completed keys for all the exercises.

If an exercise has been made camera-ready, we have indicated that on the double spaced copy and have attached a duplicate with the key marked in red. All materials in red are *only* for the instructors edition. Materials marked in purpel should be included in the student text.

3) A single spaced copy of the manuscript. This copy is for your reference so you can double-check the exercises if you have questions. They give a better idea of spacing then does double-spaced copy.

We have talked about many things over the course of the books development. Just as a reminder were including a brief list of suggestions to be considered in the books desing.

2

September 9, 1999

1. A gray (or other color) numbered line should be placed next to camera-ready exercises to help instructor's and students locate errors to be corrected.

2. The number of errors should also be included on the instructors key.

3. A copy of a 1999 Calender must be included in the book, preferably on the inside back or front cover.

4. A list of the rule headings should be placed at the beginning of the chapter, this can be used in place of behavioral objectives.

6. A listing of the two letter state abreviations should be placed on the inside front or back cover.

7. To add authenticity perhaps you're art department could design letterheads for some of the letters.

8. A relisting of the rules and lists might be included in a appendix. We also like the idea of a fold out list of proofreading symbols but we would have to mark them in some way so the sections agree with the exercises in chapter 1.

9. The boxes (proofreading pointers) may be designed in what ever way you feel would be appropriate. Feel free to change their name as well.

Our curiosity will be killing us as we wait to see what you come up with in the design and layout of the book. We'd love to be kept as up to date as your policy allows.

Sincerely,

Ms. Sharon A. Souder

Ms. Cherie C. White

EXERCISE 18-D *Directions:* Using standard proofreaders' marks, correct any errors in the following article. The exercise is an all-text review.

Entertainment or One-Upmanship?

Sometime near the end of 1881 or the beginning of 1982, George Washington Gale Ferris attended a banquet for engineers and architects in Chicago. Although the building director, Daniel H. Burnham, praised the beautiful buildings that had been designed for the Worlds Columbian Exposition, his only real regret was that no building equaled the Eiffel Tower, the star of the 1879 International Exposition.

Although Eiffel had offered to design something for the fair, the American planners felt that any tower built for the exposition should be designed by Americans. Always one to accept a challenge, Ferris started working on four or five ideas at a Saturday afternoon club meeting. Ferris claimed that before the day was over he had decided on the size, the construction, the number of cars, the price, and the plans for loading passengers.

The original design included two circles with railroad style cars attacted to the outer circle. Although Ferris claimed the design was completed in a day, the controversy over the feasibility of the wheel continued even after the ride opened at the Exposition. Ferris spent $25,000.00 on the plans that he submitted to the fair's directors. The idea was certainly one to surpass the Eiffel Tower, so the directors gave permission. Claims of fawlty design and feasibility of the wheel may have then caused them to question their decision because they almost immediately withdrew their approval. On November 29, 1982 the directors once again gave the go-ahead on the project. Unlike the designers of the Eiffel Tower, however, Ferris had to locate his own financing.

Ferris purchased some of the first materials on his own personal credit, but was finally able to attract investors, including a railroad magnate, and a judge. With financing assured, the major problem remaining was a lack of time. Only twenty-two weeks remained before the fair's opening in May, 1893.

Construction Problems Abound

Construction on the project required patience and persistence. Many of the parts were manufactured in Detroit, Cleveland, Youngstown, Ohio, Pittsburgh, and Bethlehem, Pennsylvania. The parts were then shipped to Chicago by rail. Concrete footers for the ride had to be poured in temperatures often below freezing; steam was used to keep the concrete from freezing.

The wheel was about as high as a 26-story building and workers had to assemble the intricate ironwork and engines in the extreme cold and wind. Powered by a coal-fired steam engine, the wheel was equipped with a westinghouse air break.

Ferris was not even in town on the day when the moment of truth arrived. He was in Pittsburgh and did not hear what was reportedly a "most horrible noise" when the wheel began to turn. It did, however, work as advertised.

A Late Beginning

On June 21 (only seven weeks late), the wheel officially opened with ceremonial speeches and the music of the Iowa State Band which occupied one of the cars. Each of the 26 gondolas had a uninformed conductor to open doors, answer questions, and calm passengers. Each car had 40 swiveling stools and standing room for another 20 passengers. The large widows could be opened for ventilation but was covered with iron grating to inhibit jumpers.

The operation was a complete success. The half-hour ride cost 50 cents, a steep charge at the time, (about the price of two men's shirts). By the time the fair closed, the wheel had brought in approximately $713,000. Ferris had spent more than $325,000 on constructions costs. An agreement with the fair board gave half of all receipts over $300,000 to the fair. In addition, Ferris had to pay wages for conductors, maintenance workers and ticket sellers.

To try to earn some extra income on the enormously expensive wheel, Ferris attempted to run the wheel on the day after the fair closed, November 1. Security guards tried to keep the riders away and police were eventually called to restore order. Abandoning the original cite, Ferris moved the wheel to another location in Chicago. Tickets were to expensive, however, and the view was less than breathtaking. Although the Ferris Wheel Company attempted to regroup, the original wheel was eventually sold at auction to the Chicago House Wrecking Company; the wheel was destroyed after one final run in St. Louis.

The Spirit Lives On

Several smaller wheels were constructed and were run profitably, and one larger wheel was built by the French for the Paris International Exposition of 1900. The most enduring legacy of the wheel came via William E. Sullivan of Roodhouse, Illinois who had ridden the original wheel at the fair. He developed and marketed the smaller portable wheel seen at almost every county fair in the summer. What started as one-upmanship with the French has become a symbol of entertainment to Americans.

CHAPTER

19 Abbreviations

CHAPTER OUTLINE	RULES
Common Abbreviations	Rules for Abbreviations
	19.1 Spacing After Periods
	19.2–19.4 Titles Before Names
	19.5 Initials
	19.6–19.8 Abbreviations Following Names
	19.9 Time
	19.10 Days and Months
	19.11 Measurements

We live in such a busy and fast-paced world that most of us try to cut as many corners as we can. Abbreviations and acronyms are ways of saving some time and space in writing. Unfortunately, we probably see many abbreviations and acronyms we don't understand. Have you ever been puzzled by any of the following?

- I need the forms for MBOs ASAP.
- When I do my YTD report, I am sure to use a WYSIWYG word-processing program.
- The MADD meeting will begin at 7 p.m.

➤ I will be taking FORTRAN and COBOL this quarter.

➤ TGIF!

In general, abbreviations are avoided in business and formal writing. However, when used sparingly, they can be part of an effective communication if a writer analyzes the intended audience's vocabulary, the writing situation, and the proper rules of abbreviation.

RULES FOR ABBREVIATIONS

Spacing After Periods

19.1 Space once after a period following an abbreviation unless the abbreviation falls at the end of a sentence and the period serves as ending punctuation or is immediately followed by the ending punctuation.

➤ We nominated John Smith Jr. He should be an exceptional candidate.

➤ Does Dixie Gregg have an M.B.A.?

Titles Before Names

19.2 Abbreviate personal courtesy titles used before names.

Ms. Kosco *Dr.* Timmons
Mr. Frisby *Mrs.* Malloy

19.3 Spell out civil, educational, military, and religious titles used before a last name when no first name is included. When both the first and last names are given, it is still preferable to spell out the title, but the title may be abbreviated to save space.

➤ *State Representative* Libben was the guest speaker at the conference.

➤ *Colonel* Joseph Timmons accepted command in April.

19.4 *Reverend* and *Honorable* are never abbreviated when preceded by the word *the.*

➤ *The Reverend* Joanna Cummings officiated at the wedding.

Initials

19.5 Initials used in a name are abbreviations. Each initial is followed by a period and a space.

➤ The chair of the finance committee is *R. J.* Bender.

Abbreviations Following Names

19.6 Abbreviate the words *junior* (*Jr.*), *senior* (*Sr.*), and *esquire* (*Esq.*) when they follow a first and last name. These words are not used following a last name when no first name is present. A courtesy title may also precede a name followed by *Jr.* or *Sr.* but is never used with *Esq.*

➤ These people were on the men's athletic committee: Tray Barsalou *Jr.*, James Jones *Sr.*, and Austin Stoecker *Esq.*

➤ *Mr.* Lewis Caldwell *Sr.* will be retiring next month; Caldwell has been employed 35 years.

19.7 Abbreviate or spell out *Inc.* (*Incorporated*) and *Ltd.* (*Limited*) when they are included at the end of a company name; follow the preference of the company if it is known. Abbreviate these words if the company preference is unknown.

➤ Wise *Inc.* has been here for only 13 years. Widgets *Limited* has been in business for 25 years. (*Limited* is a company preference.)

19.8 Omit courtesy titles before a name when an academic degree follows the name.

➤ The college president is Lynn Willett, *Ph.D.*, and the vice president of instruction is Dolores Floria, *Ed.D.*

EXERCISE 19–A

Directions: Using standard proofreaders' marks, make all necessary corrections in the following sentences. This exercise covers Rules 19.1 through 19.8.

1. Mr. Bruce Cline Esq. and Mr. Jim Sorrels Jr. will be accepting the positions as consultants next month.
2. Mr. Sorrels Jr.was previously employed by Haskins & Sons Inc.
3. Bruce Cline Esq. had been the senior consultant for Wolfe Advertising Ltd.
4. Dr. Dixie Stone, Ph.D., will be the commencement speaker.
5. The Hon. Linda M. Lillie and the Rev. David Caldwell will cosponsor the exchange student this year.
6. Lt. Jane Bender will be visiting her parents in Sheridan, Montana, next week.
7. Dr. Debbie Henderson and Dr. Jane Allwardt will be coediting the newsletter.
8. Ms Lynn Alexander and Col. Robert Dunavant have announced their engagement.
9. Ms. Sue Gibson, CPA, and Ms. Deb Wilson, M.B.A., have opened Accounts & Taxes Limited.
10. Mayor Quinn presented the trophy to C.A. Kolpitcke.

EXERCISE 19-B

Directions: Using standard proofreaders' marks, make all necessary corrections in the following memorandum. This exercise covers Rules 19.1 through 19.8.

MEMORANDUM

TO: Dr. Kay Roach, Ph.D.

FROM: Susan Henderson, Chair

DATE: September 22, 1999

SUBJECT: Selection of Student Enrollment Task Force

Since the college is always concerned about enrolling and maintaining students, the faculty has decided to form a communitywide student enrollment task force. We want to make sure this committee includes representatives from every level of the college and from the community.

After receiving many recommendations and reviewing the tasks for this coming year, we are asking these individuals to serve on the committee: Becky Anderson, M.B.A.; Judy Barnhardt, RN; Randy Hutchinson Junior; the Rev. Beverly Janke; Dr. Elizabeth Libben, M.D.; Mr. Samuel Manford Senior; Don Neumann, Ed.D.; Lt. Judy Ore; Dr. Stephen Rostek Esquire; JoAnne Smith, Ph.D.; and Father Harlan Soppe.

The meeting will be held in the conference room of Manford Manufacturing Inc. on Monday, October 11, at 7:30 p.m. State Sen. Deb Stockwell has graciously agreed to speak to us about the state's educational and fiscal concerns for the upcoming year. Caring Caterers Ltd. will be serving dessert. You are most welcome to attend our kickoff meeting.

Thank you.

lk

Time

19.9 Write the abbreviations for time (*a.m.* and *p.m.*) in lowercase letters followed by periods with no internal spacing. The abbreviation *o'clock* (of the clock) is used only in formal writing.

➤ Cindi Clifton has an appointment at *9 a.m.* this coming Tuesday.

➤ The Reverend Daniels requests the honor of your presence for the opening ceremonies at *7 o'clock.*

Days and Months

19.10 Do not abbreviate the days of the week or the months of the year in general writing. The abbreviations listed below may be used only in tables, lists, and charts.

DAYS OF THE WEEK

WORD	STANDARD ABBREVIATION	1- OR 2-LETTER ABBREVIATION
Monday	Mon.	M
Tuesday	Tues.	Tu
Wednesday	Wed.	W
Thursday	Thurs.	Th
Friday	Fri.	F
Saturday	Sat.	Sa
Sunday	Sun.	Su

MONTHS OF THE YEAR

WORD	STANDARD ABBREVIATION	1- OR 2-LETTER ABBREVIATION
January	Jan.	Ja
February	Feb.	F
March	Mar.	Mr
April	Apr.	Ap
May	May	My
June	June	Je
July	July	Jl
August	Aug.	Ag
September	Sept.	S
October	Oct.	O
November	Nov.	N
December	Dec.	D

Measurements

19.11 In general, spell out units of measure, although they may be abbreviated in tables, forms, and invoices. No period follows the abbreviation; the same abbreviation represents both singular and plural units of measure.

➤ The desk measures 3 *feet* 7 *inches* and weighs 72 *pounds.*

➤ Object	Length	Height	Width/Depth	Weight
Desk	3 ft 7 in	2 ft 10 in	2 ft 3 in	72 lb

PROOFREADING POINTER

Acronym or abbreviation? Acronyms are words formed from the initial letters of a series of words. They generally are written in capital letters. Unlike regular abbreviations, acronyms are pronounced as one word.

EPCOT	Experimental Prototype Community of Tomorrow
PIN	Personal Identification Number
SADD	Students Against Drunk Driving
ZIP	Zone Improvement Plan

Common Abbreviations

Many commonly used abbreviations are included in the following table. A standard dictionary is the best source for correct abbreviations if you cannot find what you need in the list. Abbreviations vary in capitalization, punctuation, and spacing; be sure to consult a source for accuracy.

Word	Abbreviation
account	acct.
accounts payable	AP
accounts receivable	AR
Acquired Immune Deficiency Syndrome	AIDS
Alcoholics Anonymous	AA
all but dissertation	ABD
also known as	aka
American Automobile Association	AAA
American Civil Liberties Union	ACLU
American Standard Code for Information Interchange	ASCII
anno domini	A.D.
anonymous	anon.
ante meridiem	a.m.
as soon as possible	ASAP
assistant	asst.
associate	assoc.
associate of arts	A.A.
association	assn.
attention	attn.
attorney	atty.
audiovisual	AV
automated teller machine	ATM
auxiliary	aux.
average	avg.
bachelor of arts	B.A.
bachelor of education	B.Ed.
bachelor of science	B.S.
bale	bl
bedroom	bdrm.
before Christ	B.C.
before the Common Era	B.C.E.
Beginner's All-Purpose Symbolic Instruction Guide	BASIC
Better Business Bureau	BBB

Word	Abbreviation
bill of sale	B/S or BS
binary digit	bit
Boulevard	Blvd.
brigadier general	B.G. or Brig. Gen.
British thermal unit	Btu
brothers	bros.
building	bldg.
Bureau of Indian Affairs	BIA
bushel	bu
carbon copy	cc
care of	c/o
cash (or collect) on delivery	COD or c.o.d.
cathode-ray tube	CRT
Celsius	C
centimeter	cm
central daylight time	CDT
Central Intelligence Agency	CIA
central processing unit	CPU
Central Standard Time	CST
certificate of deposit	CD
Certified Professional Secretary	CPS
Certified Public Accountant	CPA
characters per inch	cpi
characters per second	cps
chief executive officer	CEO
citizens band	CB
colonel	Col.
common business-oriented language	COBOL
community antenna television	CATV
compact disc–read-only memory	CD-ROM
company	Co.
computer-aided design	CAD
computer-aided manufacturing	CAM
computerized axial tomography	CAT
consumer price index	CPI
continued	cont.
copyright	cop.
coronary care unit	CCU
corporation	corp.
credit	cr.
cubic centimeter	cc
data processing	DP
Daughters of the American Revolution	DAR
daylight saving time	DST
dealer	dlr.
delivery	dlvy.
demilitarized zone	DMZ
department	dept.
Department of Defense	DOD
deputy	dept.
desktop publishing	DTP
direct current	DC or dc
discount	dis.
disk operating system	DOS
distributor, distribution, distributed	distr.
district	dist.
dividend	div
division	div.
doctor of dental surgery	D.D.S.
doctor of veterinary medicine	D.V.M.
document	DOC
double	dbl.
down	dn.
dozen	doz.
Eastern Standard Time	EST
electrocardiogram	EKG
electron	e
elementary	elem.
emergency medical technician	EMT
enclosure	enc.
engine	eng.
England	Eng.
English as a second language	ESL
ensign	Ens.
Equal Rights Amendment	ERA
Equal Employment Opportunity Commission	EEOC
esquire	Esq.
estimated time of arrival	ETA
et alii (and others)	et al.
et cetera (and so forth)	etc.
executive	exec.
extrasensory perception	ESP
facsimile transmission	FAX
Fahrenheit	F
Federal Bureau of Investigation	FBI
Federal Housing Administration	FHA

Word	Abbreviation
figure	fig.
first in, first out	FIFO
fiscal year	FY
Food and Drug Administration	FDA
foot	ft
for example	e.g.
formula translation	FORTRAN
for your information	FYI
forward	fwd.
free on board	f.o.b. or FOB
gallon	gal
grade-point average	GPA
gram	g
Grand Old Party (Republican)	GOP
gross	gr.
gross national product	GNP
headquarters	hdqrs. or HQ
health maintenance organization	HMO
height	hgt.
Her or His Majesty's Ship	HMS
high school	H.S. or HS
highway	hwy.
horsepower	hp or HP
Housing and Urban Development	HUD
I owe you	IOU
ibidem (in the same place)	ibid.
identification data	ID
inches	in
including	incl.
incorporated	Inc.
individual retirement account	IRA
integrated circuit	IC
intelligence quotient	IQ
intensive care unit	ICU
Internal Revenue Service	IRS
introduction	intro.
Juris Doctor (Doctor of Laws)	J.D.
Justice Department	JD
karat	k
kelvin	K
kilogram	kg
kilometer	km
kilowatt	kW
last in, first out	LIFO
Library of Congress	L.C.

Word	Abbreviation
limited	Ltd.
local area network	LAN
lowercase	lc
magnetic resonance imaging	MRI
management information system	MIS
manufacturing	mfg.
Master of Business Administration	M.B.A.
master of ceremonies	M.C.
maximum	max.
Medicinae Doctor (Doctor of Medicine)	M.D.
memorandum	memo
merchandise	mdse.
mile	mi.
miles per gallon	mpg
miles per hour	mph
military police	MP
milligram	mg.
milliliter	ml
minimum	min.
minute	min
miscellaneous	misc.
Modern Language Association	MLA
monosodium glutamate	MSG
month	mo.
mortgage	mtg.
Mountain Standard Time	MST
National Aeronautics and Space Administration	NASA
National Basketball Association	NBA
National Football League	NFL
National Organization for Women	NOW
net in 30 days	n/30
New York Stock Exchange	NYSE
not applicable	N/A
not in my backyard	NIMBY
nota bene (note well)	N.B.
notary public	N.P.
Nuclear Regulatory Commission	NRC
number	no.
Occupational Safety and Health Administration	OSHA
okay	OK
operating room	OR
optical character recognition	OCR

Word	Abbreviation
Organization of Petroleum Exporting Countries	OPEC
ounce	oz
over the counter	OTC
overdose	od
Pacific Standard Time	PST
package	pkg.
page, pages	p., pp.
paid	PD.
parcel post	PP
part	pt.
personal computer	PC
personal identification number	PIN
Philosophiae Doctor (Doctor of Philosophy)	Ph.D.
pint	pt
port of entry	POE or p.o.e.
post meridiem	p.m.
post office	P.O.
postscript	PS
pound	lb
pro tempore	pro tem.
prepaid	ppd.
public relations	PR
public address	PA
quantity	qty.
quart	qt
quarter	qtr.
radio detecting and ranging	radar
random-access memory	RAM
read-only memory	ROM
ream	rm.
received	recd.
regarding	re
registered	reg.
registered nurse	RN
répondez s'il vous plaît (please reply)	RSVP
research and development	R&D
revised	rev.
revolutions per minute	rpm
route	Rte.
Royal Canadian Mounted Police	RCMP
rural delivery	RD
save our ship	SOS
savings and loan association	S&L
Scholastic Aptitude Test	SAT
second	sec
secretary	sec.
Securities and Exchange Commission	SEC
self-addressed, stamped envelope	SASE
self-contained underwater breathing apparatus	scuba
Small Business Administration	SBA
sound navigation ranging	sonar
square inch	sq in
standard	std.
standard operating procedure	SOP
standing room only	SRO
Students Against Drunk Driving	SADD
Tactical Air Command	TAC
television	TV
tender, loving care	TLC
that is	i.e.
trademark	TM
transaction	trans.
transfer	tfr.
treasurer	treas.
trinitrotoluene	TNT
ultraviolet	UV
unidentified flying object	UFO
United Press International	UPI
United Nations	UN
United Service Organizations	USO
United States	U.S.
United States Department of Agriculture	USDA
universal	UNIV.
Universal Product Code	UPC
university	Univ.
versus	vs.
very important person	VIP
Veterans Administration	VA
vice versa	v.v.
video display terminal	VDT
voice mail	VM
volume	vol.
weight	wt.
what you see is what you get	WYSIWYG
wholesale	whsle.
Wide-Area Telecommunications Service	WATS
with	w/
Women's Army Corps	WAC
word processing	WP

Word	Abbreviation	Word	Abbreviation
words per minute	wpm	year	yr.
World Health Organization	WHO	year of birth	YOB
World War I	WWI	year to date	YTD
yard	yd	Zone Improvement Plan	ZIP

EXERCISE 19–C

Directions: Write the correct standard abbreviation. This exercise covers Rules 19.9 through 19.11.

1. ________ Master of Business Administration
2. ________ Zone Improvement Plan
3. ________ doctor of philosophy
4. ________ standard operating procedure
5. ________ United States Department of Agriculture
6. ________ not in my backyard
7. ________ quantity
8. ________ June
9. ________ sound navigation ranging
10. ________ compact disc–read-only memory
11. ________ route
12. ________ what you see is what you get
13. ________ self-addressed, stamped envelope
14. ________ secretary
15. ________ Thursday
16. ________ second
17. ________ individual retirement account

EXERCISE 19-D *Directions:* Using standard proofreaders' marks, indicate on the comparison copy any differences between this letter and the comparison letter found on the following page. There could also be errors in this letter. This exercise is a text review.

January 23, 1999

Ms. Vickie George
Travel Time
7895 Whitlington Way
Zanesville, OH 43701

Dear Ms. George

I was delighted to read your humorous suggestions on how to survive the teenage years. I've always felt I would need a sense of humor if I lived to see my teen's adulthood arrive. Basically, all went well until the sixteenth year, which has its own brand of torture and requires a special set of rules. I'll borrow a phrase from my daughter and call this the year I developed "autotransportaphobia."

I thought *Travel Time* might find the suggestions contained in the article enlightening. I've attached a copy that you might like to include in an issue of your magazine just to assure other adults that while the disease may be contagious, it usually is not fatal.

Just for sake of fairness, I've included a copy of the "other" side of the issue. My daughter has written her impressions on the subject. Some of the teens in the audience might enjoy this article.

Neither of us wants to be paid for the articles. We merely want to help enlighten others who may soon face the same ordeal. We would like bylines on the articles if they are published.

Sincerely,

Ms. Sharon Souder
Autotransportaphobia Victim

Enclosures (2)

COMPARISON COPY 19-D

January 23, 1999

Ms. Vicki George
Travel Time
7895 Whitlingten Way
Zanesville, OH 43701

Dear Ms. George

I was delighted to read your humorous suggestions on how to survive the teenage years. I've always felt I would need a sense of humor if I lived to see my teens adulthood arrive. Basic-ally, all went well until the sixteenth year which has its own brand of torture and requires a special set of rules. I'll coin a phrase from my daughter and call this the year I developed "autotransportaphobia."

I thought the Travel Time might find the suggestions contained in the article enlightening. I've attached a copy that you might like to include in an issue of your magazine just to assure other adults that while the disease might be contageous, it usually is not fatal.

Just for sake of fairness, I've included a copy of the "other" side of the issue. My daughter has written her impressions on the subject. Some of the teens in the audience might enjoy this article.

Neither of us wants to be paid for the articles. We meerly want to help enlighten others who may soon face the same ordeal. We would like bylines on the article if they are published.

Sincerely yours,

Ms. Sharon Souder
Autotransportaphobia Victim

EXERCISE 19-E *Directions:* Proofread the following article using standard proofreaders' marks to indicate needed corrections. This exercise is a text review.

AUTOTRANSPORTAPHOBIA

By Sharon Souder

One day almost 17 years ago, I have birth to an adorable, bald girlchild who was going to grow up to save the world, or at least be president of the United States. Maybe she will, but she'll probably have a hard time getting elected when her past comes out during the election campaign. How many adults will vote for a president who was the "Autophoid Lynn" of the automobile set? She spread "autotransportaphobia" to everyone over the age of twenty-one who road in a car with her.

The interesting thing about this disease is that it comes on suddenly. I know I always told my daughter that she could never drive my car; I was just kidding. The first symptoms of the disease appeared at around the age of fourteen when all her friends in the band were driving. that year I started noticing the accidents on Maple Avenue involving—yes, you guessed it—teenagers. Then I heard the stories about the students who had lost there licenses for speeding. Not to worry—Lynn was only fourteen. I did, however, give her friends my "You Have My Child's Life in Your Hands" lecture before I would let her ride in the car with them.

When she turned fifteen, I suddenly realized that the adorable girlchild was only a year away from the wheel of my car. The first twinges of panic started to set in. They weren't uncontrollable yet, but they were present. I would wake up in the night when a siren sounded and run to her room to make sure she was their. I would give brief lectures on "A Car Is a Deadly Weapon" while I was driving her to school. I'd point out articles in Reader's Digest about young drivers who had died because they weren't paying attention. Subtle I probably wasn't, but then panic isn't a subtle emotion.

The dreaded year finally came, and—surprise— I was granted a reprieve! Remember those lectures on "A Car Is a Deadly Weapon?" They worked for about four months. She didn't even ask to take driver's education. She told someone she didn't want to drive because she might kill someone. I was elated. I even stopped complaining about having to take her to band practices and social events.

I couldn't be lucky forever. November was the month she became "Autophoid Lynn". The weakening of the fear of driving—or maybe it was having a few fee hours in her schedule—found her in a driving class. I wasn't thrilled, but at least she was in a building; she didn't have a permit—yet. December found her at the driver's license bureau while I sat in my car and prayed she would fail the premit test. I didn't want her to be disappointed; I just wanted her to be alive. I knew I was in trouble when she opened the car door, sat down, gripping an imaginary steering wheel, and said, ""Varoom, varoom." She was ecstatic; I was near hysteria.

Lynn couldn't convince me to let her drive home. I has valid excuses. She hadn't done her road work for driving class. It was a Saturday before Christmas. The roads were busy. I finally worked up my nerve and let her drive from a deserted college parking lot to a friend's house about a half mile away. It was then I developed a full-blown case of autotransportaphobia. In the time it took her to drive that short distance, I learned to grip the window ledge in the car (no small feet in a subcompact) and to put on my brakes—you know, the ones on the passenger's side of the car. I also found that I wasn't able to make a simple correction when she made a mistake. I had to tell her everything that could possibly happen when she made the type of error she did.

I could tell she was not amused. I tried to control my use of the passenger's side brake by holding down my brake foot with my other foot so I wouldn't be able to put on the imaginary brake. Unfortunately, I found I was drawing in huge gasps of air every time she did something wrong. She was even less amused. When I talked to my friends about getting crash helmets, I realized it had to be the fault of "Autophoid Lynn." I was the rational adult; she was the teenager.

As a rational adult, I analyzed the situation and found that I was right, of course. I had to put on the break because she wasn't stopping soon enough. Everyone starts stopping a block before the stop sign, right? I had to grasp for air because she didn't understand you had to follow the same rules in parking lots that you had to follow on the road. I always stop at the stop sign in a deserted parting lot at 11 p.m. Surely everyone else does the same. And every ratiional driver learns to watch the taillights of the cars ahead, right?

Once I realized she was the problem, I finally realized there is no solution. she was determined to learn to drive and I, being the responsible parent I am, would have to teach her. I do have a couple of suggestions for those who follow me thru the various stages of this dreaded disease.

1. Let others teach the teen to drive. Friends should not be the teachers since they are a part of the problem. Grandparents who like to spoil the child is a good answer. They are better able to handle "I wasn't going to hit that car" then are the parents.
2. Pay to have your child's birth certificate altered so the birth certificate will say fourteen when the child is sixteen. then you'll ahve an extra two years.
4. Play "A Car Is a Deadly Weapon" speech every night of the child's life, starting at birth. (If you supply a bland tape, Ill make you a copy of mind.) Hearing the tape over and over

> for 15 years should keep the child from wanting the permit until about the age of nineteen. If you plan carefully, you can then sent the child to a college that restricts the use of cars on campus and you may never face the problem. (I can also supply you with a list of colleges with these restrictions.)

If all else fails, tie you feet to the floor, wear a gag to keep from gasping for breath, close your eyes, and hope he child can't get in the required driving hours until the age of twenty-one. I'm told the child is no longer contagious by the age of twenty-one so if I can just hold out until then, . . . It may be had, She's almost seventeen and talking about making an appointment for her test. I'm afraid to find out what terrible symptoms will appear the first night she takes my car somewhere. Still, I'm told this disease is not fatal. Well see!

EXERCISE 19–F *Directions:* Proofread the following article using standard proofreaders' marks to indicate needed corrections. This exercise is a text review.

AUTOTRANSPORTAPHOBIA

By Lynn Souder

The dreams of a teenager all have some things in common—driving. A bright red car with a sunroof, sunglasses on, crusing down Maple Avenue, and checking out the guys. At least that was my dream. But like all good things, my dreams abruptly vanished when I learned my mother had a serious desease. Its name is "Autotransportaphobia.

I realize the name is fairly complicated, but the disease itself is very uncomplicated. It is simply the fear your parents have about letting you take the "big step" and get behind the wheel. the symptoms are clear. The first signs can appear as early as your fourteenth birthday. Your parents immediately begin telling you that you'll never drive their car or get a license for that matter. A definite symptom, one you get your permit, is when the parent is found gripping the car window or slamming a foot into the floorboard while you are driving (as if these desperate measures will do them any good). when you are driving, they may also say such things as "When the light is red, you can go," or "Stop at the stop sign."

The severity of the disease varies. It can result in severe damage to the parent and the teenager. I've seen cases where teenagers get their licenses and their parents don't let them drive. They are forced to do such things as call every half hour—supposedly to make sure no accident has occurred in the last 29 minutes. Some teens are never permitted to get their licenses at all.

I feel that my mother has the worst case in the history of the disease. She began telling me at the age of ten that I would never get my license. When I turned fifteen she was already telling me that just because I was turning sixteen in a year didn't mean I would be able to drive. Then I turned sixteen in June. Until October she wouldn't even allow me to take driver's education. When I got my permit in December, she wouldn't even let me drive for two weeks. The first time she finally did let me drive, I thought she was going to go int shock or something. In a two- block trip she tired to use her imaginary break by stomping on the floor, steering for me by reaching through my arms, almost cause me to wreck anyway, and turning on the turn signal in the same mannor.I couldn't believe it.

Once I was with a friend, and he let me drive. I thought I did a respectable job. The next morning my mother said she saw me driving and that I could have killed everyone in a two-mile radius. (We were site-seeing in the countryside.)

Once I recognized what my mother's symptoms were, I immediately began researching to see what the problem was and what could be done about it. I looked in a book about diseases of the mind. when I read the symptoms of Autotransportphobia, I knew that was it. Tragically, there is no "cure". The only thing you can do is wait it out and hop for the best. In my case, I'm still waiting; I'll be seventeen in a couple of months.

I decided to try a couple of my own ideas to cure her; I couldn't wait forever to drive. First, I thought that maybe if I drove very carefully when she was in the car, never making mistakes, she would trust me. That didn't work. No matter how careful I was, she was sure I was going to kill her or someone else. Then, I decided to confront her about her problem. All that did was anger her. she told me I was crazy and that was probably why I was such a terrible driver. I didn't know what else to do, so I gave up. I'm still waiting.

Even though I've had my permit for two months, nothing has changed. In fact, I thinks its worse. Last night she actually pushed a whole in the floorbored trying to put on the breaks. Oh well, I hope neither you nor anyone you know ever has to go through such an ordeal just to get one of the simple pleasures all people need . . . driving.

I only ask one thing of you. The next time you see a teenager in the car with an adult who looks terrified, give the teenager an encouraging smile or wave. Trust me—the teen needs it!

CHAPTER

20

A Final Look

All good things must come to an end. This chapter is just that—the end of this book. Although it is the last time you will proofread exercises in this text, it certainly isn't the last time you will be proofreading. If you are to be successful, you will need to keep your proofreading skills finely honed. You will proofread everything you do, whether it's your own personal correspondence, a term paper, or work your employer entrusts to you. The rules in this text are appropriate for all levels of writing; indeed, they are required if you want to do your work correctly. Remember, *you get only one chance to make a first impression; make it a good one!*

The following exercises complete the minisimulation for Glascow Computers Inc., which began in Chapter 16. Make all necessary corrections. The exercises review the following major topics:

Abbreviations	Other punctuation
Apostrophes	Parallelism
Capitalization	Pronouns
Colons	Reading for meaning
Commas	Run-on sentences
Comma splices	Semicolons
Divisions	Sentence fragments
Document format	Spelling
Document layout	Subject-verb agreement
Enumerations	Troublesome words
Number usage	

PROOFREADING POINTER

When in doubt, check it out!

EXERCISE 20-A *Directions:* Correct this letter using standard proofreaders' marks.

GLASCOW
COMPUTERS
INC.
1714 Mobeetie Road
McLean, TX 79057

April, 5, 1999

Mrs. Brenda Preslicka
79034 Effie Drive
McLean, TX 79051

Dear Mrs. Preslicka:

This letter will confirm our telephone conversation on April 2 regarding arre offer of employment as a computer software specialist. Our discussion included the following;

1. The duties of the job include, but are not limited to software selection, training, and installation.

2. The salary for the position will be $32,000 per year, with a two-week vacation the first and second years, a 3-week vacation the third and fourth years, and a 4 week vacation beginning in the fifth year.

3. The schedule work hours for the position are 8 a.m. to 5 p.m. with a one hour lunch.

4. Standard company benefits are provided with the job.

5 The travel will be substantial during the first 3 months of the job, with consultations at all district corporate headquarters. After the initial coprorate survey, the travel should be limited to one week every other month.

A copy of the contract for the position is included with this letter. If you have any additional questions, call me at 555-7269, Ext. 242. We expect to hear from you within one week from the date of this letter.

Sincerely

Terri Martin
Personnel Manager

mw

EXERCISE 20–B *Directions:* Correct this letter using standard proofreaders' marks.

GLASCOW COMPUTERS INC.
1714 Mobeetie Road
McLean, TX 79057

April 14, 1999

Mr. Justin Braddock
450 Farling Road
Amarillo, TX 79105

APPLICATION FOR COMPUTER SOFTWARE SPECIALIST

We thank you for the time and effort you took in coming to Glascow Computers, Inc. for an interview for the Computer Software Specialist position we had open. We enjoyed the interview and we were especially impressed with several faucets of your credentials.

It is always difficult to make a selection when you have several qualified job applicants for only one position. We certainly had trouble making a selection in this search. After the interviews, however we felt that one of the other candidates were best suited for the job.

It is our company policy to keep employment applications on file for six months. We wish you luck in your job search, and we hope you will apply again for other position openings with Glascow Computers, Inc. If you should see and advertisement for a position matched with your qualifications, simply call me at 555-7269, Ext, 247, and ask us to reactivate the file.

SINCERELY

MS. TERRI MARTIN
HUMAN RESOURCES MANAGER

mw

EXERCISE 20-C *Directions:* Correct this memo using standard proofreaders' marks.

April 14, 1994

Anton Schneider

THANKS FOR A JOB WELL DONE!

I received your recommendation for the computer software specialist position on March 25, and I was pleased to see the committee had selected the same candidate I would have chosen.

I contacted Brenda Preslicka early last week and discussed the position, making her an offer. We received her response today when she brought in a signed contract. Her first day will be April 19. We will be having a juice and coffee welcome that morning, and since you are in her department, I would like to ask that you meet her at the front gate and show her to her office. She should arrive at 7:45 p.m.

We appreciate the extra time and energy it takes to serve on these Search Committees. Thanks again for serving on the committee.

Mr. Terri Martin
Personnel Manager

c Employee Permanant File

EXERCISE 20-D *Directions:* Correct these minutes using standard proofreaders' marks.

MINUTES

Computer Software Specialist Search Committee

April 4, 1999

The final meeting of the Computer Software Specialist Search Committee was held on April 14, 1999 at 10 a.m. in the Greenery Conference Room. Members present were: Barb Davis, Anton Schneider, Sara Gibson, and Gayle Jenkins. Ron Redfern was excused. Terri Martin was present as a guest.

The minutes of the previous meeting were read and approved. A memo from Joe Christie, CEO, was read to announce Brenda Preslickas acceptence of the computer software specialist position. Mr. Christie complemented the committee on their selection of an outstanding employee.

The committee made the following recommendations concerning future searches. 1) The members of the committee felt one committee member should be responsible for escorting the candidate through all stages of the interview. This should reduce the stress level and make the candidate feel more comfortable. 2) All candidates should be allowed about five minutes of casual conversation before the actual interview begins. This would give the candidate a chance to size up the group and feel more comfortable; A group of five to seven strangers immediately firing questions at the candidate can shake some candidates who might be good employees. 3) Copies of the applicants' materials should be made available to all interviewees during the interview. 4) More immediate feedback should be given to the candidates not being called for an interview.

The committee thanked Terri Martin for her assistance in answering questions and scheduling interviews. They also commended Mark Watton for his help with minimising the paperwork during the search process. Serving on search committees is always a real challenge, but Mark and Terri kept things moving efficiently and smoothly.

Terri Martin officially discharged the committee at 10:45 p.m.

Respectfully submitted,

Anton Schneider

hg

EXERCISE 20-E *Directions:* Correct this news release using standard proofreaders' marks.

N E W S R E L E A S E

For Immediate Release

For additional information contact
Teri Martin
Personnel Manager

Brenda Preslicka has been hired as a computer software specialist, effective April 19, 1999. She will be replacing Rob Wright; Rob is leaving to join his wife in California.

Brenda is a graduate of Reston High School in Resten, Virginia. She received an associate degree at Hawkeye Technical Institute and a Bachelor's Degree in Office Administration from Western Michigan University in Ohio. Her previous work experience will include: four years of teaching with Edison State Community College, three years of sales in the computer software field and five years of experience as a software evaluation technician with Software House .

Brenda was a member of Business Professionals of America, serving as a state and national officer; she placed first in the national data specialist contest held in Louisville, KY. Brenda is currently a member of the National Software Specialist Association and the Computerized Office Management Organization.

In addition to her professional activities Brenda is active in local community organizations, including Toastmasters, Business and Professional Women, and the University Womens' Organization. Her hobbies include speed walking and playing computer games. Brenda and Cale, her husband, enjoy "playing at amateur archaeology" at area sights, and are particularly looking forward to helping with the excavation of a mastadon discovered in their back yard hear in Amarillo.

EXERCISE 20-F *Directions:* Correct this letter using standard proofreaders' marks.

May 24 1999

Roy B.Worstall
Travelers Associates
17 South Street
Amarillo, TX 79105

CORPORATE RESERVATIONS FOR BRENDA PRESLICKA

Glascow Computers, Inc. has recently hired a new employee for the postion of computer software specialist. Mrs. Brenda Preslicka will be traveling to our regional offcies to meet with software users from our company.

We have been pleased with the professional service we have received from your organization in the passed. It is always a pleasure to deal with a company with an outstanding attitude.

We have listed below the dates for Belinda's trips to the seven regional offices . Brenda will be traveling alone, except for the trip to Kona, when her husband Cole will be accompanying her. The travel dates and the hotel we prefer to use has also been included. Could you begin making travel reservations for Brenda, keeping in mind that transportation to the hotel and back to the airport will also need to be included in the travel plans. We prefer to use the Air Care Cozy Class rates. If you are unable to book with Air Care, any carrier with comparible rates are acceptable.

June 27–29	Des Moines, Iowa	Inner City Inn
July 2–5	Reno, Nevada	The Barn
July 12–17	Kona, Hawaii	The Sunshine BeachHotel
August 4–7	Boston, Massachusetts	Boston Gardens
August 12–15	Tallahassee, Flor.	The Piazza
August 18–21	Denver, Colorado	Su Casa

Roy B. Worstall
May 24, 1999
Page 2

The reservations at the hotels should be for a single room, (a double in Kona) corporate rates. Our corporate identification number is GC-7632-8976TX. Once you have made the arrangements, notify Edna Roberts in the purchasing department, and he will file the appropriate forms for handling the financial arrangements. Ednas number is 555-6001, ext. 291. She can also answer any other questions you might have. If our plans change, we will, of course, let you know immediately.

Glascow Computers, Inc. has enjoyed wording with you in the past, and we look forward to our continued busness association.

JOE CHRISTIE
PRESIDENT

df

EXERCISE 20–G

Directions: Compare the two schedules. Make all necessary corrections on the typewritten schedule.

TRAVEL SCHEDULE FOR BRENDA PRESLICKA

July and August 1999

Date	Destination	Departure	Arrival	Contact
June 27	Des Moines, Iowa	8:20 a.m.	11:07 p.m.	Fran Brilla
July 2	Reno, Nevada	10:32 a.m.	2:23 p.m.	Carol Krieger
July 12	Kona, Hawaii	3:01 a.m.	5:53 p.m.	Angelina Ruppel
Aug. 4	Boston, MA	10:01 a.m.	4:53 p.m.	Don Nauer
Aug. 12	Talahassee, Florida	3:00 p.m	5:32 p.m.	Jeff Everett
Aug. 18	Denver, Colorado	9:00 a.m.	Noon	Tracey Klinehoffer

TRAVEL SCHEDULE FOR BRENDA PRESLICKA

July and August, 1999

DATE	Departure	Destination	Arrival	Contact
June 27	8:20 a.m.	Des Moines, Iowa	11:07 a.m.	Fran Brilla
July 2	10:32 a.m.	Reno, Nv	2:23 p.m.	Carole Krieger
July 12	3:01 a.m.	Kona, Hawaii	5:53 p.m.	Angelina Ruppel
Aug. 4	10:01 a.m.	Boston, Massachusetts	4:53 p.m.	Don Nauer
Aug 12	3:00 p.m.	Talahassee, Florida	5:32 p.m.	Jeff Everett
Aug 18	9 a.m.	Denver, Colorado	Noon	Tracey Klinehoffer

EXERCISE 20-H *Directions:* Correct this itinerary using standard proofreaders' marks.

ITINERARY FOR

Brenda Preslicka

June 12

3:01 a.m.	Departure from Oklahoma City International Airport aboard Flight 4561 (Unified Airlines.) The flight should allow you to get some sleep on the first part of the trip. This is a nonstop flight to Honolulu. Your luggage has been checked throught to Kona Airport
3:50 p.m.	Arrive at Honolulu International Airport. No customs check is necesary upon arrival from mainland cities. Your flight to Kona departs at 5:30 p.m. from Concourse B via Island Airlines.
5:53 p.m.	Report to Spiffy Car Rental Desk at terminal B to pick up keys for your rental car. Spiffy will have a midsize car waiting by the luggage exit when you pick up you luggage. Directions to the Royal Lahina Condominiums will be left on the front seat of the car.
9 p.m.	Dinner with Martin Mahali in the dining room at the Royal Lahina. Its known for its seafood entrees.

July 13

9:15 a.m.	Meet with Angelina Ruppel in the lobby of the Royal Lahina. She will escort you to Glascow Computer building to show you the route you will need to follow on Thursday. The remainder of the day has been left free so you and Cale will have time to adjust to the time shift. Meals will be charged to the company charge card you received with the travel papers.
July 14	No activities are scheduled for July 14.

July 15

9:30 a.m.	Tour of Kona Office. You will meet Angelina Ruppel at the main door of the Kona Plant. After a breakfast with the Ezekial Dresdent, president of the Pacific Regional operations, you and Angelina will tour the facilities.
11 a.m.	Meet with Marla Gentle, office manager for the main office. Marla will be briefing you on special operations and procedures for this district. She also has a problem with a database she is trying to design. No, you don't have to solve it on the spot but you can

Itinerary for Brenda Preslicka
Page 2
June 12–17

bring the specifications back with you. This database she is working with, is vital to the company and will be one of your first major projects.

Noon — Meet with Andrew Roquemore, Sales Manager for the Pacific region, for a working lunch. Although the sales inventory is connected to a Lantie network system. We often have to download information for special projects. Andrew has a project in the works and is looking for direction for the project.

2 p.m. — Meet with Etana Wilhila. She will escort you to the Kilauea Volcano area for publicity pictures; we'll be using one of the shots taken here for the company newsletter, Corporate Policy and for local press releases. The company thought this would be a good way to promote our Atlantic operations.

You should plan to have Cale join you at the office at 2 so that he can go along. You'll be driving your rental car. Following the pictures, you and Cale will be free to tour the area. The helicopter tour you requested is reserved for 5 p.m. with Lani Heli Tours. Directions and a brochure are included in your travel packet.

For he remainder of the day and evening you are on your own.

July 16 — No activities are scheduled for July 16.

July 17

6:10 p.m. — Meet with Ezekial Dresdent and his wife for dinner at their home. You and Cale should have your luggage in the car. We have scheduled a late departure, you should be able to sleep on the fligt back to the mainland.

11:00 p.m. — Be at Spiffy Car Rental to drop off the rental car. Spiffy will take you to the Kona airport for the shuttle flight to Oahu.

12:45 a.m. — Depart for Oklahoma City International Airport aboard Unified 4562. You should arrive in Oklahoma City at 4 a.m. on July 19.

ALOHA!

Index